CW01197485

MASTERS OF
FASHION
ILLUSTRATION

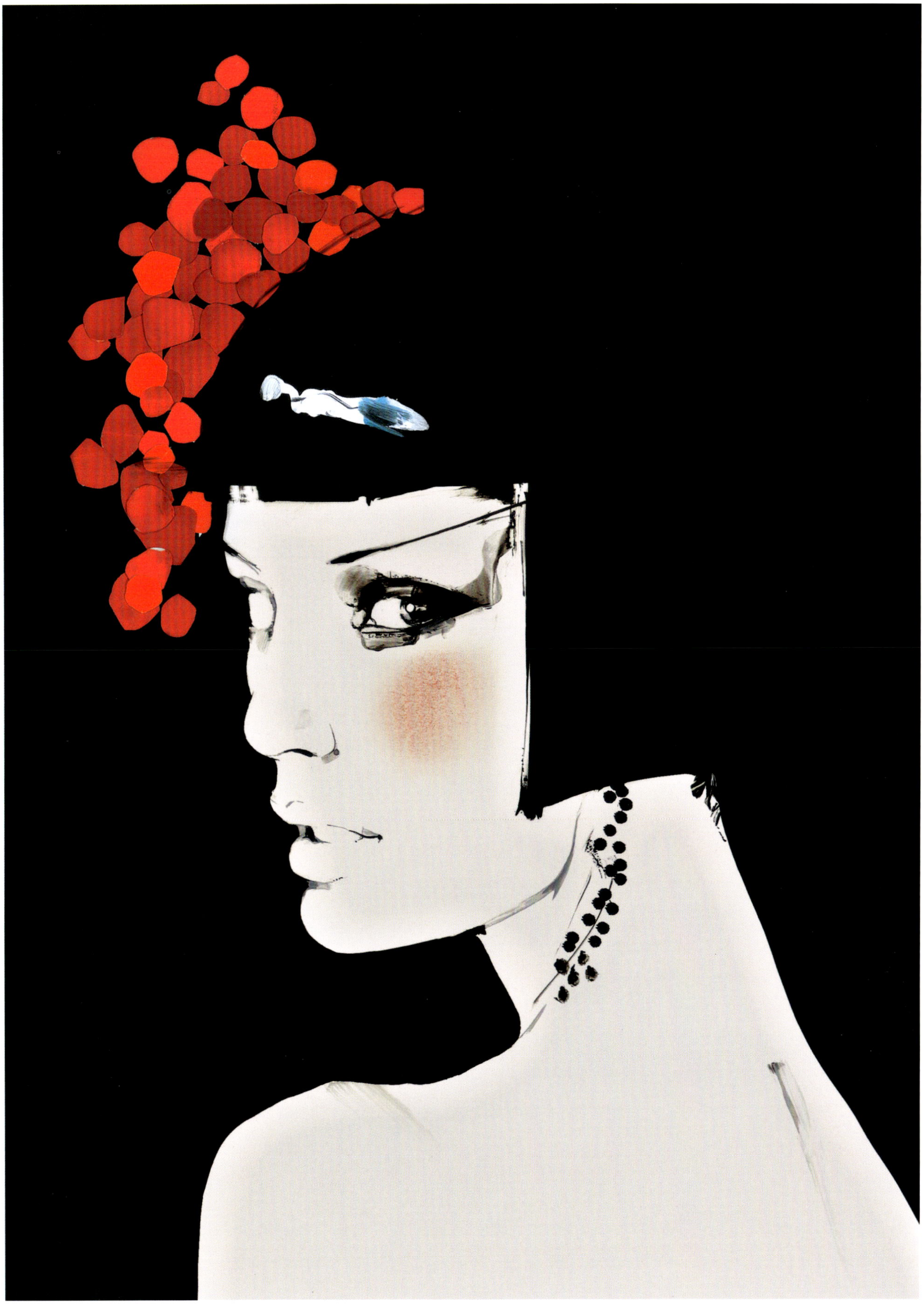

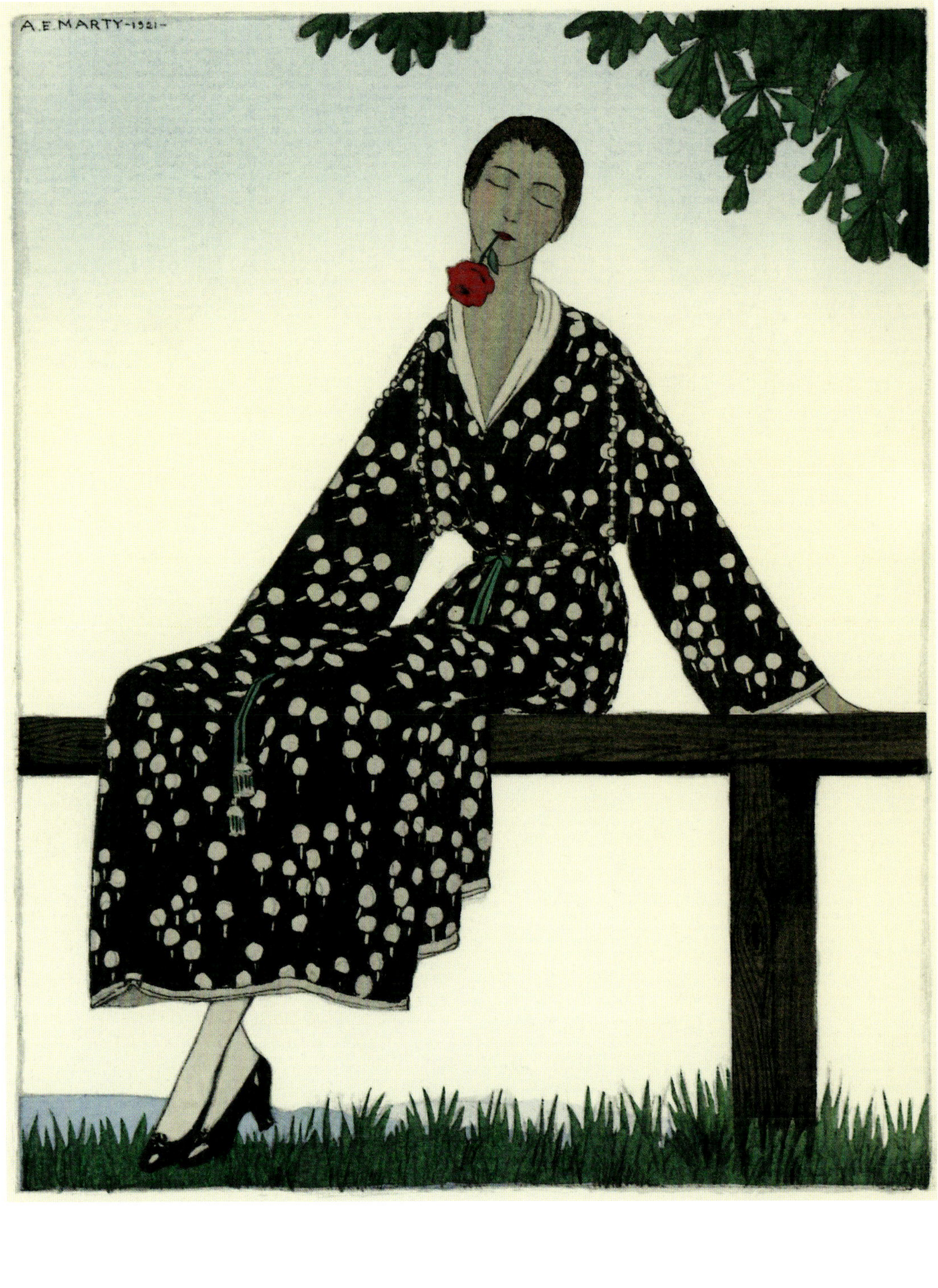
A.E. MARTY-1921-

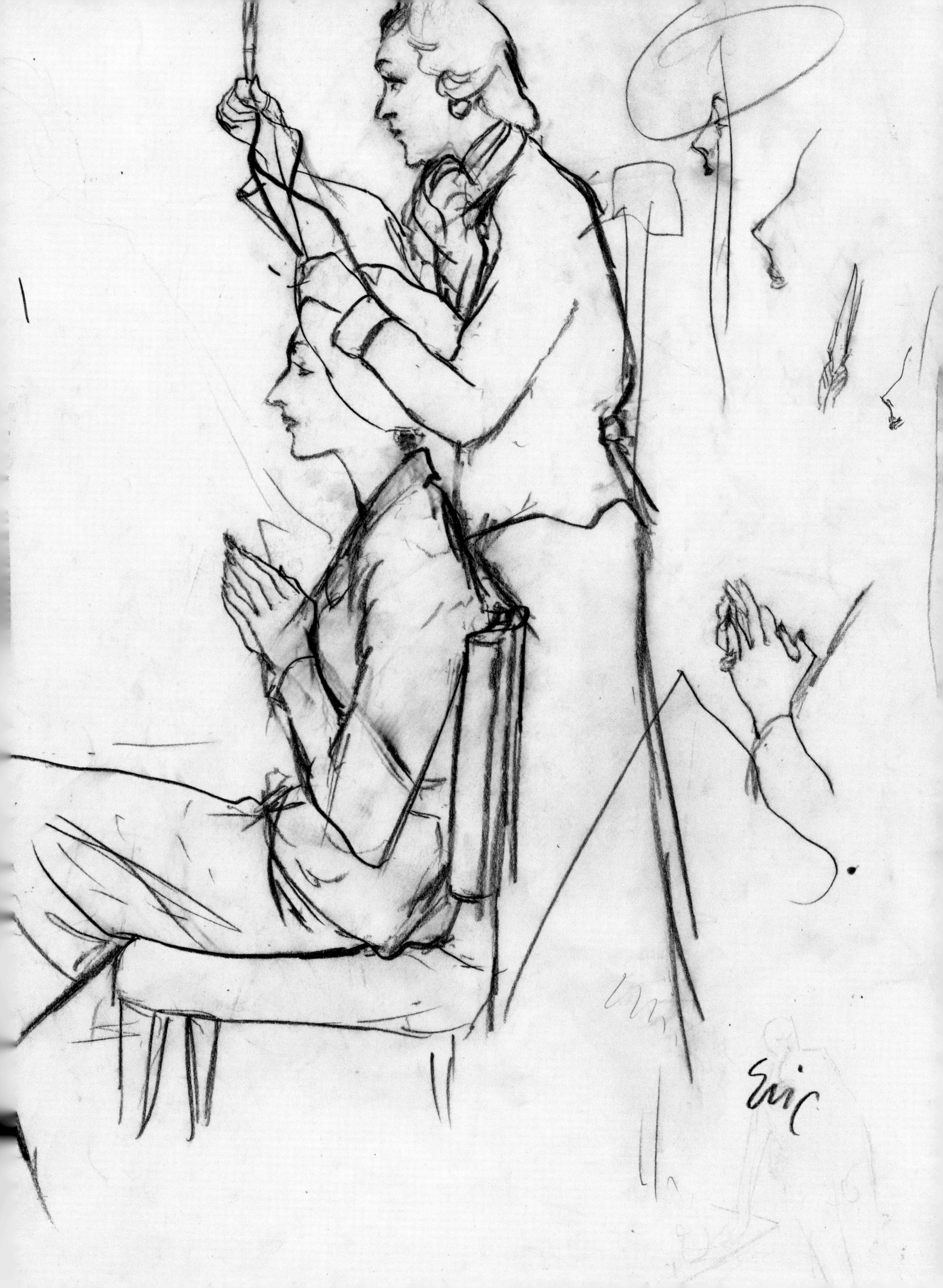
Eric

Suzy's sugar-pink twill toque.

P

G

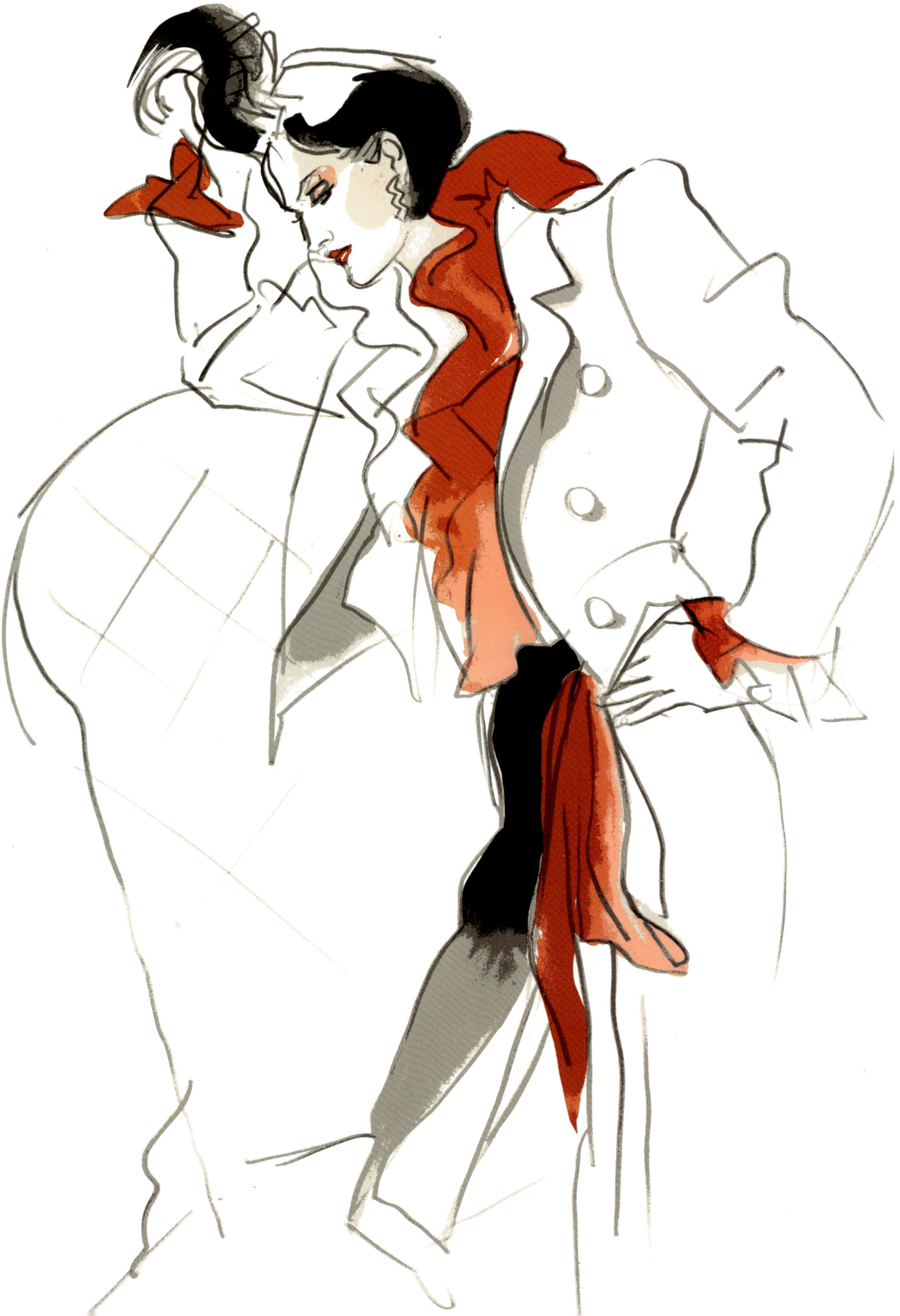

9

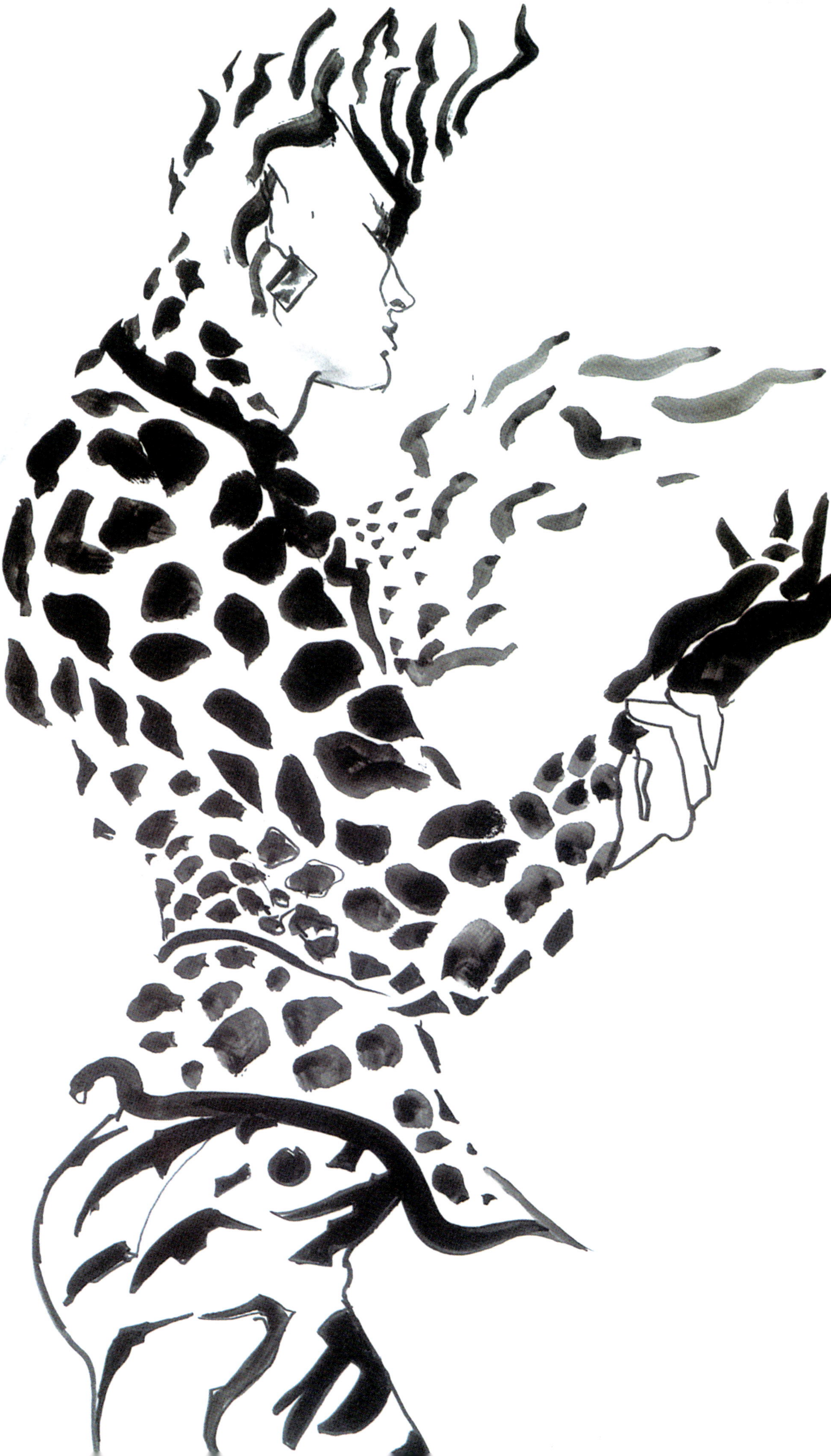

11

12

3
DAVID DOWNTON
Christian Dior Haute Couture, 2006.
Artist's collection

4
ANDRÉ-EDOUARD MARTY
Pochoir plate from *Gazette du Bon Ton*, 1921.
Courtesy Tony Glenville

5
CARL ERICKSON
Sketch, circa 1940.
Courtesy The Museum of Fine Arts, Boston

6
MARCEL VERTÈS
Illustration for *Harper's Bazaar*, 1938.
Courtesy The Mary Evans Picture Library

7
TOM KEOGH
Illustration for *Dictionnaire Des Femmes*, 1961.
Private collection

8
ANTONIO LOPEZ
Portrait of Paloma Picasso for *Vanity* issue 9, January 1984.
Copyright Estate of Antonio Lopez and Juan Ramos/ Courtesy Galerie Bartsch & Chariau, Munich

9
ÉTIENNE DRIAN
'Pagode' illustration for *Costumes Parisiennes*, 1914.
Courtesy The Collection of Joanne Bergen/Artophile

10
TONY VIRAMONTES
Jean Louis Scherrer, for *La Mode En Peinture*, 1984.
Courtesy Estate of Tony Viramontes

11
BERNARD BLOSSAC
Evening coat by Jacques Fath, circa 1948.
Courtesy Galerie Bartsch & Chariau, Munich

12
RENÉ BOUCHÉ
Fashion illustration, circa 1953.
Courtesy Galerie Bartsch & Chariau, Munich

DAVID DOWNTON

MASTERS OF FASHION ILLUSTRATION

LAURENCE KING PUBLISHING

LAURENCE KING

Published in 2010 by Laurence King Publishing Ltd
361–373 City Road
London EC1V 1LR
United Kingdom

Tel: + 44 20 7841 6900
Fax: + 44 20 7841 6910
e-mail: enquiries@laurenceking.com
www.laurenceking.com

Copyright © text 2010 David Downton

David Downton has asserted his right under the Copyright, Designs, and Patent Act 1988, to be identified as the Author of this Work.

All rights reserved. No part of this publication may be reproduced or transmitted in any form or by any means, electronic or mechanical, including photocopy, recording or any information storage and retrieval system, without prior permission in writing from the publisher.

A catalogue record for this book is available from the British Library

ISBN: 978 1 85669 704 0

Design: Karen Morgan
Picture Research: Claire Gouldstone
Senior Editor: Clare Double
Commissioning Editor: Helen Rochester

Printed in China

CONTENTS

Foreword by Carmen Dell'Orefice	19
Introduction by David Downton	20

THE AGE OF OPULENCE

Giovanni Boldini	24
J.C. Leyendecker	32
Gazette Artists	38
Étienne Drian	46
Erté	54

AN EMERGING LINE...

Carl Erickson	62
Marcel Vertès	72
Francis Marshall	80
Bernard Blossac	88
Tom Keogh	96

THE NEW *GRAPHISME*

Coby Whitmore	104
Bob Peak	114
Andy Warhol	124

FROM THE SALON TO THE STREET

René Bouché	134
Kenneth Paul Block	144
Antonio Lopez	152
Tony Viramontes	162

DAVID DOWNTON IN CONVERSATION

David Downton Interviewed by Tony Glenville	174
Fashion	178
Portraits	198

Further Reading	217
Index	218
Picture Credits	221
Acknowledgements	224

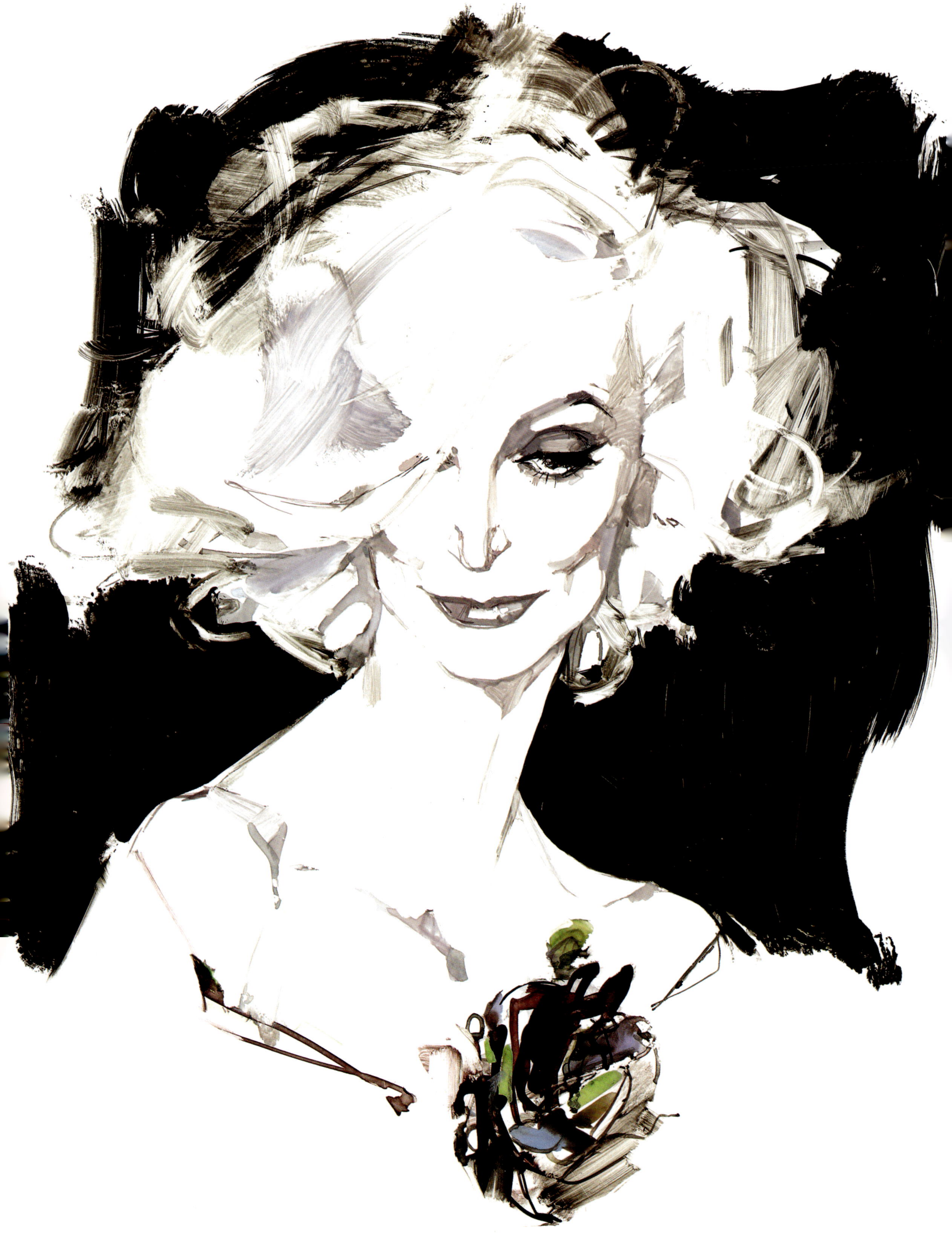

CARMEN
Carmen Dell'Orefice portrait by David Downton,
London, May 2003. *Artist's collection*

FOREWORD BY CARMEN DELL'OREFICE

Looking through this beautiful book I realize a decade and some has passed since my first encounter with David Downton in Paris, after one of John Galliano's fabulous fashion shows. Since then we have worked together continuously, developing a delightful professional intimacy. David's inner eye is something he was born with, and he has honed his skills over the decades to breathtaking perfection. I was aware of his special talent because for more than sixty years, I have posed for some of the greatest illustrators and artists of the times.

I began working at *Vogue* right after World War II, before television was commonplace and before photography became the art form it is today. There were a number of artists at the magazine in those days and when a job came up I would rollerskate over to Central Park South, where many had their studios. Working with artists was very different to working with photographers; it was up close and personal, with much less fuss and folderol. And no hot lights! But I got the same fee – $12.50 an hour. Looking back it was all very easy. I was booked for half a day, and we were done… I felt like I was stealing money!

Eric, I remember in particular, was quiet and considerate, but clear about what he wanted. If we were doing a specific fashion story there would be an editor present – Baron Nicky de Gunzburg, Scully Montgomery or Barbara Cushing Mortimer (later Babe Paley), the great arbiters of taste and style of those times – to make sure the pearls were on, or the fox fur or hat were adjusted properly. In those days we did not have hairdressers or make-up artists; women designed themselves. Eric would sit by a window with an enormous pad of paper propped on his knee. He let me play around a bit with the pose and then he would say 'Hold it!' and I did. I was used to working with photographers like Penn and Erwin Blumenfeld, who used 8 x 10 bellows cameras with long exposures so you had to pose like a statue. You needed stamina to do it, but I was young and of course I'd had ballet training, which helped.

In 1946, Cecil Beaton introduced me to Salvador Dalí after a photo shoot at *Vogue*. Dalí painted me and we developed a friendship that lasted until his death. I also worked with Bouché and Vertès, two of the best-known illustrators of that time, and later Michael Werboff, Fred Greenhill and, of course, Joe Eula, who was a friend. Like these great master artists, David is first and foremost a gentleman. He is a disciplined romantic with a unique ability to capture the essence of his subjects.

Sometimes I feel like the last link to a golden era. I've watched the popularity of fashion illustration wax and wane. But I'm happy to say – and this book bears me out – that it never goes away; it just keeps coming back, like a familiar melody.

INTRODUCTION BY DAVID DOWNTON

In July 1996, when I was sent to draw at the Paris haute couture shows by the *Financial Times' How to Spend It* magazine, I was a moderately successful illustrator, wagging my tail when the phone rang, delighted to be making my living by drawing. I certainly didn't consider myself a fashion illustrator (although I'd had fashion commissions). In fact, I was happy doing whatever came along; maps and menus, textbooks and cookbooks and, in the early days at least, much too much romantic fiction. But I was old enough (I was 37) and smart enough to recognize that I was being handed an opportunity.

As instructed, I presented myself at the Ritz Hotel in the Place Vendôme, where the great Roman couturier Valentino had set up temporary court. In a mirrored salon heavy with the sweet, sad smell of lilies, the maestro was adjusting liquid folds of material on the semi naked body of the most beautiful woman I had ever seen, Amber Valletta. Later that evening, at my first couture show, one of the last designed by Gianni Versace (he was murdered the following year), Linda, Naomi and Kate stormed the catwalk, ablaze in primary colour. It was like being given the keys to Narnia.

I may have been a fashion rookie but I did know and love the work of the great fashion illustrators: Antonio, Eric, René Gruau. To me they were artists; artists whose subject was fashion. I don't believe there is a frivolous subject for art (although there are undoubtedly frivolous artists) and these superb draughtsmen were masters of the fluid, reductive line that I loved and tried so hard to emulate. They told not just the 'story of the dress,' but the story around the dress, describing the time, the place and the woman with an economy and flair that photography, however striking, could never match.

This book is a chance to celebrate and share the work of my favourite artists. Some have transcended the world of fashion and need no introduction; others, mysteriously and unaccountably, have slipped from public view. I should say straight away that this is not a directory, and is not intended to be comprehensive (there are gaps and omissions, but more of that later). And, like all endeavours of this kind, it is shot through with prejudice. Perhaps prejudice is the point. I have tried to convey something of the flavour of each artist's work and of *l'air du temps*, but in essence this is a book about drawing and will, I hope, be its own reward; a magic lantern show of changing times and the way they were interpreted by brilliant artists.

Fashion illustration is only 'superficially superficial' – to mangle a quote from Max Ophüls' *Madame de...* – it deals with the truth of line and the power and the illusion of beauty; complex themes perhaps, but all in a day's work for these masters of fashion illustration.

THE AGE OF OPULENCE

At the turn of the twentieth century, in Paris and in New York, the first generation of fashion artists had much to reflect upon, from the heady exoticism of the Ballets Russes and the radical shake-ups in the art world, to the privations of World War I and the gold rush of its aftermath, the 'Roaring Twenties'.

Boldini
1901

CLÉO DE MÉRODE
Boldini painted the dancer and international fascinator Cléo de Mérode with customary panache in 1901, when she was 26 and at the height of her fame. She would also sit for Toulouse-Lautrec, Gustav Klimt and the photographer Félix Nadar.
Courtesy Topfoto

GIOVANNI BOLDINI

Firstly of course, Giovanni Boldini was not a fashion illustrator. He was a pre-eminent social portraitist of the belle époque who rejoiced in the epithet 'the master of swish'. But consider the way his dramatic, large-scale canvases combine a love of attenuated proportion, a sensuous delight in haute couture and a pulsating energy that keeps his subjects on the move, as though life in Paris at the turn of the century were a never-ending catwalk. He may have lacked the restraint (and at times, it must be said, the taste) of his peers Whistler, Helleu and Sargent, but his bravura portraits reflected the optimism, glamour and self-confidence of the age and would have a lasting effect on the grand manner fashion artists of the first half of the twentieth century – Drian, Eric and especially Gruau.

He was born Giovanni Gusto Filippo Maria Boldini in Ferrara, Italy, in 1842. Showing early promise, he trained initially with his father, a painter and picture restorer, and in 1862 he enrolled in L'Accademia di Belle Arti in Florence. Boldini's social antennae were already finely tuned: while still a student he found early patrons among the wealthy British expatriates living in Tuscany, including Sir William Falconer, for whom he created murals, and Sir Alfred Cornwallis West.

By 1871, Boldini had established himself in Paris. His prolific output of small-scale genre scenes quickly found favour with the public and brought him to the attention of the eminent art dealer Adolphe Goupil, with whom he signed an exclusive contract that would run until 1888. His debut at the Salon de Mars in 1874 consolidated his success and, ever upwardly mobile, Boldini moved to a house at Versailles with his model/fiancée Berthe in tow. He enjoyed his early popularity, travelled widely, and exhibited in Berlin, London and Florence. His ebullient personality and prodigious talent led him to form friendships with the leading artists of the day, including Degas, Whistler, Lautrec and Sargent, all of whom he would paint during this period.

In May 1884, Sargent unveiled his *Portrait of Madame ***** (later known as *Portrait of Madame X*) to widespread condemnation. The artist's depiction of the American-born Virginie Gautreau, with her plunging *décolletage* and coolly detached sexuality, infuriated critics and enraged the public. 'My daughter is ruined!' wailed the sitter's mother, who tried to get the painting removed from view. Later that year, as the criticism rumbled on, Sargent left Paris for London where he would re-establish his reputation, and in 1886 Boldini took over the lease of Sargent's former studio and apartments at 41 Boulevard Berthier.

In 1888, Boldini's portrait of Emiliana Concha de Ossa, the daughter of a Chilean diplomat, signalled a turning point. Scaled to match the heroic proportions of Sargent's work and with more than a passing debt to his friend Degas, the portrait marked the flowering of Boldini's mature style, with its flattering likeness, palpable energy and full-blown sense of style. The painting won the Gold Medal at the Paris Universal Exposition in 1889.

THE MASTER OF SWISH
Boldini's dazzling bravura style reached an explosive high point in his 1892 painting, *Fuoco d'artificio* (*The Firework Display*). *Courtesy akg-images*

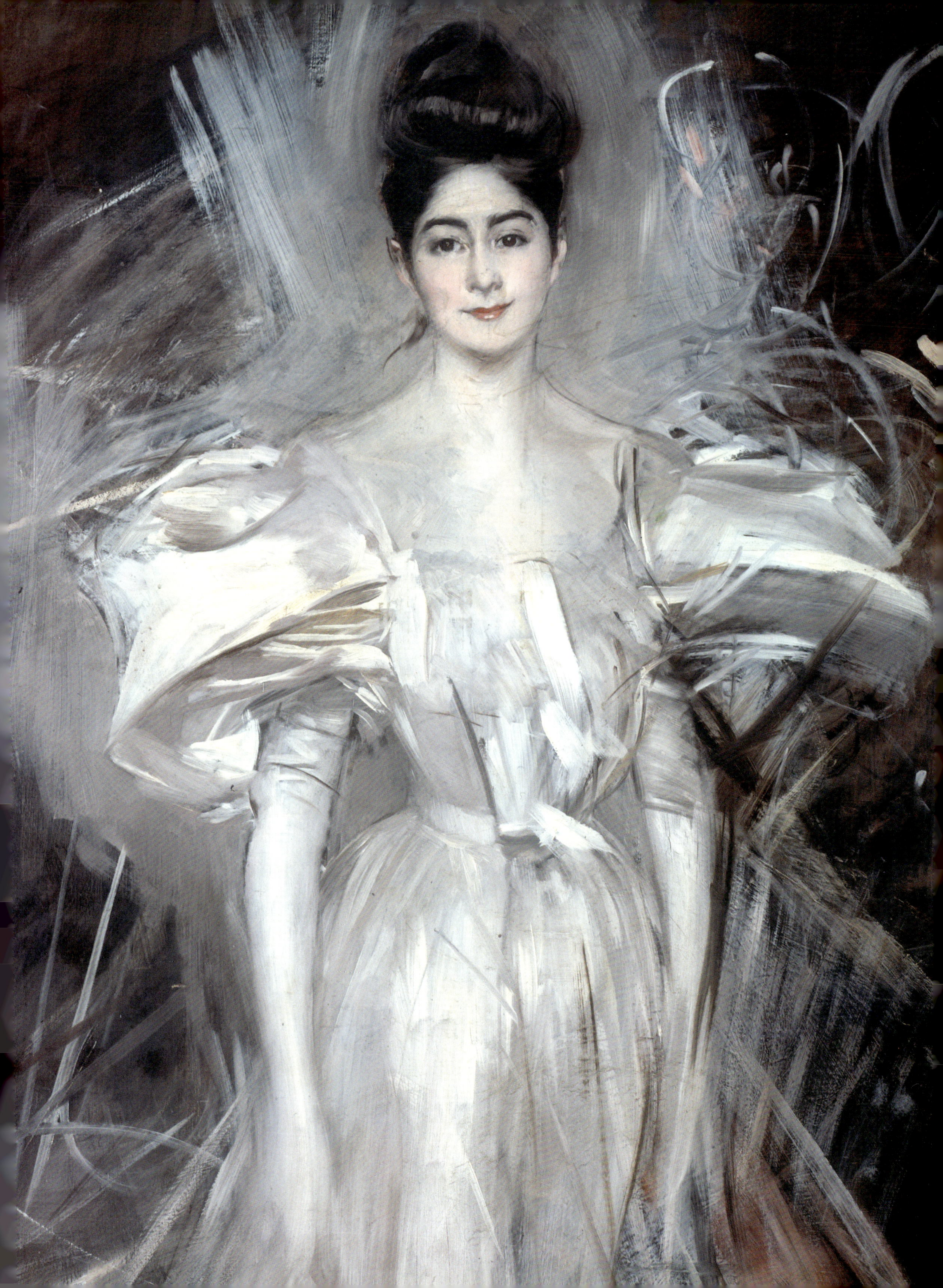

PORTRAIT OF THE ARTIST
The artist Lawrence Alexander Harrison was a friend and travelling companion of John Singer Sargent. Boldini's 1910 portrait, with its subtle palette and languid pose, has the glamour of a modern Gainsborough. *Courtesy akg-images*

LADY COLIN CAMPBELL
Lady Colin Campbell's direct gaze and self-confident air suggest that her scandalous divorce (her husband sued on the grounds of adultery, naming as co-respondents a duke, a surgeon, a general and London's fire chief) is long behind her in Boldini's 1897 portrait. *Courtesy National Portrait Gallery, London*

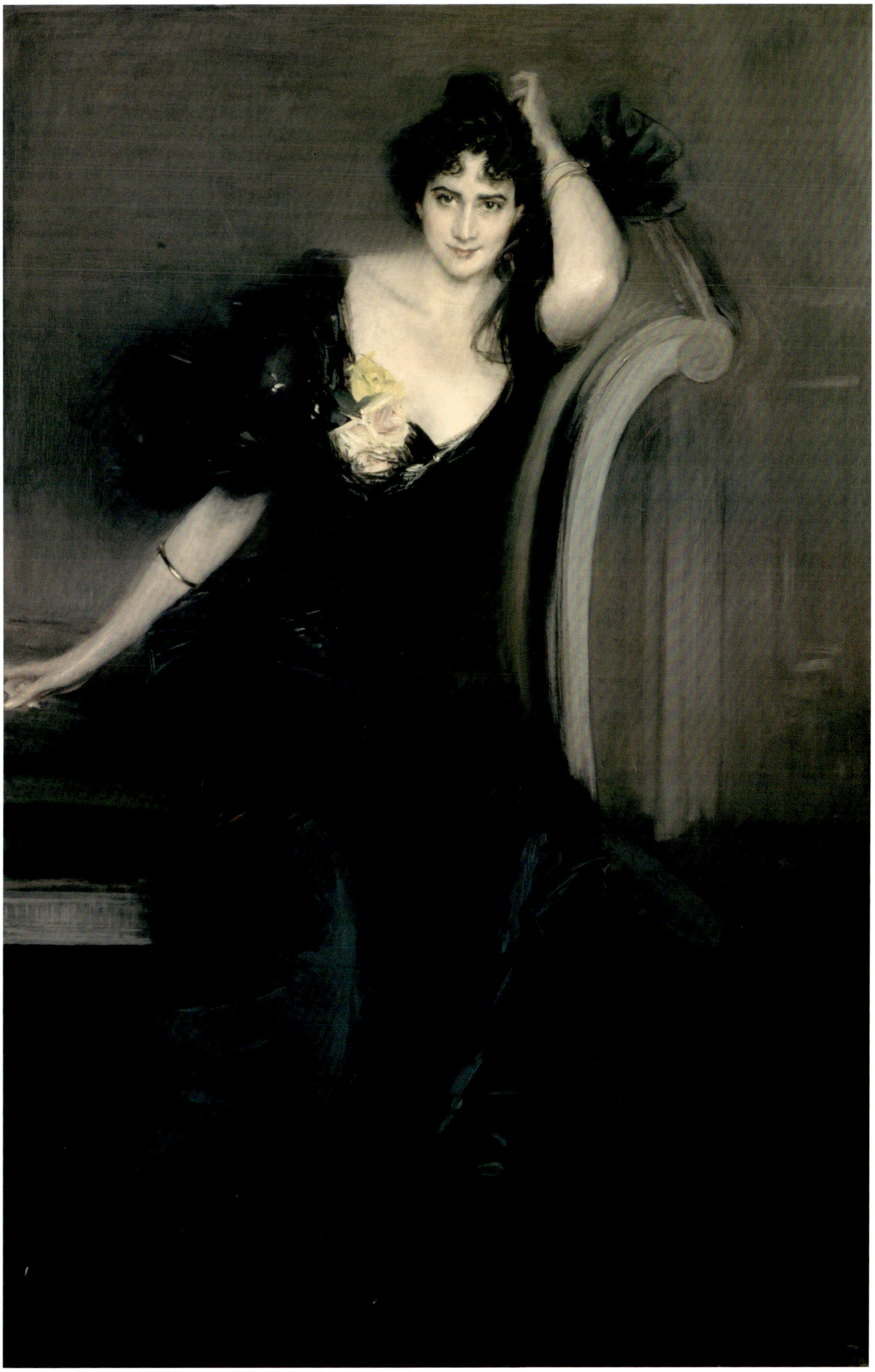

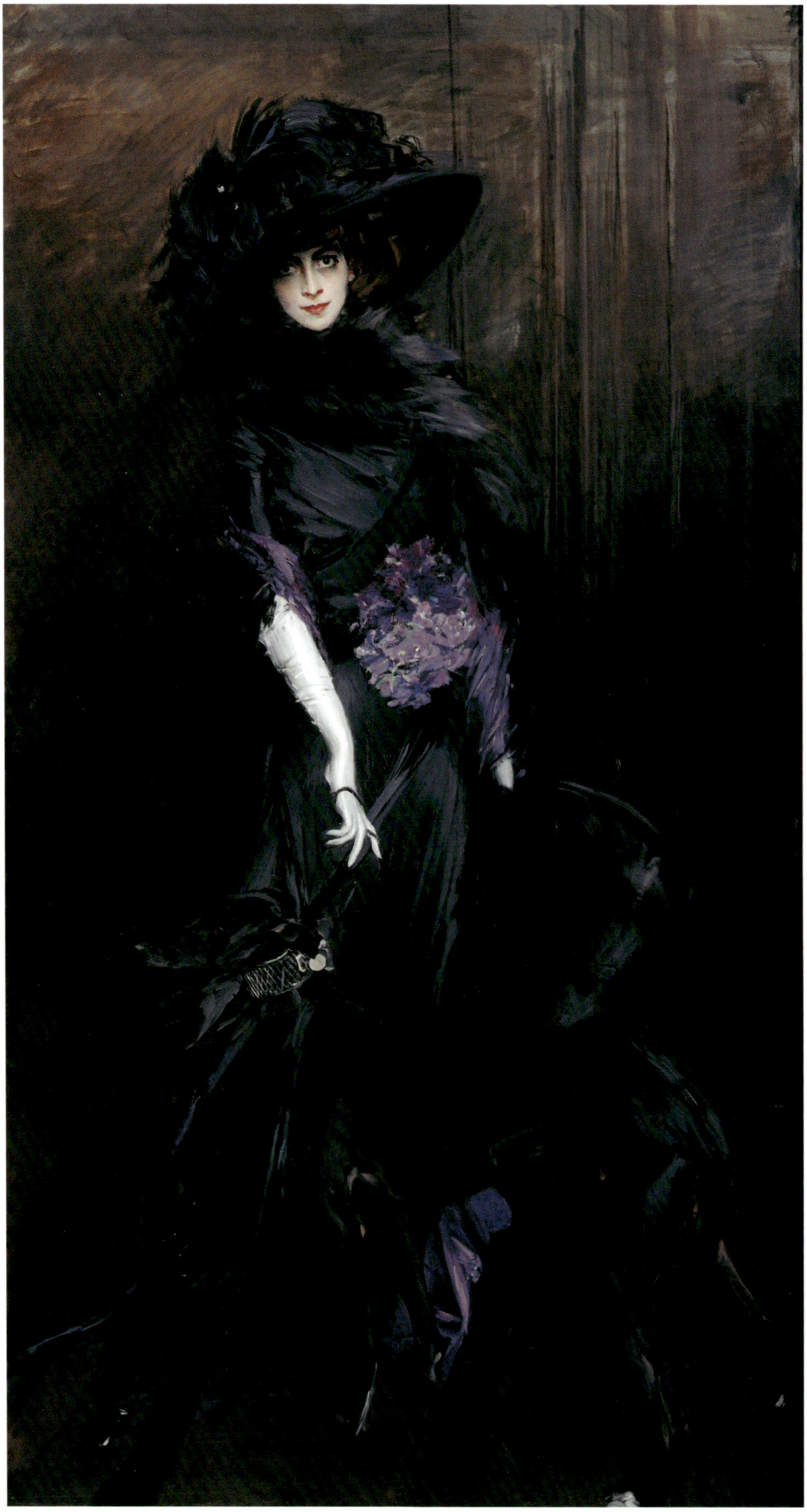

The relationship between artist, sitter and the public had been slowly evolving in the last quarter of the nineteenth century. Portraiture, once the preserve of the aristocracy, was increasingly seen as a form of social advancement by the *nouveau riche*, and as the scandal of Madame X slowly subsided it was clear that the *demi-monde* would no longer be excluded from the salon.

By the 1890s, Boldini had established himself as the most successful and sought-after portraitist of the day. Throughout the decade and beyond, a Proustian cast of actresses and heiresses, entrepreneurs and aesthetes found their way to the Boulevard Berthier studio. Commentators were divided: 'He is the magician of movement,' announced the choreographer Serge Lifar. 'The *non pareil* parent of the wriggle and chiffon school of portraiture,' sniffed Sickert. 'The artist of his age,' declared the caricaturist Sem.

It is unclear what Boldini made of the seismic shifts in the Paris art world of the early part of the twentieth century – what his reaction was to the appearance of the Fauves in 1905, or Picasso's *Les Demoiselles d'Avignon* in 1907 – and while some would later claim that his frenetic canvases marked him out as a Futurist, Boldini would certainly have deplored the outright misogyny of their early manifestos.

Boldini spent the war years in Nice and was awarded the *Légion d'honneur* in 1919. A notorious womanizer, he finally married, aged 86, in 1929; his bride, journalist Emilia Cardona, was several decades his junior. He continued to make portraits, but the florid style that had once been a barometer of the times was increasingly at odds with the Art Deco aesthetic.

Boldini died in 1931, and reviewing a posthumous exhibition in New York in 1933, *Time* magazine summed up the prevailing mood. 'He was the painter of the champagne supper and the ribbon-trimmed chemise,' it noted; 'the passing of the petticoat was the passing of his art.'

Boldini's reputation has fluctuated wildly in the intervening years. Critics outside Italy have tended to dismiss him as a sybaritic first cousin to Sargent and Whistler and tellingly, despite his work being in the collections of most of the world's great galleries, there is no monograph or *catalogue raisonné* in English. But for almost two decades Boldini captured the glimmer of the Golden Age, and how poignant his sitters look today, caught in his beautifying gaze as the world rushed towards modernity.

ARTIST AND MODEL
The caricaturist Georges Goursat (Sem) was a great friend of Boldini's, but that didn't prevent him from lampooning the diminutive and socially ambitious artist, here seen waltzing with the Marchesa Casati, circa 1914. *Private collection*

MUSE OF THE WORLD
The fabulously exotic Marchesa Casati would be immortalized by Augustus John, Kees Van Dongen and Man Ray, among many others, but it is Boldini's swirling kinetic portrait that perhaps best captures her enduring fascination (and baleful gaze). The dress is by Poiret. *Collection of Lord Lloyd Webber*

ARROW
COLLARS
& SHIRTS

J.C. LEYENDECKER

THE LEYENDECKER LOOK
With his classical sensibility and unerring eye for design, Leyendecker was one of the twentieth century's first true commercial artists. This quintessential Arrow Collar image appeared in 1923, three years after he won the first Annual of Advertising Art in the United States award. *Courtesy National Museum of American Illustration*

In the early years of the twentieth century, before audiences could put names to movie stars – before Douglas Fairbanks and John Gilbert and Rudolph Valentino flickered onto the screen, silvery pale and high on emotion – the original American idol (and fashion icon) was… a drawing.

The Arrow Collar Man made his first appearance in 1905, advertising dress collars and shirts. Handsome, athletic, firm of jaw and untroubled of brow, he bore the faint flush of someone who knew they were being stared at. He was the creation of the artist J.C. Leyendecker, who would paint him countless times over the next twenty-five years. Sometimes he appeared alone, gazing soulfully from an ornate frame; as often, he formed part of a narrative tableau, golfing, riding, sailing or dressed for the theatre. In these pursuits he is accompanied by a coterie of good-looking male friends. The barely concealed subtext, of course, was one of homosexual desire. Leyendecker's most consistent model for the Arrow Collar Man was the handsome, graceful and athletic Charles Beach, who would become his life-long partner. However, audiences in the 1910s and 1920s may hardly have noticed the simmering homoeroticism, and we should be wary of viewing the work through a twenty-first-century prism. The Arrow Collar Man worked because he was brilliantly conceived and executed by Leyendecker: women swooned over him; men dreamt of being him. He was a matinée idol, a hero, a fashion icon and a brand, and because of him, Leyendecker became the most successful and sought-after illustrator of his day.

Joseph Christian Leyendecker was born in Montabaur, in southwestern Germany, in 1874. He emigrated with his family to Chicago when he was 8, and by the time he was in his teens he already had ambitions to become an artist. Apparently it ran in the family; both his younger brother Francis 'F.X.' and his older brother Adolph would also pursue artistic careers.

Aged 15, Leyendecker was made an apprentice to an engraving firm, J. Manz & Co. He studied at the Chicago Institute at night and took what freelance work he could find. After winning a prestigious first prize for his cover of *Century* magazine in 1896, he spent a year studying with his brother Francis in Paris. There, he came into contact with a brilliant group of graphic artists including Jules Chéret and Alphonse Mucha, whose work would have a telling influence on him. While in Paris, Leyendecker also staged his first one-man show, at the Salon du Champs de Mars.

The brothers returned to Chicago the following year, and in 1900 they moved to New York. By now Leyendecker was working steadily; he had already produced his first covers for *Collier's* and *The Saturday Evening Post*, magazines with which he would become indelibly associated in later years. Gradually, his natural flair and newly acquired European polish coalesced into the recognizable 'Leyendecker Look'.

GENTLEMEN AND PLAYERS
Audiences were enthralled by the Arrow Collar Man's privileged world of refinement and ease. Leyendecker's handsome protagonists are seen here in 1914, as yet untroubled by world events. *Courtesy National Museum of American Illustration*

ACES HIGH
Leyendecker's vital (and visible) brushwork enlivens this characteristically heroic study of a World War I pilot. This painting was executed for the cover of *Collier's* magazine in 1917. Three years earlier, Norman Rockwell had dubbed Leyendecker 'The Master of the Magazine Cover'. *Courtesy National Museum of American Illustration*

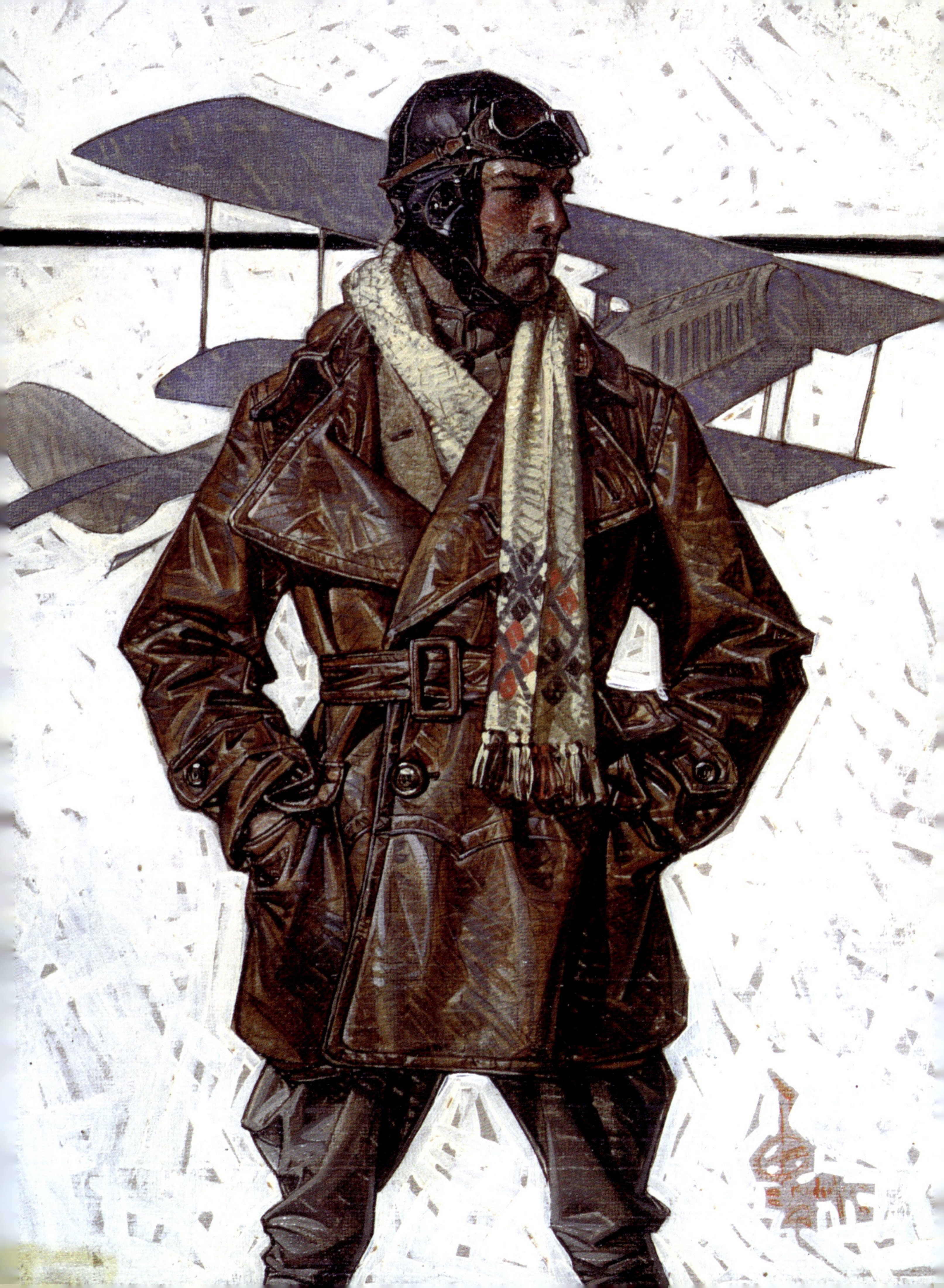

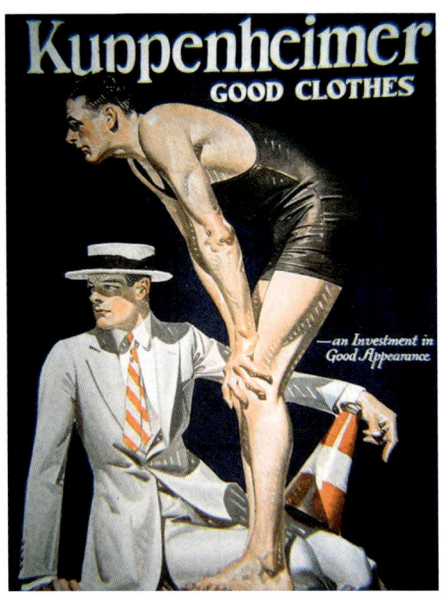

The success of the Arrow Collar campaign resulted in advertising commissions from Kellogg's and Ivory Soap, among others. At the same time, Leyendecker began to assert his dominance as a magazine cover artist. He would produce more than 300 covers for The Saturday Evening Post over a period of forty-four years, and there is no doubt that he was instrumental in creating the iconic look and feel of that magazine. His subjects were perennial: the Fourth of July, Thanksgiving, Mother's Day and Christmas. He introduced the New Year Baby, sent America's youth to two world wars and welcomed them home as heroes. He pre-dated Norman Rockwell (who idolized him) as the originator, and purveyor, of the American Dream. Though they covered much the same territory, the two artists differed significantly in their approach. For Leyendecker, everyday narratives were shot through with glamour; his sweethearts looked like movie stars, his baseball players were paragons of Olympian beauty. Rockwell, on the other hand, championed the little guy and homed in on everyday scenarios.

After a period in New York, Leyendecker moved with his brother and sister to a sprawling estate at New Rochelle, where Beach joined them in 1915. By now he was a nationally celebrated figure, wealthy and enormously prolific. Throughout the 1920s, his Gatsby-esque Arrow Collar advertisements defined the mood and the look of the time. Gradually though, the sands shifted. The Arrow Collar man was 'retired' in 1930, and Leyendecker completed his last Saturday Evening Post cover in 1943. By the time of his death eight years later, at the age of 77, he was all but forgotten and Rockwell had replaced him as America's favourite artist.

In recent years, Leyendecker's reputation has been re-evaluated, and today he is acknowledged both as a master illustrator and as the creator of a masculine ideal whose twenty-first-century descendants stare down from the billboards of Abercrombie & Fitch.

AD MAN

Kuppenheimer Good Clothes and Interwoven Socks were two long-running advertising campaigns that Leyendecker worked on, beginning in 1908. An Interwoven Socks image dating from 1921 is still used today by the American retailer Paul Stuart Clothing. *Courtesy The Advertising Archive*

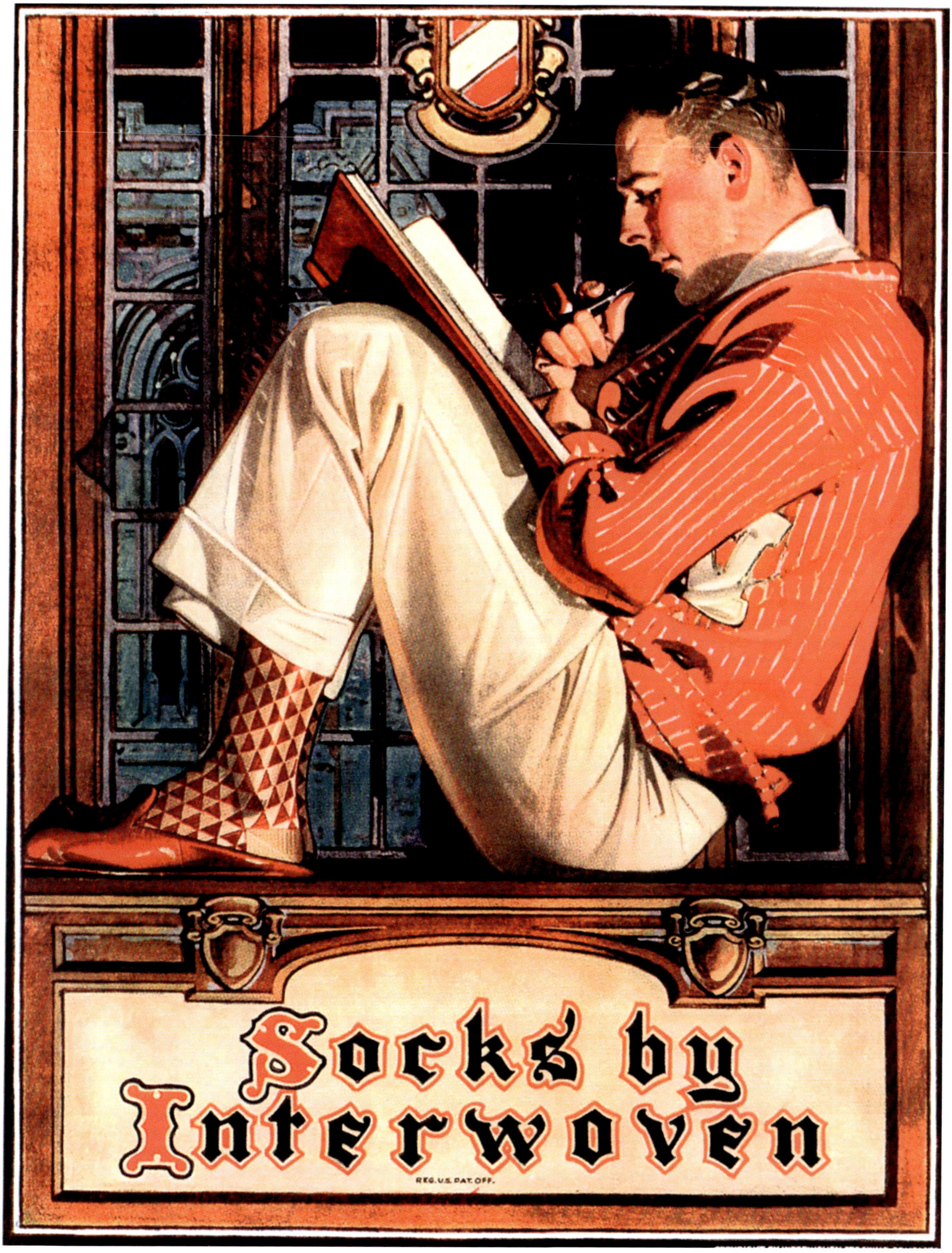
Socks by
Interwoven
REG. U.S. PAT. OFF.

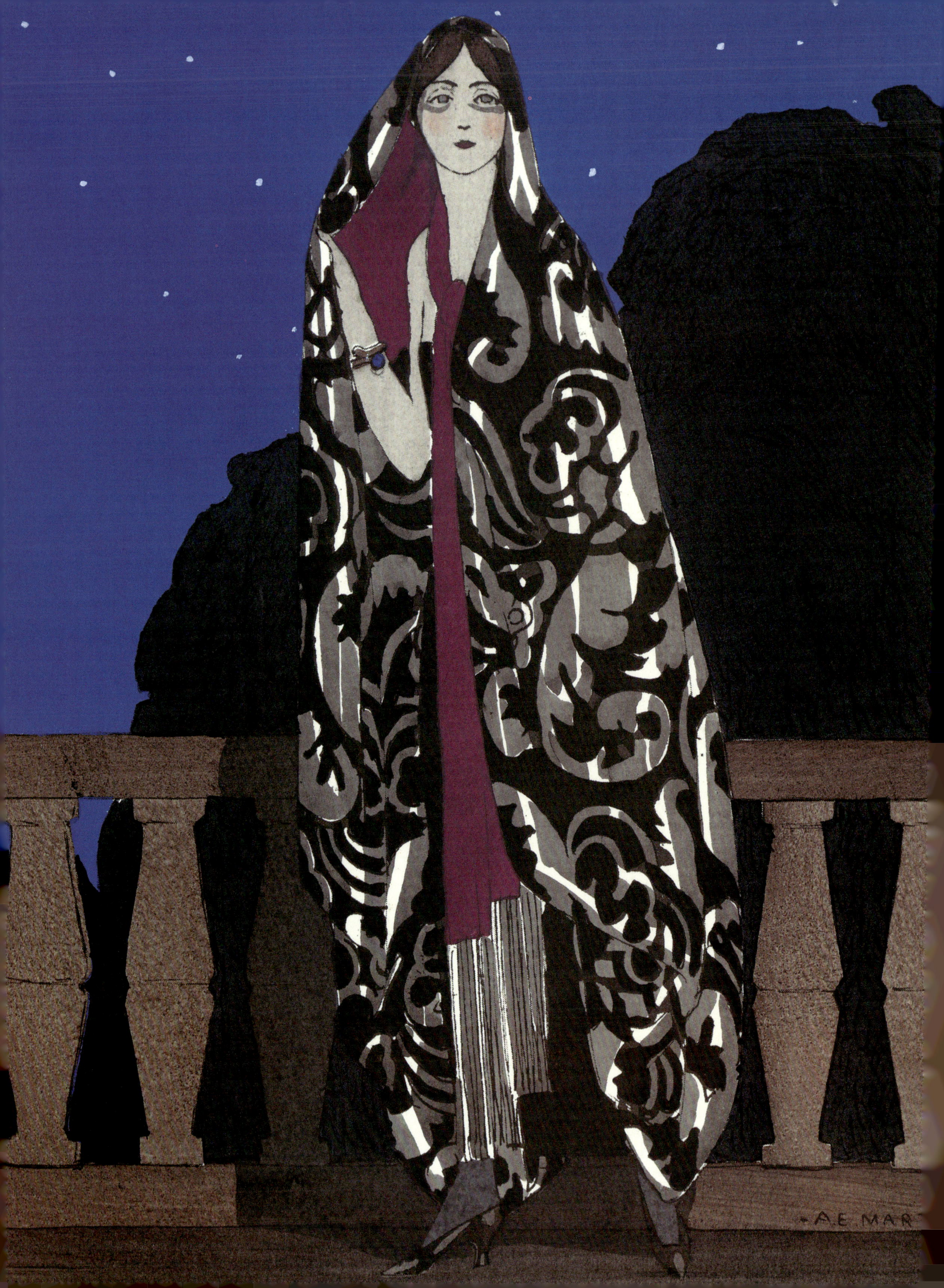
A.E. MAR

GAZETTE ARTISTS

ANDRÉ-EDOUARD MARTY
Of all the *Gazette* artists, Marty (1882–1932) was perhaps the most romantic and elegiac. He trained at the École des Beaux-Arts in Paris, and enjoyed a long career, producing designs for posters, book covers and ceramics. *C'est Moi*, pochoir plate, evening cloak by Poiret, 1922. *Courtesy Tony Glenville*

In his wonderfully self-regarding memoir, *My First Fifty Years*, published in 1930 at the tail end of his starburst career, the couturier Paul Poiret reflected that his 'most efficacious influence' could be seen in his collaborations with artists. Rising to prominence in the years before the outbreak of World War I, Poiret was known as the King of Fashion, the Pasha of Paris or simply as *le magnifique*. He was the couturier who freed women from the constraints of the corset, who echoed the swooning exoticism of Diaghilev and the Ballets Russes, and who, by aligning fashion, interiors, fragrance and accessories, became the first designer to promote the concept of 'lifestyle'. In 1908, to publicize his Directoire collection, Poiret commissioned an album of drawings by a young French graduate of the École des Beaux-Arts, Paul Iribe. The result, *Les robes de Paul Poiret racontées par Paul Iribe*, was startling. Printed in large format on heavy quality paper, Iribe's illustrations were fluid, pared down and rigorously graphic. Blocks of colour were used to delineate Poiret's tubular Empire shapes, while backgrounds were reduced to a scratchy, theatrical scrim. Prior to this, fashion illustration had been seen more as a craft than as an art form. The highly detailed (and often sumptuous) fashion plates of the latter half of the nineteenth century described the ribbon and the trim, but all too often had a lifeless 'cabinet of curiosities' quality. The collaboration between Poiret and Iribe marked the birth of modern fashion illustration. Three years later, Poiret commissioned a second album, this time from Georges Lepape, an aspiring portrait painter also from Les Beaux-Arts, and fashion illustration came of age.

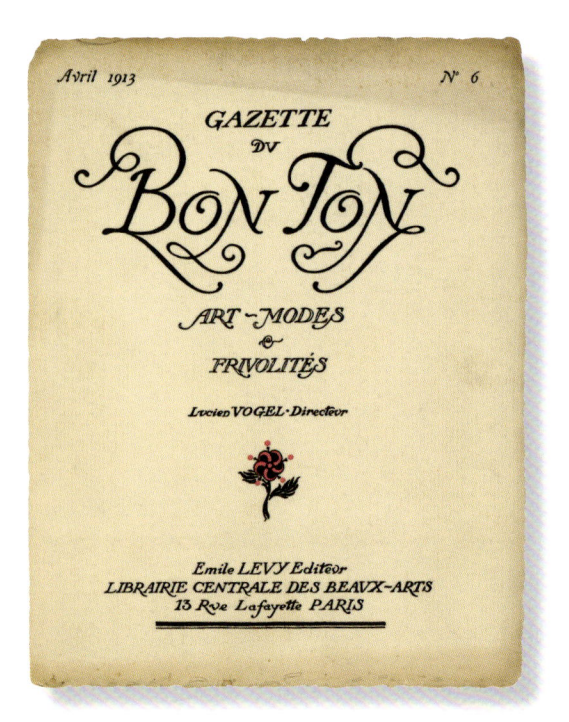

STYLE BIBLE
The *Gazette*'s beautifully simple typographic cover.
Courtesy Tony Glenville

**BERNARD BOUTET
DE MONVEL** (overleaf, left)
Boutet de Monvel (1884–1949) was the son of the celebrated illustrator Maurice Boutet de Monvel. Born in Paris, he worked for *Vogue* and *Harper's Bazaar* before turning to portraiture. His early illustrations for the *Gazette* had a distinctive, linear clarity. *Le Choix Difficile*, pochoir plate, 1914. *Courtesy Tony Glenville*

PIERRE BRISSAUD (overleaf, right)
Brissaud (1885–1964) was the cousin of Bernard Boutet de Monvel and, like many of his peers, he trained at the École des Beaux-Arts. His illustrations had a great density and narrative wit. He would later work for *Vogue* and *House and Garden* as well as illustrating several books, including Flaubert's *Madame Bovary*. *A l'Opéra*, pochoir plate, 1920. *Courtesy Tony Glenville*

It was at an exhibition to promote the launch of Lepape's album in 1911 that Poiret met publisher and art director Lucien Vogel. Vogel was a young man in a hurry. Inspired by the success of Poiret's albums, he was planning to launch a new review, the *Gazette du Bon Ton*. The *Gazette*, which would be broadly based on a nineteenth-century periodical called *Le Journal des Dames et des Modes*, had a bold ambition: to commandeer the skills of the most talented and innovative artists, writers and couturiers, and produce an unashamedly elitist – and expensive – journal celebrating fashion, travel, interiors and *les arts du vivre* (a rough equivalent today would be a combination of *Vogue*, *Vanity Fair* and *World of Interiors*). To that end, Vogel had already enlisted the artists André Marty and Pierre Brissaud; now he added not only Lepape, but his circle of friends and associates from the École des Beaux-Arts – George Barbier, Charles Martin and Bernard Boutet de Monvel. As a group they were celebrated as the 'Beau Brummels of the Brush' and the 'Knights of the Bracelet'. In a further coup, Vogel also enlisted the help of the leading couturiers of the day: Beer, Cheruit, Doeuillet, Doucet, Lanvin, Paquin, Poiret, Redfern and Worth, who agreed that an exclusive design would be unveiled in each issue.

The *Gazette* was launched in 1912, and was printed in a smaller format than Poiret's albums, but on similarly luxurious paper. It contained editorial, illustrations and advertising, but at its heart were the loose-leaf fashion plates created by its core group of artists. There were up to ten in each issue, seven promoting the couturiers' designs and three showcasing clothes designed by the artists themselves – the most emphatic blurring yet of the boundary between art and fashion. The plates had witty or elliptical captions and, like Poiret's albums before them, were realized using the laborious pochoir process. This involved cutting a stencil in zinc or bronze for each colour, and then applying paint (usually gouache) in layers by hand. As many as thirty or forty stencils might be necessary to replicate the artist's original for a single plate. A new typeface, Cochin, designed by Georges Peignot, was utilized, and the strapline '*Art, Modes et Frivolités*' underlined the *Gazette*'s areas of interest. 'When fashion becomes an art, a fashion gazette must itself become an arts magazine, such is *Gazette du Bon Ton*…,' announced an editorial in the first issue. The *Gazette* was an instant success; aimed unequivocally at the social elite (but happy to send it up), it was beautifully mounted, witty, erudite and, above all, glorious to look at.

CHARLES MARTIN
Martin (1884–1934) trained at the École des Beaux-Arts and at the Académie Julian in Paris. He contributed regularly to the *Gazette* and also to its rivals *Le Journal des Dames et des Modes* and *Modes et Manieres d'Aujourd'hui*. He went on to design for the theatre and the ballet. *Hindoustan*, pochoir plate, fashion by Poiret, 1920. *Courtesy Tony Glenville*

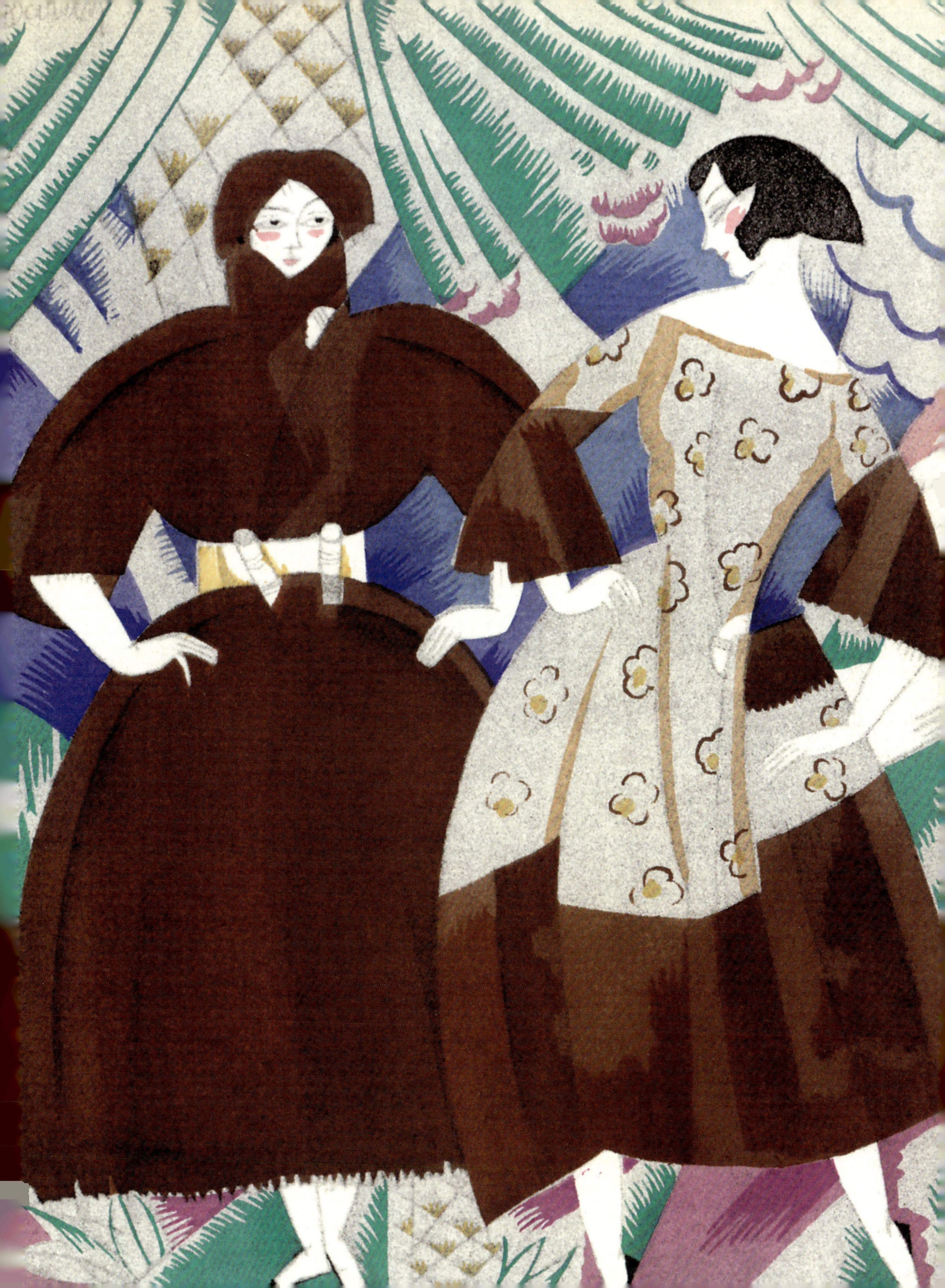

LE CHOIX DIFFICILE

Manteau du soir de Worth

Gazette du Bon Ton. — N° 4   Avril 1914. — Pl. 40

A L'OPÉRA

Manteau et robe, pour le soir, de Jeanne Lanvin

N° 10 de la Gazette du Bon Ton   Année 1920. Planche 77

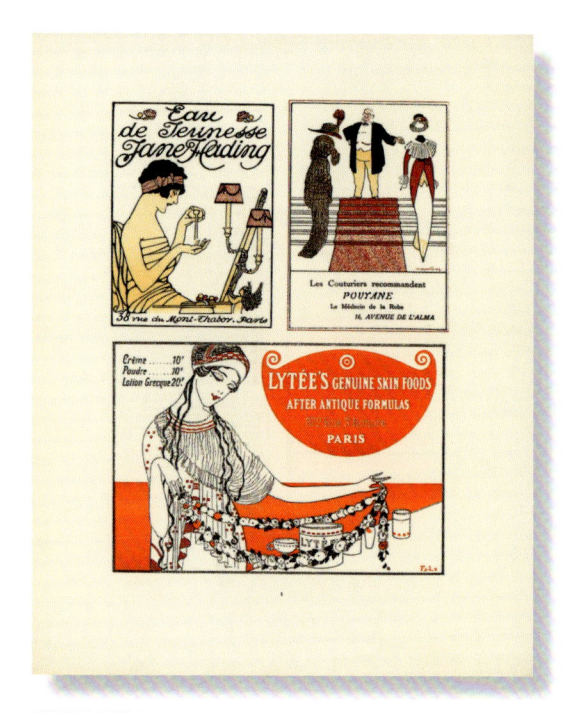

SOFT SELL
Even the *Gazette*'s advertisements were beautiful.
Courtesy Tony Glenville

The *Gazette* proved to be a perfect showcase for its artists. Channelling the creative *air du temps*, they embraced the drama of Nijinsky, the colour palette of the Fauves and the restrained rigour of Japanese prints. In May 1914, the *Gazette*'s couturiers held a dinner in the gardens of Poiret's rue Auber mansion, celebrating 'eighteen happy months' of publication. There were dancing girls (in neoclassical tunics, naturally) and fireworks. Within months, however, the outbreak of World War I closed down publication. A special, single edition went out in 1915, patriotically talking up the success of Paris' designers in America. Drian contributed a stunning suite of drawings (see pages 46–49) exploring the poignant dislocation between the privations of war and the world of high fashion. An editorial set out the *Gazette*'s attitude: 'As a contribution to the heroic struggle, Paris has created its own brand of wartime elegance, a gay, sporty and casual style allowing complete freedom of movement, be it in lifting the unfortunate wounded or even wielding a weapon... and since Latin taste is fighting Teutonic barbarity, was it not a good thing that Paris should take the lead as always over the Spring fashions?'

Gazette du Bon Ton was relaunched in 1920. Its aims were as lofty as before, but there had been a slew of imitators and the world had changed inexorably. Vogel himself was turning his attention elsewhere; he published *Les Feuillets d'Art* in 1919 and *L'Illustration des Modes* in 1920. He sold the *Gazette* in 1921 and joined Condé Nast, becoming art director of French *Vogue*. Later he would launch two new magazines, *Lu* and *Vu*; significantly, both utilized photography rather than drawing.

The last issue of *Gazette du Bon Ton* was published in 1925; in all there were twelve volumes and sixty-nine issues. The artists scattered. Many worked in America for *Vogue* and *Harper's Bazaar* and for Hollywood and Broadway. They designed costumes and backdrops, painted portraits and illustrated books. All would go on to productive careers, but never again would one publication unite so many dazzling and disparate talents.

GEORGE BARBIER
Barbier (1882–1932) was a brilliant decorative artist, designer and writer. Highly prolific and endlessly inventive, in addition to contributing to the *Gazette* he illustrated books and designed costumes for the movies (including Valentino's *Monsieur Beaucaire*), the ballet and the theatre. *La Fontaine de Coquillages*, pochoir plate, dress by Paquin, 1914. *Courtesy Tony Glenville*

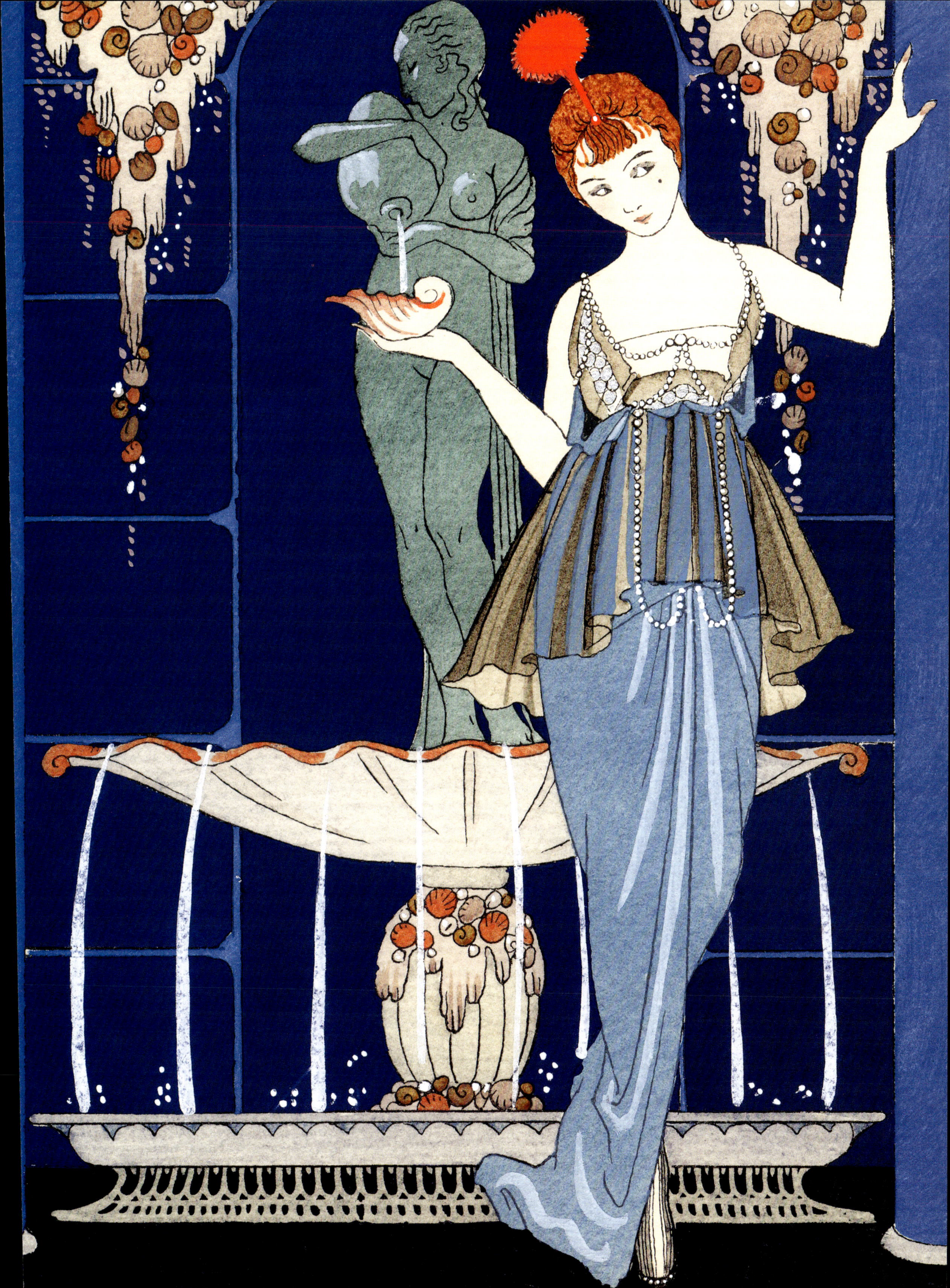

Drian

GRAPHIC MASTER
Drian's superb illustrations for a special wartime issue of *Gazette du Bon Ton* in 1915 *(left and overleaf)* utilized all his skills as a draughtsman and graphic artist. These brilliantly composed images anticipate René Gruau by almost three decades.
Courtesy Tony Glenville

ÉTIENNE DRIAN

Of all the fashion artists who rose to prominence in Paris before World War I, Drian was the one who kept his head. While Barbier, Marty and Lepape embarked on ever more daring experiments with perspective, colour and surface design, Drian drew what he saw. Working from life, his models are notable for their elegant – but distinctly flesh and blood – beauty. As his peers embraced Orientalism and dreams of *1001 Nights*, Drian explored the inherent possibilities of line. In many ways, his gestural brushwork and grand manner marked him out as a natural successor to Boldini, while his fluid line and controlled graphic sensibility anticipated the masters of the next generation, Eric and Gruau.

SANS SA VOITURE

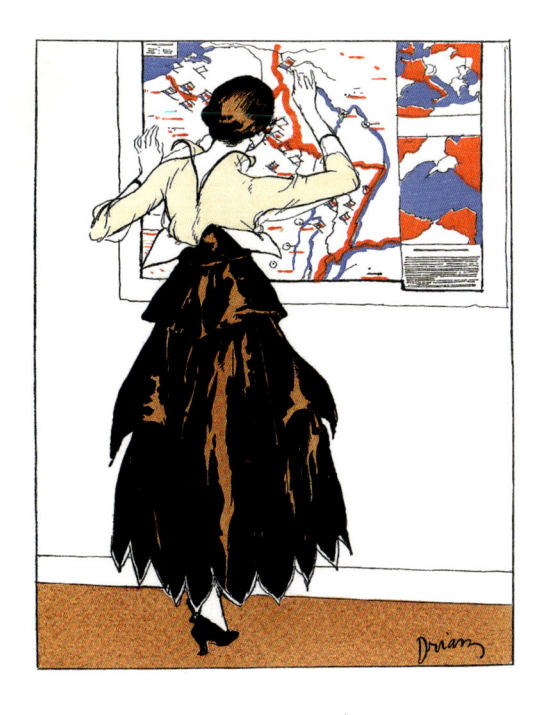

EN SUIVANT LES OPÉRATIONS

LE COMMUNIQUÉ

BOUQUET TRICOLORE

LA MARSEILLAISE

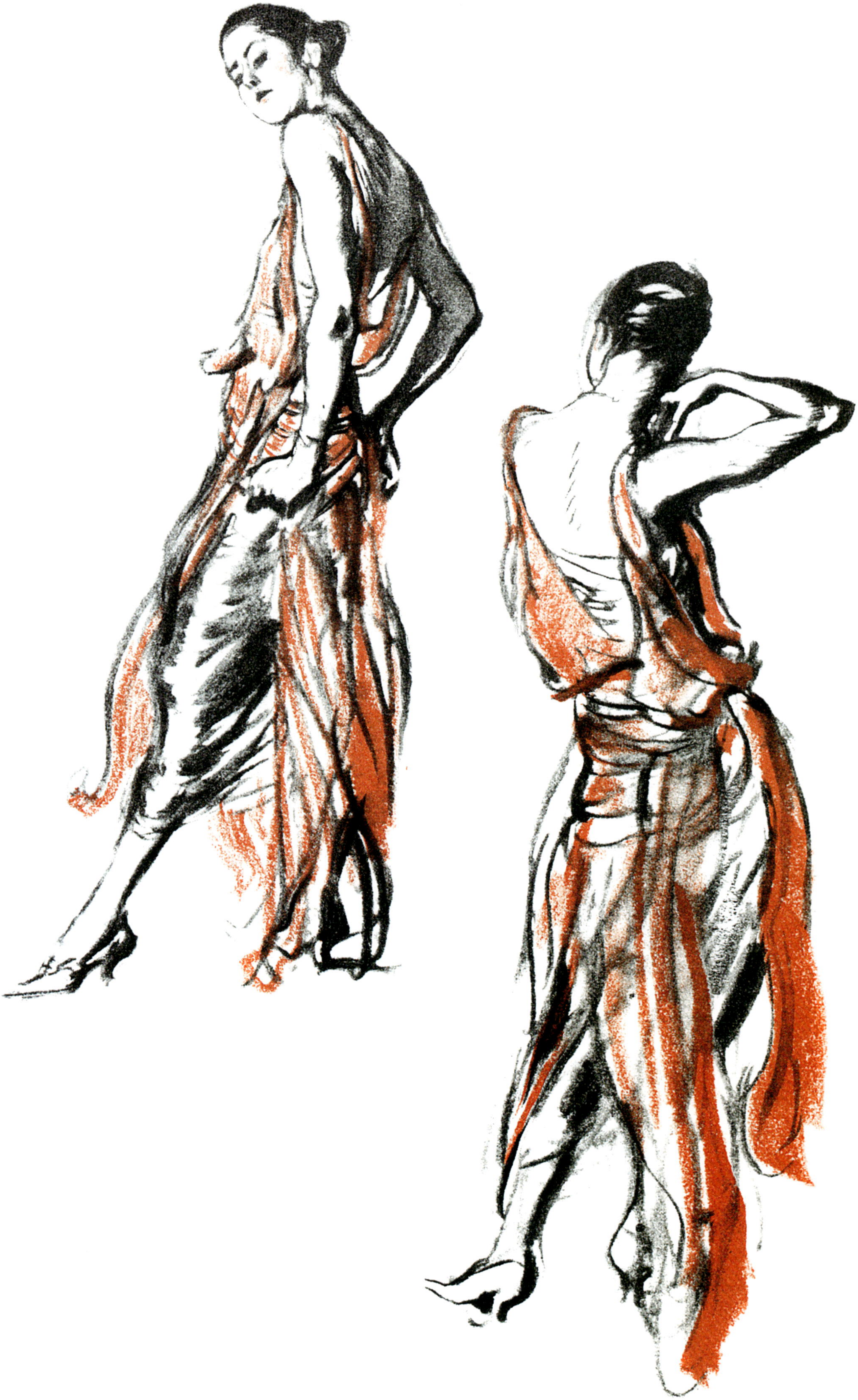

Drian was born Adrien Désiré Étienne, in Bulgnéville in the Lorraine region of France, in 1885. After studying at the Académie Julian in Paris, where he adopted the pseudonym Drian, he quickly established himself as one of the leading illustrators in the growing number of exclusive publications dedicated to fashion and *les arts du vivre*. He was not among the seven original 'Knights of the Bracelet' brought into *Gazette du Bon Ton* by Lucien Vogel, but he became a regular contributor, as he would to Vogel's short-lived *Les Feuillets d'Art* and Tom Antongini's *Le Journal des Dames et des Modes*.

After the war, Drian continued to work with the leading fashion magazines such as *L'Illustration* and *Femina* in France and, in 1921, he was introduced with some fanfare to the American readers of *Harper's Bazar* (the second 'a' was added only later, in 1929). 'He has consented,' announced a gushing editor's letter, 'to illustrate frequent short stories, and to present his intimate glimpses of Parisian life.' At the same time, Drian began illustrating novels, fairy tales and short stories by Perrault, Jean Lorrain and Sacha Guitry, among others.

As his reputation as an artist and taste-maker grew (in his book *The Glass of Fashion*, Cecil Beaton claimed that Drian was 'one of the few who had a genius for knowing exactly where to place furniture in a room'), Drian took on a broad range of commissions: he designed windows for the department store Lord & Taylor in America; a spectacular mirrored office for the couturier Molyneux in Paris; and murals and screens for the legendary interior designer Elsie de Wolfe. (Drian's delirious portrait of de Wolfe bestriding the Atlantic gazed down from the ceiling of her Versailles home Villa Trianon.)

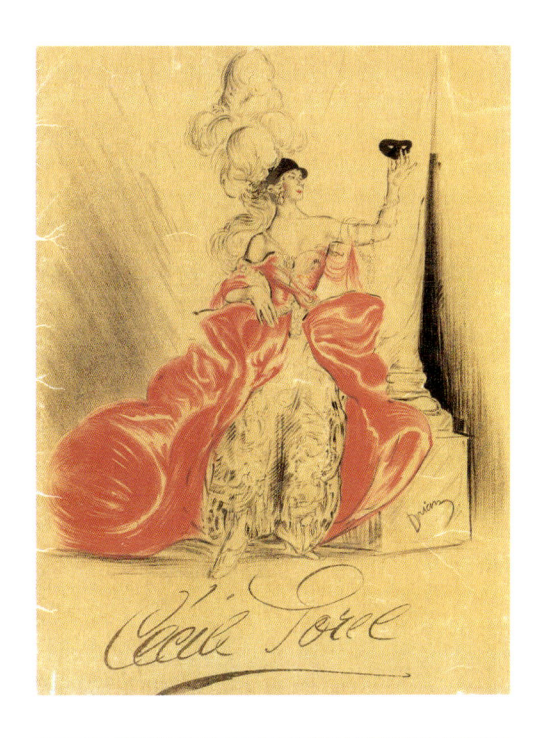

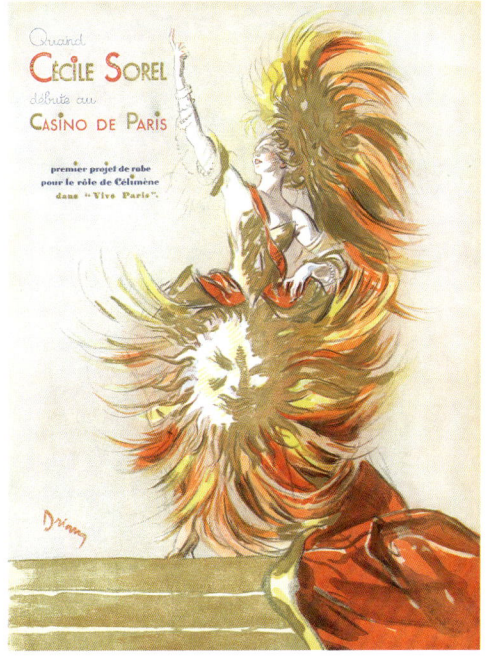

CÉCILE SOREL
In June 1933, at the age of 60, Cécile Sorel gave a farewell performance as a tragedienne at the Comédie Française. By October that year, she had reinvented herself as a musical comedy star and opened at the Casino de Paris. Drian designed the programmes for both productions. 'What does the Arc de Triomphe care if a dog pisses on it!' was her memorable riposte to critics. *Courtesy Tony Glenville*

LA PARURE DU GESTE
A typically convincing drawing (note the way the beautifully posed feet take the weight of the body) for the French magazine *Femina*, in 1922.
Private collection

Drian never entirely abandoned the world of fashion; in 1937, for example, he recorded what may have been the first celebrity fashion show, when Gloria Guinness and Lady Thelma Furness – 'It Girls' of their day – designed and modelled a collection at Harrods in London. With an ever-expanding network of social contacts, it was perhaps inevitable that Drian spent the last phase of his career principally as a portrait painter, and his large-scale oils of society beauties – and occasionally their families – were as flattering as they were popular.

Drian, who died in 1961, holds a unique place in the history of fashion illustration, bridging the gap between the great stylists of the pre-World War I era and the studied ease of the mid-century masters. 'To me, he is the greatest,' said René Gruau; '…a span ahead of the others: Eric, Lepape, Marty, Benito.'

UNE PARISIENNE
This witty illustration, circa 1923, shows Drian's mastery of high-contrast black and white.
Private collection

WALLIS SIMPSON
The Duchess of Windsor was a perennial favourite with fashion illustrators, from Cecil Beaton to Antonio Lopez. Drian's full-blown romantic portrait, in what Suzy Menkes memorably described as 'sweet pea colours,' was painted in 1938. Later the Duke and Duchess bought Drian's country home, Moulin de la Tuilerie, near Paris, and transformed it into a corner of France that would be 'Forever England'. *Courtesy The Bridgeman Art Library*

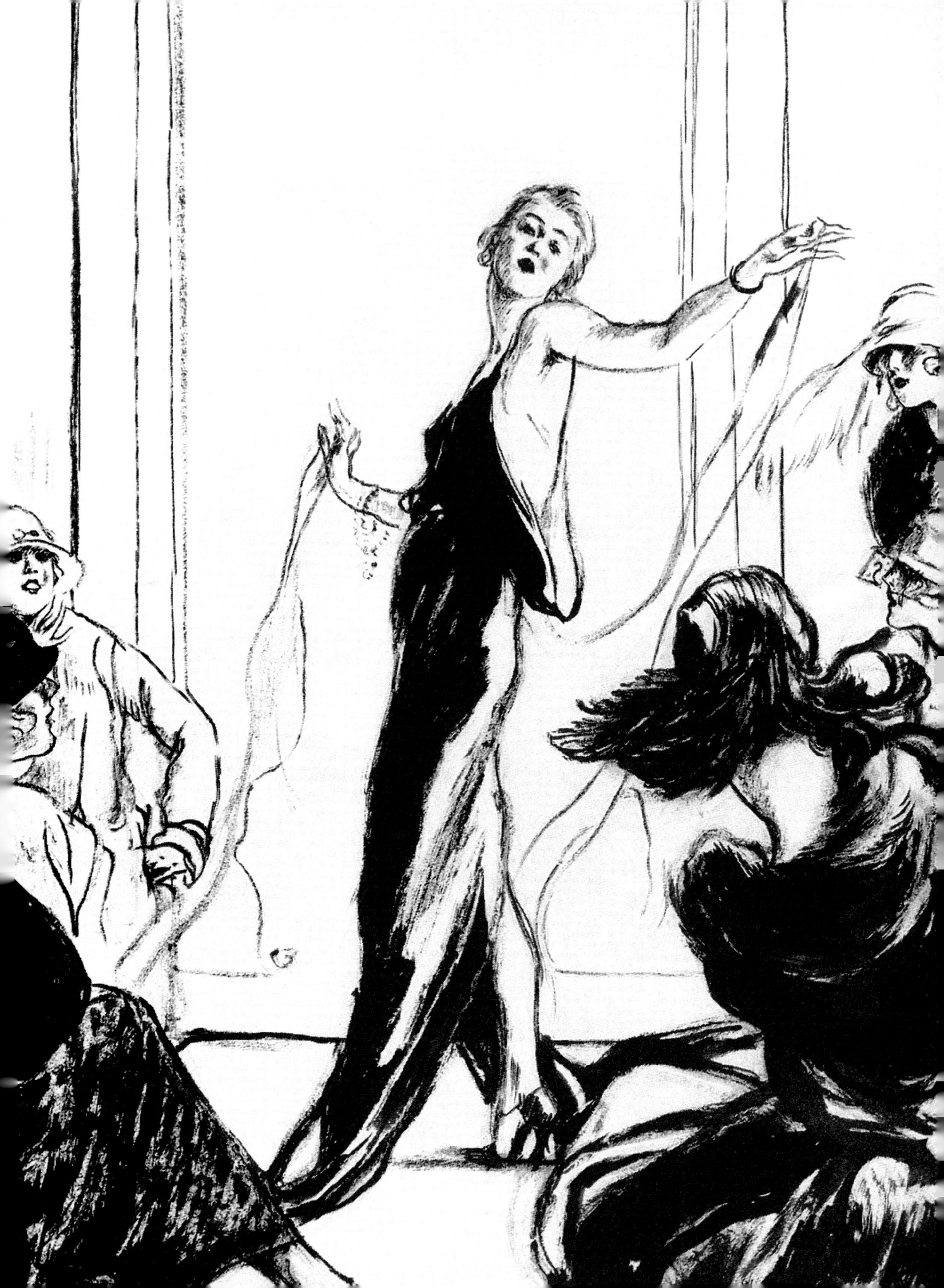

HARPER'S BAZAAR

INCORPORATING "VANITY FAIR"

JUNE 1931

EARLY SUMMER
FASHIONS

ERTÉ

As a fledgling designer for Paul Poiret in pre-World War I Paris, Erté designed costumes for Mata Hari. At his 90th birthday party in New York, in 1982, he was photographed by Andy Warhol and serenaded by Diana Ross; a testament to his astonishing longevity and enduring fame. For almost eight decades, Erté's singular vision, unshakable work ethic and seemingly unstoppable flow of ideas set trends and, just as frequently, defied fashion.

He was born Romain de Tirtoff (Erté is the phonetic French pronunciation of his initials 'R' and 'T'), into a distinguished family in St. Petersburg, in 1892. The cultural and theatrical life of that pre-revolutionary city would exert a life-long influence, but by 1912, when it was obvious that he would not be following in the family naval tradition (his father was an admiral), Erté's parents were persuaded to let him go to Paris. He enrolled at the Académie Julian, with the idea of becoming a portrait painter. But by the following year, perhaps inevitably, he had found his way to Paul Poiret's *atelier*. Poiret, recognizing Erté's love of theatricality and excess, hired him on the spot. Through Poiret, Erté met Lucien Vogel, and his first signed fashion illustrations appeared in *Gazette du Bon Ton* in 1913.

In 1914, a virulent and potentially dangerous bout of scarlet fever prompted Erté to leave Paris for a healthier climate and he set up house in Monte Carlo, with his cousin Prince Nicholas Ouroussoff. In need of income, he submitted a series of sketches to *Harper's Bazar* (the second 'a' was added only later, in 1929) in America and the following year his first cover appeared, the beginning of a twenty-two-year association. In all Erté would produce 240 covers for the magazine.

HARPER'S BAZAAR
As shiny as shellac and throbbing with jewel-like colour, Erté's covers for *Harper's Bazaar* in the 1930s are masterpieces of Art Deco design.
Courtesy The Mary Evans Picture Library

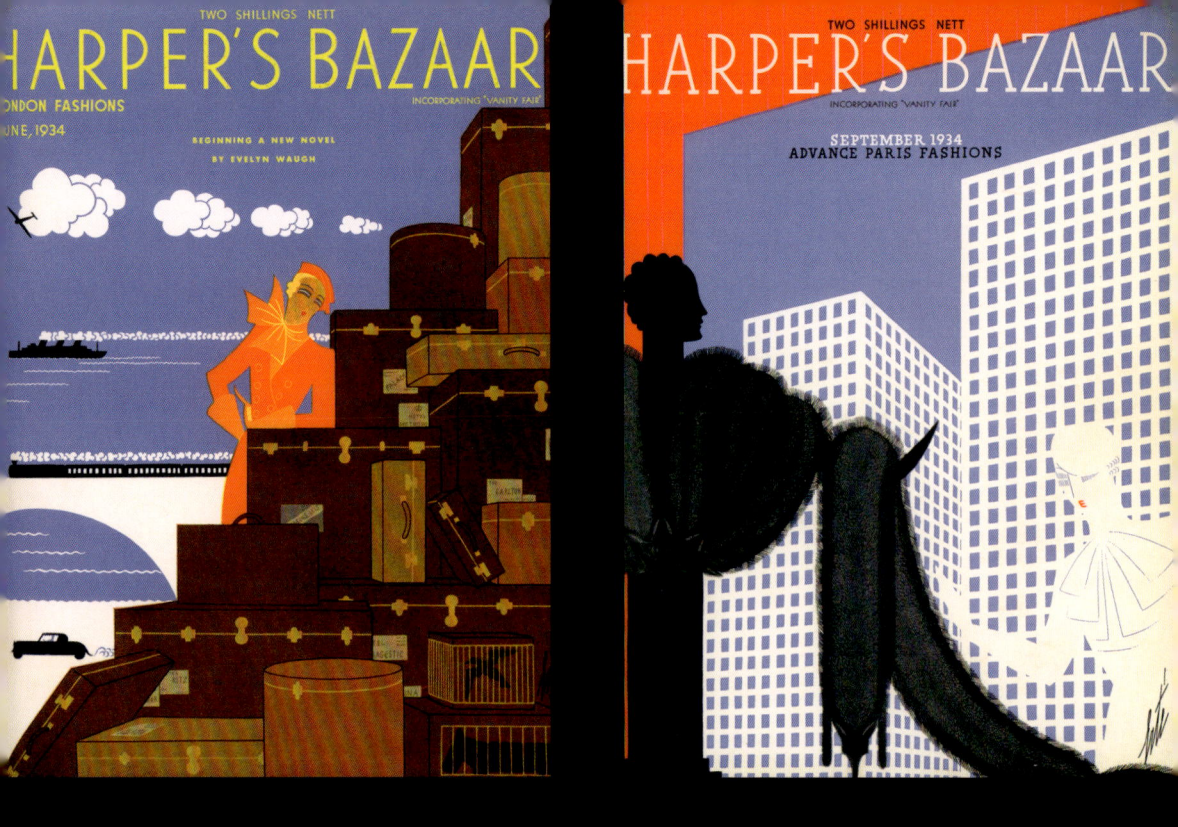

HARPER'S BAZAAR
TWO SHILLINGS NETT
LONDON FASHIONS
JUNE, 1934
BEGINNING A NEW NOVEL BY EVELYN WAUGH

HARPER'S BAZAAR
TWO SHILLINGS NETT
INCORPORATING "VANITY FAIR"
SEPTEMBER 1934
ADVANCE PARIS FASHIONS

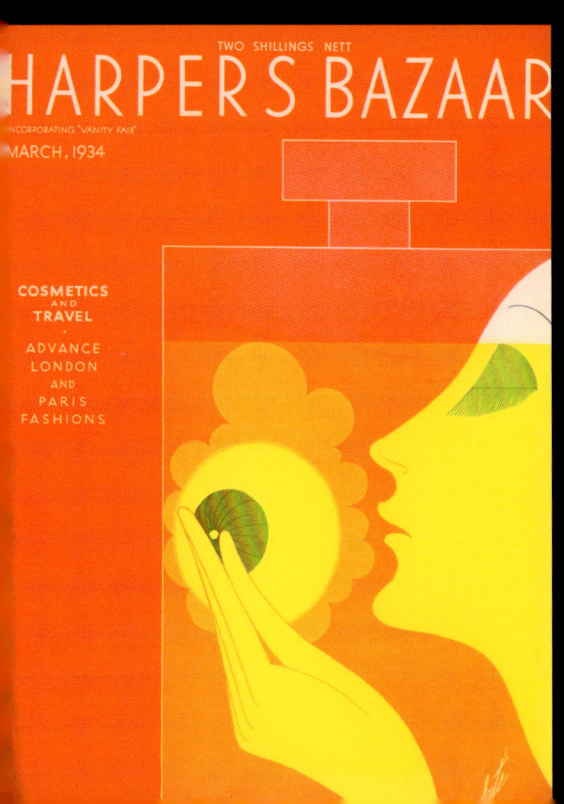

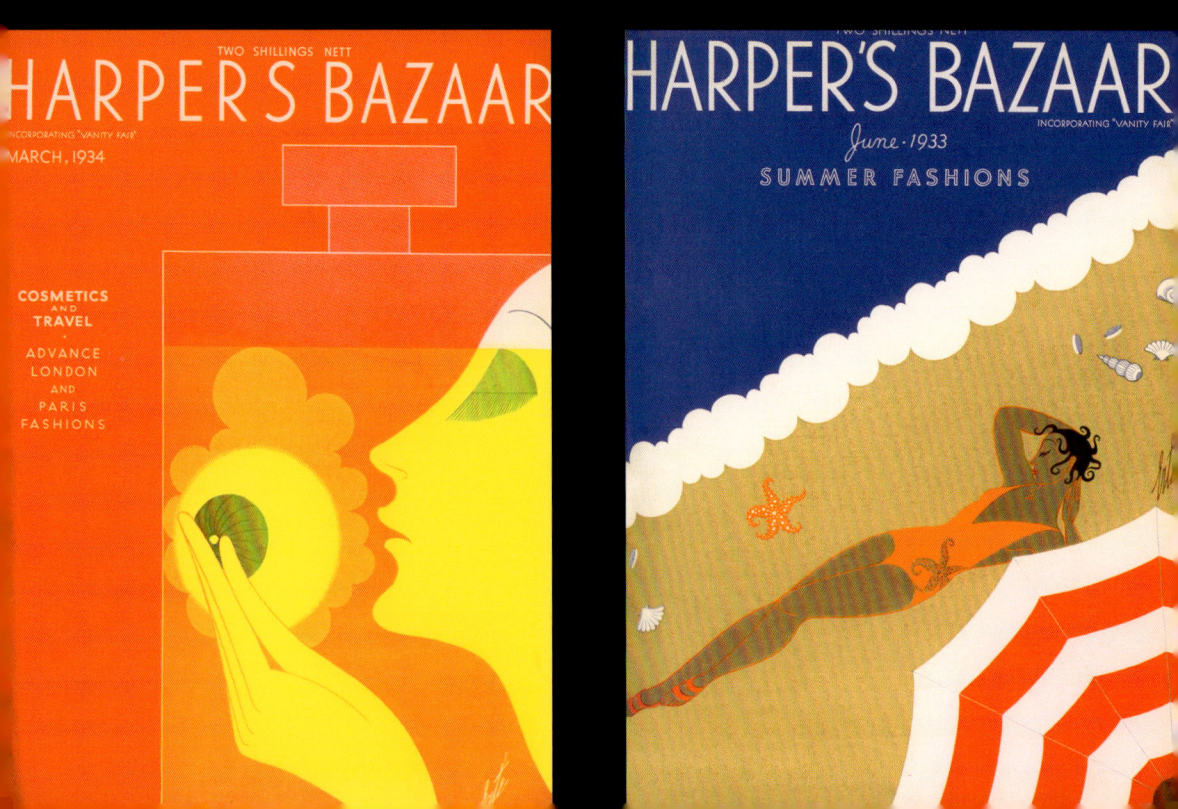

HARPER'S BAZAAR
TWO SHILLINGS NETT
INCORPORATING "VANITY FAIR"
MARCH, 1934
COSMETICS AND TRAVEL
ADVANCE LONDON AND PARIS FASHIONS

HARPER'S BAZAAR
INCORPORATING "VANITY FAIR"
June · 1933
SUMMER FASHIONS

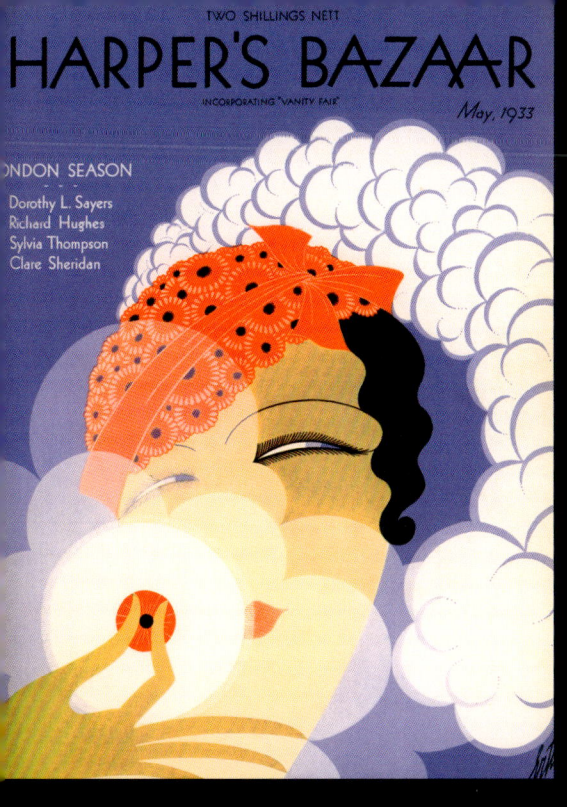

HARPER'S BAZAAR

TWO SHILLINGS NETT
INCORPORATING "VANITY FAIR"
May, 1933

LONDON SEASON
Dorothy L. Sayers
Richard Hughes
Sylvia Thompson
Clare Sheridan

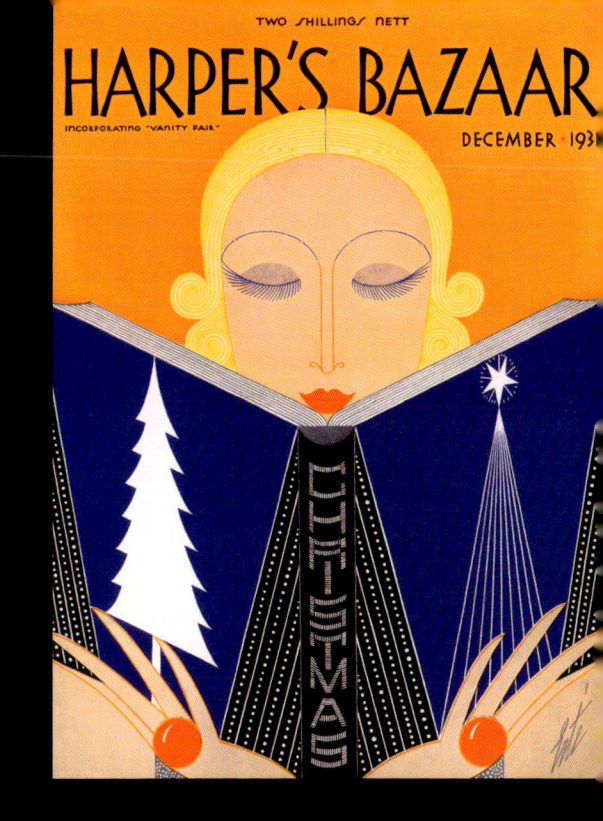

HARPER'S BAZAAR

TWO SHILLINGS NETT
INCORPORATING "VANITY FAIR"
DECEMBER · 1931

CHRISTMAS

HARPER'S BAZAAR

TWO SHILLINGS NETT
March, 1933
INCORPORATING "VANITY FAIR"

LONDON FASHIONS

HARPER'S BAZAAR

TWO SHILLINGS NETT
SUMMER TRAVEL   JULY, 1934
INCORPORATING "VANITY FAIR"

LOUIS GOLDING
CLARE SHERIDAN
JOHN COLLIER
EVELYN WAUGH

By the 1920s, largely thanks to *Bazar*, Erté was famous. The magazine dubbed him 'The foremost designer of original fashions in the world'; they serialized his autobiography, published airy missives from the Riviera and even encouraged him to share the inspiration behind his covers. 'My imagination has taken me, this time, to a shady park, where summer sings its love songs with the buoyant warbling of birds…' began one such fulsome article in 1922.

By now he had established the distinctive Erté style, contrasting a rigorous graphic simplicity with intricate surface design and an all-pervading exoticism. His influences ranged from Persian miniatures to Russian icons and, of course, the Ballets Russes. Though he later confessed that he preferred the high style of the pre-war years, Erté seemed made for the 1920s. His costumes and sets for Broadway, for the Ziegfeld Follies and for the Folies Bergère became ever more extravagant and, in this heady period, his wildest fantasies could be realized. The artist George Barbier marvelled at the 'networks of diamonds throbbing on nude bodies' and the curtains 'woven with ostrich feathers or heavy with fur.' A spell in Hollywood in 1925 was less successful, though Erté dutifully informed his *Bazar* readers that he had submitted to 197 interviews en route to the film capital.

The Wall Street Crash of 1929 not only wiped out Erté's personal fortune, it effectively put an end to the grandiose productions that had made his name. Erté cut his cloth. He worked on a smaller scale for revue, for the ballet and operetta. In 1935, he moved to a sixth-floor apartment overlooking the Bois de Boulogne in Paris (which he would maintain until his death), and the following year he finally terminated his association with *Harper's Bazaar* after some acrimonious exchanges with the new editor, Carmel Snow. Erté's replacement was the French poster artist Cassandre. 'I do not know of anybody who could do worse, unless it be Picasso,' wrote William Randolph Hearst, the magazine's owner. Erté stayed on in Paris throughout the occupation and after World War II went wherever the work took him, including, incongruously, to Blackpool, which he pronounced 'ghastly'.

In 1967, a wildly successful exhibition of his drawings at the Grosvenor Gallery in London sparked an interest that became a fully fledged revival. 'If Michelangelo were to come back from the dead he could hardly have greater or more eulogious publicity,' observed the critic John Russell Taylor. His last years were spent receiving honours, attending retrospectives and enthusiastically embracing new challenges, ranging from taking up sculpture to designing covers for *Playboy* and labels for a mineral water deliciously named 'Eau Erté'. He died in 1989, aged 97, one of the twentieth century's true magicians.

DEFINING DECO *(previous pages and right)* In 1916, William Randolph Hearst, the owner of *Harper's Bazar*, offered Erté an exclusive ten-year contract (which would later be renewed). From then on the magazine unashamedly promoted its protégé. 'To glance at an Erté drawing is amusing. To look at one is interesting. To study one is absorbing. That any human being can conceive – and execute – such exquisite detail is positively miraculous…' ran an editorial in 1917. In addition to covers, Erté contributed fashion drawings and designs for accessories and interiors. *Courtesy The Mary Evans Picture Library*

HARPER'S BAZAAR

NOVEMBER, 1933   INCORPORATING "VANITY FAIR"   LONDON FASHIONS

AN EMERGING LINE...

In the 1930s, fashion illustration discovered a new mood: relaxed, witty, informative, and eager to explore the infinite possibilities of line. Whether describing the rarefied atmosphere of the couture salon, or life on the streets of Nazi-occupied Paris, fashion artists raised reportage to an art form.

VOGUE

BEAUTY NUMBER   PRICE WITH VOGUE PATTERN BOOK

THE CONDÉ NAST PUBLICATIONS LTD   MAY·15·1935 (10)

VOGUE, COVERED
Eric's 1935 *Vogue* cover, with its echoes of Matisse, was as daring and reductive as he would ever be.
Courtesy British Vogue

CARL ERICKSON

Eric

Carl Erickson – who was universally known as Eric – was unquestionably the most influential fashion artist to emerge in the 1930s. A master of descriptive line, he recorded the theatre of high fashion – the Paris collections, a Broadway opening or cocktails at the Ritz – with an effortless ease and assurance. His art was essentially that of reportage. Unlike the great stylists of the 1910s and 1920s – Erté, Barbier and Lepape – who viewed the world from an artful distance (as though through lorgnettes), Eric relished his insider's perspective. Elegant, incisive and unfailingly charming, his drawings graced the pages of *Vogue* for more than thirty-five years, a record unmatched by any other artist.

SOPHISTICATED LADY
Eric's bravura technique is beautifully demonstrated in this cover illustration for *Vogue* (who advised its readers to be 'up to your eyes in Leopard this season') in 1940, and in the effortlessly relaxed study *(right)* for Crown Tested Rayon Taffeta the following year. *Above, Courtesy British Vogue. Right, Private collection*

Eric was born Carl Oscar August Erickson, in Joliet, Illinois, in 1891 to Swedish immigrant parents. He studied at the Academy of Fine Arts in Chicago and by 1914 had made his way to New York, to pursue a career as a commercial artist. 1916 saw his first appearance in *Vogue*, and four years later he married a successful staff illustrator there, Lee Creelman. By 1925 he too was on staff. Eric's rise was slow but inexorable through the late 1920s. His advertising clients included Buick, Rayon and Stehli Silks, while *Vogue's* increasingly high-profile editorial assignments found him sketching at the Venice Lido and in the nightclubs of Montmartre.

By the time his first *Vogue* cover appeared in 1930, when he was almost 40 years old, Eric was living in Paris. His expressionistic style, with its echoes of Van Dongen and Degas, was directly at odds with the highly graphic work of Georges Lepape and Benito, *Vogue's* undisputed cover stars of the previous decade. It was a timely change of emphasis. A debate was playing out at the magazine: editor Edna Woolman Chase was becoming increasingly irritated by the lack of reality, the lack of *clothes* depicted on the magazine's cover. 'I don't see why it should be so irksome to modern-day fashion artists to let a subscriber see what the dress she may be interested in buying is really like,' she wrote. Condé Nast, the magazine's proprietor, agreed. From now on, 'mere novelty, or art value, or surprising "modernism" would be unacceptable.'

Eric's practised ease and all-observing eye quickly came to dominate *Vogue*, and his wife jealously guarded his position. When a rival, such as the equally brilliant René Bouët-Willaumez, appeared, he was quickly dispatched to London at Lee's behest. Eric drew at the races and on the Riviera; he was at home at the couture salon and the private dress show. Gradually, the stout and socially insecure Midwesterner evolved into a 'St. James' Street *boulevardier*' according to his friend, the photographer Norman Parkinson, 'dressed in perfect dark navy English tailoring, handmade shoes and shirts, finished off with a sincere Sulka tie and, of course to crown it all, a fine bowler hat from Lock's.'

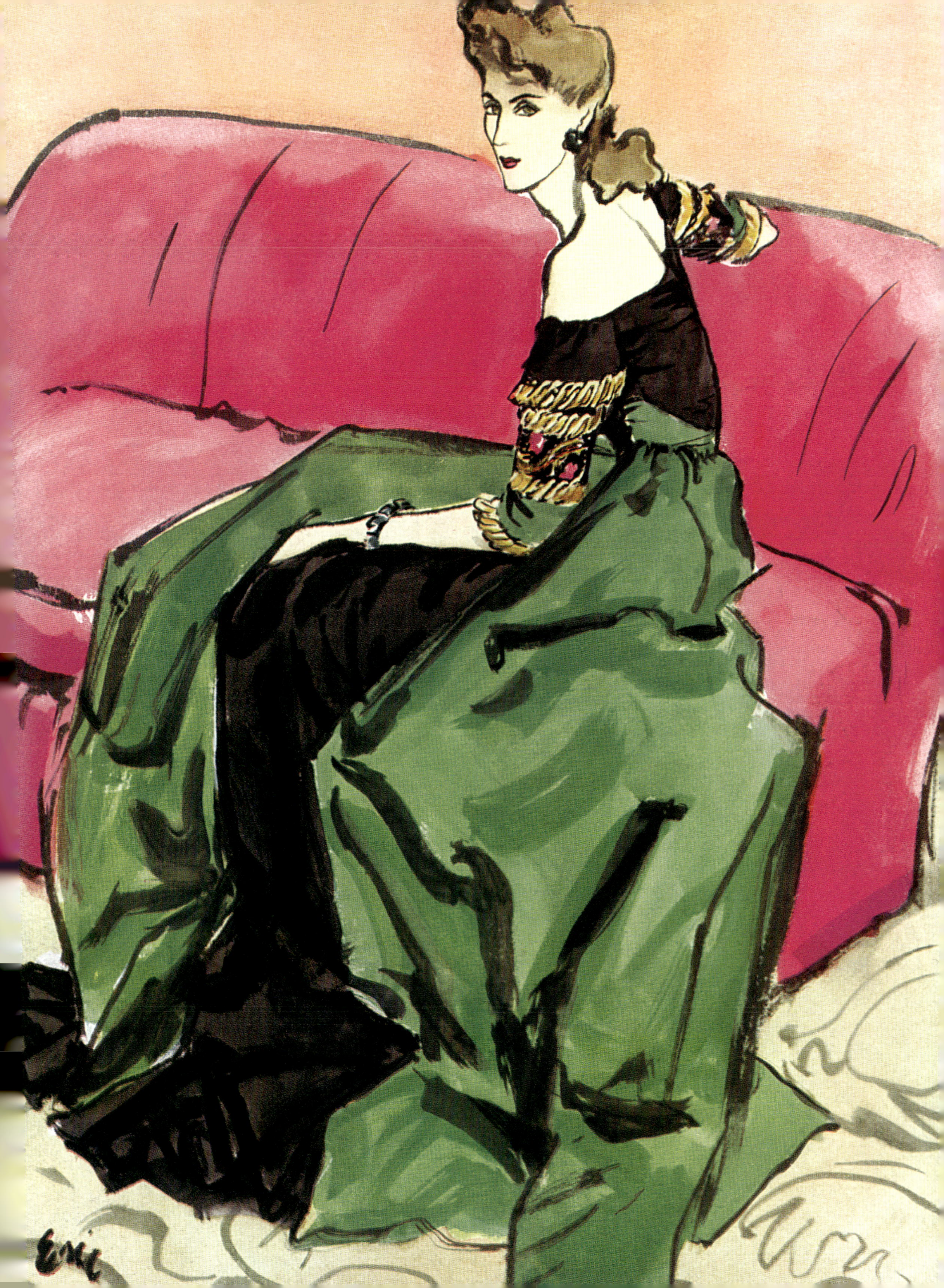

LINE KING
Eric's elegance set him apart from even his closest rivals, whether he was describing the rigours of a beauty routine in 1946 *(this page, Courtesy British Vogue)* or an agonizing choice over shoes in 1943. *Courtesy Condé Nast Archive*

67

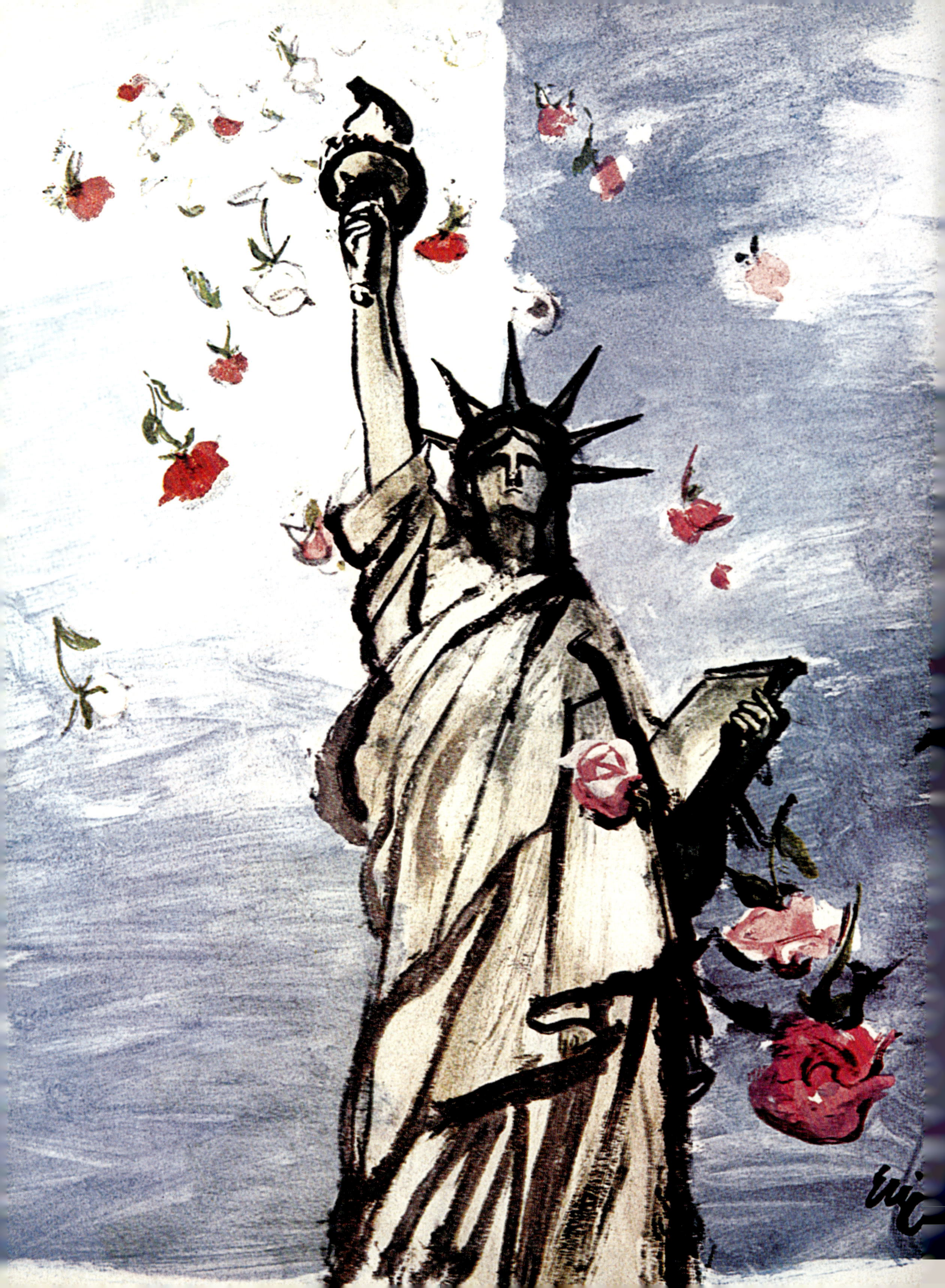

Although under contract to American *Vogue*, throughout the 1930s Eric worked frequently for its French and British counterparts and was unquestionably a star at all three magazines. During the winter of 1939, as the 'phony war' dragged on, Eric drew his wife playing backgammon in their bomb shelter while the Chinese servants and their poodle Fez looked on. As the Germans advanced, his family (Eric and Lee had a daughter, Charlotte) were forced to leave their farmhouse in Senlis, north of Paris. Their journey to Bordeaux was brilliantly described in a letter to *Vogue* by Lee, published in July 1940, and illustrated by Eric (below).

Back in New York, Eric continued to record the social round, but now he supplemented it with drawings of returning GIs, or the Service Man's lounge at Grand Central Station. VJ Day was marked by a confetti of roses swirling around an impassively triumphant Statue of Liberty.

WAR ARTIST
Eric and his family left France after the fall of Paris. '…we joined a slowly moving mass of carts, wagons, camions and cars piled high with bedding and families, refugees on foot…' his wife wrote in a letter to *Vogue* in 1940. Five years later in New York, Eric created a suitably joyful and symbolic image for VJ Day (*left*). *Courtesy Condé Nast Archive*

COTY
During the 1940s, in addition to his work for *Vogue*, Eric produced a number of lively advertisements for the cosmetics firm Coty. *Private collection*

After the war, still very much in harness at *Vogue*, Eric divided his time between Paris and New York. Always a heavy drinker, he now slipped into alcoholism. Norman Parkinson claimed that, sober, Eric was unable to perform to his own exacting standards. Parkinson described one sitting with his wife, Wenda. Supporting himself against a wall, Eric 'lunged' at the paper and drew a single eye and, lower down on the page, an ankle. Then, as an astonished Parkinson looked on, he joined the two together; 'he scratched up the calf, behind the knee, along the hips, the waist, and suddenly conjured from the air an arm, a hand and its bracelet, the shoulders, the neck, and now his bent stick of charcoal circumnavigated the skull, with miracle intention enclosing in its correct position the original eye.'

Fred Smith, a prolific New York-based illustrator in the 1950s, also remembered Eric with affection; 'Never sober, but never disreputable either,' standing in the middle of the street at Lexington and 57th directing traffic with his newspaper on his way to a morning martini on Third Avenue. From the mid-1950s on, Eric's appearances in *Vogue* became more sporadic, his illness (and his attempts to cure it) accounting for long absences. But Eric was still a master, and his late drawings, when they did appear, were as vital and as keenly observed as ever.

Eric died in 1958 and *Vogue* saluted an irreplaceable, long-term contributor with a wistful obituary. 'He has left his mark on *Vogue's* history, as on the times. And for that we are grateful,' it concluded. It was the end of an era.

ALWAYS IN VOGUE
Four years before his death in 1958, and already in poor health, Eric had lost none of his relaxed grand manner. *Courtesy Dean Rhys Morgan Collection*

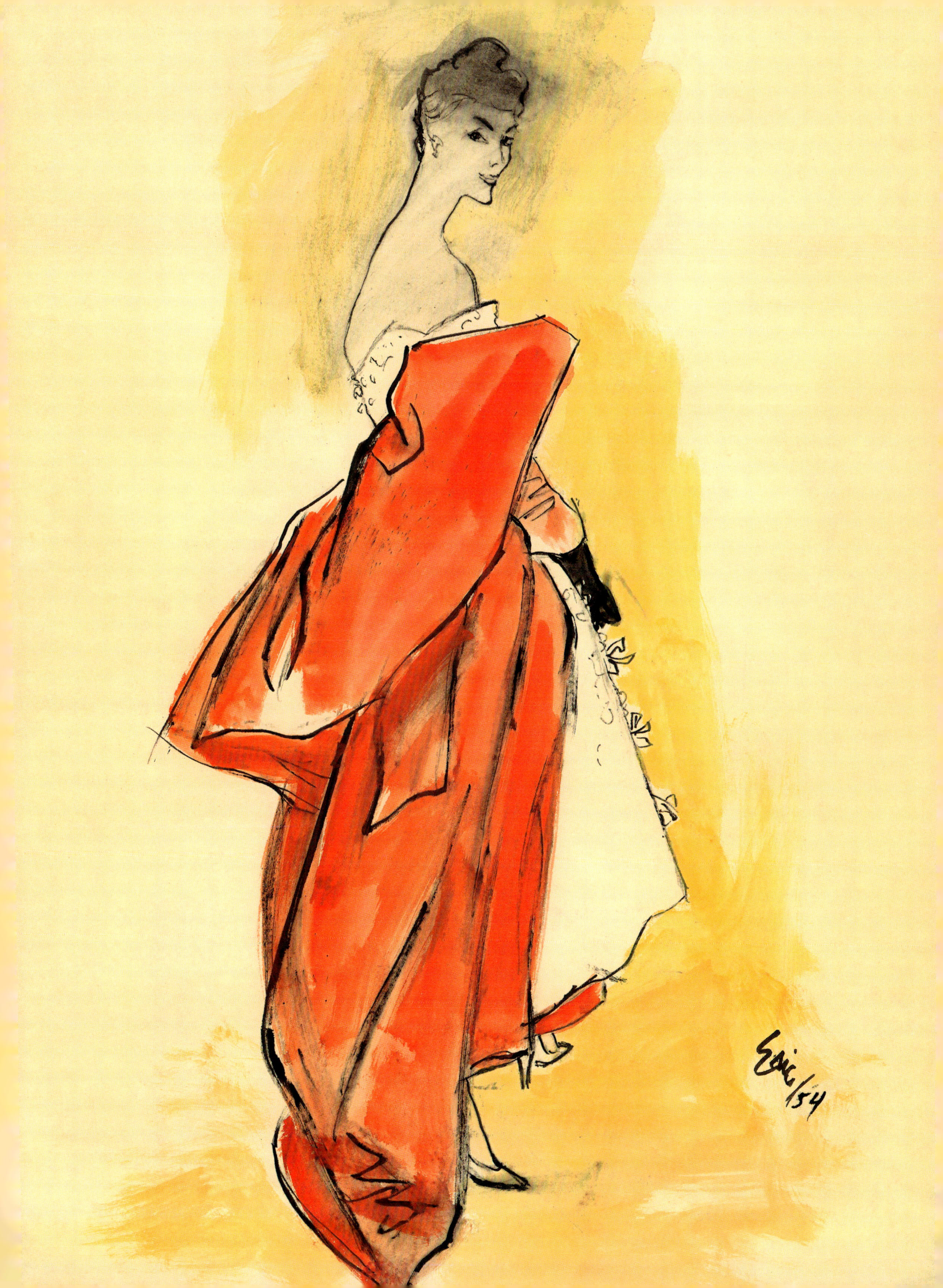
Eric/54

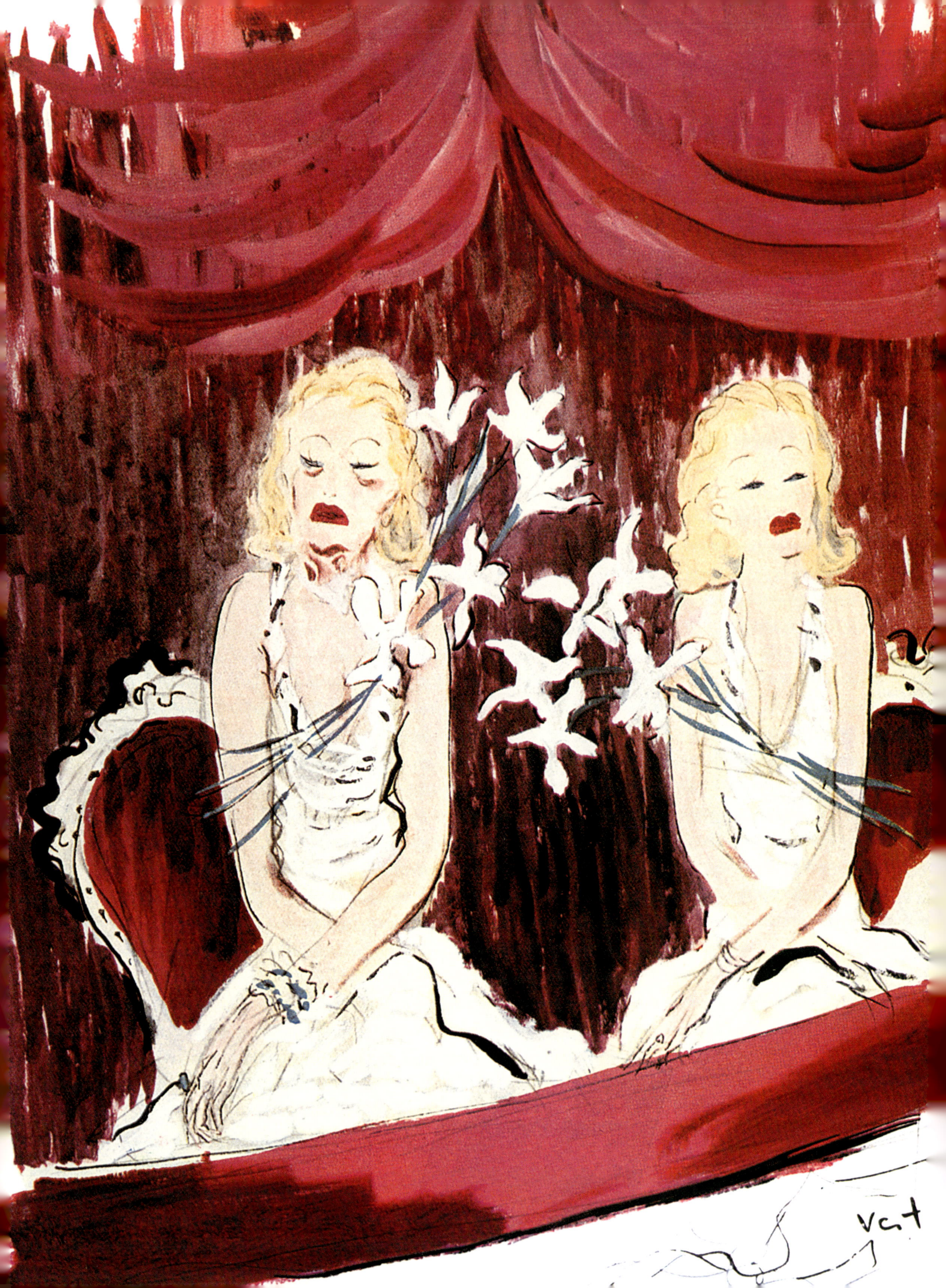

MARCEL VERTÈS

Vertès [signature]

Some artists defy categorization. In a long and industrious career, Marcel Vertès variously assumed the mantle of fine artist, portraitist, muralist, satirist, ceramicist, author, illustrator, printmaker, and costume, fabric and set designer. He may never have developed the frenetic versatility of, say, Antonio Lopez, but did anyone else work across so many disciplines with such aplomb?

Given all that, it is interesting how often Vertès returned to the world of fashion, I suspect because it gave him licence to revisit his favourite subject: women. 'There is nothing more gratifying,' he told a reporter in the 1940s, 'than to encounter, here or there in the smoky New York streets, charming creatures who applaud me for having picked out colour combinations for their clothes which make them look even prettier.' Vertès may have been enthralled, but he was seldom fooled. Few artists could exploit the gap between our real and imagined selves with the relish of his 1936 mother-and-daughter illustration for *Vogue* (opposite). Of course, humour had always been a part of the fashion artist's repertoire, from Sem's (mainly) benign, bemused caricatures, to the slyly subversive captions in *Gazette du Bon Ton*. But Vertès went further; his drawings of the *beau monde* shimmer with gleeful malice, while his dancing line and joyful Dufyesque colours diverted the eye and soothed the very egos they ruffled. If Vertès never explored the nihilistic territory of Grosz and his ilk (and it is not too big a step to think he might have), it is because what he sought, and frequently found, was enchantment.

LIKE SISTERS REALLY!
Vertès could be delightfully malicious, as here, sending up the 'distinct recent phenomenon, the perpetually adolescent mother and her daughter' in 1936. *Courtesy British Vogue*

73

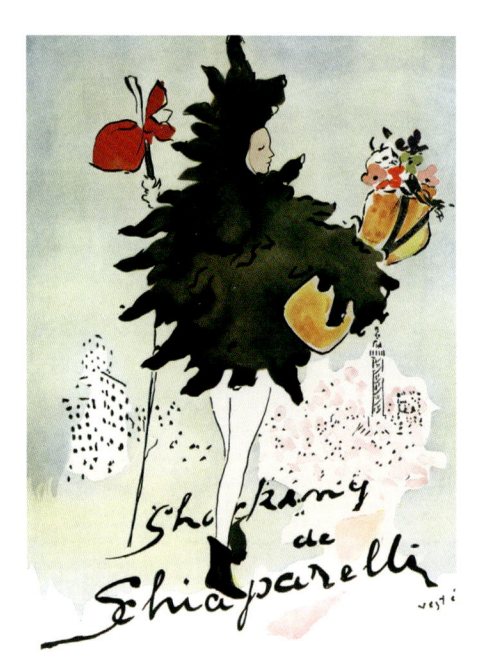

Vertès was born in Budapest in 1895. After serving in his country's army during World War I, he abandoned plans to study law and made his way to Paris with the idea, he later told *Vogue*, of becoming an artist 'with animal skins and divans and mandolins on the studio walls,' and, of course, 'women in the nude' to paint. The latter ambition was quickly achieved: in 1920 he published *L'heure exquise*, a suite of startlingly erotic etchings, followed by another equally charged portfolio, *Le pays à mon gout*. Rumour has it that Vertès financed himself during his formative years in Paris by becoming an expert forger of Toulouse-Lautrec; certainly by the mid-1920s his subject matter – the circus, the dancehall and the brothel – indicate that this might not have been a stretch. Whatever the truth, Vertès soon turned his attention elsewhere, principally to illustrating classic texts, including Zola's *Nana* and Colette's *Chéri*.

By the mid-1930s, Vertès' work was appearing in both *Vogue* and *Harper's Bazaar*, an unusual, if not unique, feat given the well-known rivalry between those magazines. He reached an apotheosis, at least in fashion terms, when Elsa Schiaparelli asked him to design the advertising for her first perfume produced in France, 'Shocking'. The bottle, a naked woman's torso (apparently modelled on Mae West) was indeed shocking in 1937, and perhaps only Vertès could have made palatable a sailor's approach to it on a park bench (above left), or a *boulevardier* tucking it into his coat.

SHOCKING

Vertès had a long and lively association with the 'Empress of Fashion' Elsa Schiaparelli. In addition to working on the advertising for her perfumes, Shocking, Zut, Sleeping and (the first fragrance for men) Snuff, he designed fabrics, painted a suitably dashing portrait, and documented her wartime lecture tour of the United States for *Harper's Bazaar*. Private collection

Shocking de Schiaparelli

76

STRAIGHTEN YOUR TIE!
Vertes could never resist sending up fashionable society. This illustration appeared in *Vogue* in 1936.
Courtesy British Vogue

LILY DACHÉ
Famous as a colourist, Vertès could be equally authoritative in black and white, as in this drawing for the milliner Lily Daché, circa 1948. *Private collection*

Vertès was briefly assigned to the 221st Workers' Regiment of the French Army in 1939. Discharged the following year, he moved south to Biarritz, where a depleted fashion industry had set up temporary quarters. There he received a cable from *Harper's Bazaar* requesting that he 'Draw page in color Schiaparelli's little pink hat with beige veil. Stop. Wish to use as cover.' But by then the German army had reached Bordeaux and the project was abandoned. The absurdity of the situation was not lost on him, and Vertès resolved to join the growing exodus of artists and writers leaving Europe. Making it over the border to Spain, he boarded a cargo ship headed for New York, with his wife, his dog and a Buick full of luggage.

Starting again in America only inspired Vertès to greater productivity. He set up a studio on West 57th Street and continued to work with Schiaparelli, *Vogue* and *Bazaar*; he painted murals for the stripper Gipsy Rose Lee and for the Café Carlyle; he wrote a lively discourse on *Art and Fashion*; held exhibitions (*Time* magazine reported that a dozen *gendarmes* were required to control the crowds at a Paris opening in 1947); won two Oscars (fittingly enough, for the sets and costumes for *Moulin Rouge*, John Huston's 1952 biopic of Toulouse-Lautrec); and designed posters for Broadway and costumes for the ballet, most notably Fokine's *Bluebeard* and Balanchine's *Helen of Troy*. Vertès was unapologetic about the scope of all this activity, claiming it made no difference whether his work appeared 'on a wall, a canvas, a sheet of paper or a China plate'. To another journalist he confessed that even if he were to win the lottery, he would never give up his commercial projects. 'It is through them,' he said, 'that I stay in touch with life.'

If women were his greatest inspiration, Vertès' other enduring love was Paris. He returned to the city in the late 1950s and it was there, in 1961, that he died, having recently served on the jury of the Cannes Film Festival. He was still unclassifiable, still an artist in full flow.

GOODBYE CHARLIE
Vertès had known Lauren Bacall since her early years as a *Bazaar* model. His portrait was one of the few memorable aspects of *Goodbye Charlie*, a 1959 farce that irritated critics and lasted 109 performances on Broadway. *Private collection*

ALL IN THE MIND
Published in 1948 in an edition of 3,500, *It's All Mental* was Vertès' characteristically astringent take on the growing obsession with psychiatry and the headlong rush to the analyst's couch, 'where a man goes in a mouse and comes out the hero (or heroine) of his own favourite thriller,' according to Anita Loos, who wrote the foreword. *Courtesy Tony Glenville*

WESLEY SIMPSON
In typically insouciant mood, Vertès advertises his own scarf designs for the textile manufacturer Wesley Simpson circa 1948. *Private collection*

Schiaparelli - page 65

SCHIAPARELLI
Marshall described Elsa Schiaparelli as a 'strange, exotic, excitable genius,' after painting her portrait for *Vogue* in 1936. *Courtesy Volker and Ingrid Zahm Collection*

FRANCIS MARSHALL

Francis Marshall is the only British artist in this book. I'm not sure why that should be relevant, nor am I sure that it was helpful to Marshall. Although he had a contract with British *Vogue* for a dozen or so years, he seldom worked for the swankier French or American versions. Nor has his reputation endured like that of Eric, say, or Gruau. Perhaps there is something a little too English, a little too *Spring in Park Lane* about him. But let's be clear: Marshall was brilliant. As a draughtsman and as a master of line, particularly in black and white, he was equal to any of his peers. He had a light, lyrical and wonderfully descriptive style and, as an observer and recorder of life in London between the wars, he was unique. Fashion and society engaged him in two distinct phases: in his work for *Vogue* from 1928 until the war, and thereafter for the *Daily Mail* for almost twenty years.

Marshall was born in London in 1901, to an English father and a Dutch mother. Aged 12, he was sent to train as a sea cadet, and from there joined the Royal Navy at the outbreak of World War I, while still a teenager. He was torpedoed more than once, and ended the war as a gunnery officer. Aged 20, he resigned his commission, intent on becoming an artist. He studied at the Slade from 1921 to 1923 under Henry Tonks. In 1925, he began work as a commercial artist at the Carlton Studios (for ten shillings a week) and through a friend was introduced to *Vogue*, which he joined as a staff artist in 1928.

The 1930s at *Vogue* were halcyon days for Marshall. He had always been an inveterate diarist, note-taker and keeper of sketchbooks, and *Vogue's* preoccupation not only with fashion but also with the London Season suited him perfectly. He presented himself at the Royal Ballet, at Covent Garden or at Ascot, sketchbook in hand (a boring opera was, he advised, best for sketching). Unlike Paris and New York, London also had the ceremony of the Court to engage him, and Marshall eagerly and respectfully recorded the Jubilee of King George V and, following the abdication, the Coronation of George VI, in 1937. By the late 1930s, married to Margaret Chambers and with a suitably stylish address on Regent's Park, Marshall was unquestionably Britain's leading fashion artist. In addition to his commitments at *Vogue*, he worked for Elizabeth Arden and for Jaeger. At the decade's end he wrote and illustrated a book, *London West*, an elegy to a privileged life in W1, that 'straggling little pleasure resort somewhere in the middle of the world's largest city'. Due to paper shortages, the publication was held up until 1944. By then, Marshall had updated it, describing a life and a cityscape radically altered by war. 'Mayfair,' he concluded, 'could take it.' He signed up as a camouflage officer at the Admiralty and continued to work sporadically for *Vogue* throughout the conflict, moving to Bath after his London flat suffered bomb damage. In 1942 he wrote another book, *Fashion Drawing*, a practical guide for aspiring fashion artists. 'Never fumble about on the paper without some idea in your head,' he cautioned. 'Scribbling on desk blotters may be quite amusing, but it is no use when you are trying to think out a complicated drawing.'

LONDON PRIDE
Always happiest when sketching the London social scene, Marshall nevertheless described the Coronation of King George VI in 1937 as a 'Heaven and Hell for the fashion world' and got up at 4.30am to secure a good vantage point *(below)*. A few years later, a morale-boosting image for Jaeger *(right)*.
Below, Courtesy Tony Glenville. Right, Courtesy The Advertising Archive

Only the brave deserve the fair

and the fair deserve
JAEGER

Stork Club

THE STORK CLUB
A characteristically authoritative and complex drawing of the fabled Manhattan Stork Club, published in Marshall's 1949 book *An Englishman in New York*. Among the diners are Hedy Lamarr, Orson Welles, Oscar Hammerstein and gossip columnist Walter Winchell (far right).
Private collection

85

DRAWING FASHION
'With verve you must "feel" the fabric in your mind otherwise you won't convey its character in your drawing,' counselled Marshall in his book *Fashion Drawing*, first published by The Studio Publications in 1942. *Private collection*

Marshall joined the *Daily Mail* after the war as their fashion and society correspondent, a post he held until 1963. He reported on the couture shows in Paris, Rome and Milan as well as on social events at home, and his emphatic, descriptive, black and white brushwork was ideally suited to the newspaper medium. In addition to his work for the *Mail*, he wrote and illustrated *An Englishman in New York* in 1949, a companion piece to *London West*; exhibited at the Wells Gallery in London; illustrated stories for *Reader's Digest* Condensed Books in America; and painted portraits for *Woman and Beauty* magazine

After leaving the *Mail*, Marshall, now in his sixties, embraced the life of a freelancer with predictable zeal. His sketchbooks suggest that he still avidly recorded the world around him, however changed; one from 1967 is labelled 'Ascot, Hippies, Teenagers.' In 1966, Marshall met the indomitable novelist Barbara Cartland at a literary luncheon, and at her invitation began to design the covers of her best-selling romances, whose florid titles included *The Bored Bridegroom*, *A Virgin in Paris* and *No Castanets at the Ballet*. Marshall researched the period settings (many were set in the Regency), and invested the covers with a dash and sophistication that perhaps only he could have managed. Combining observational drawing and tongue-in-cheek glamour, Marshall created a delirious world of wide-eyed heroines and square-jawed heroes in which virtue always prevailed. In all, he would produce more than 200 covers for Cartland's romantic fables and was still working on them in 1980, at the time of his death. For Marshall, the association with Cartland proved to be a sustained and lucrative swansong, but perhaps most importantly it kept him where he most loved to be: at his drawing board.

QUEEN OF THE WORLD
Dame Barbara Cartland wrote more than 700 books, making her the twentieth century's most prolific author. Marshall's suitably triumphant portrait did duty as her 1978 Christmas card.
Courtesy Cartland Promotions

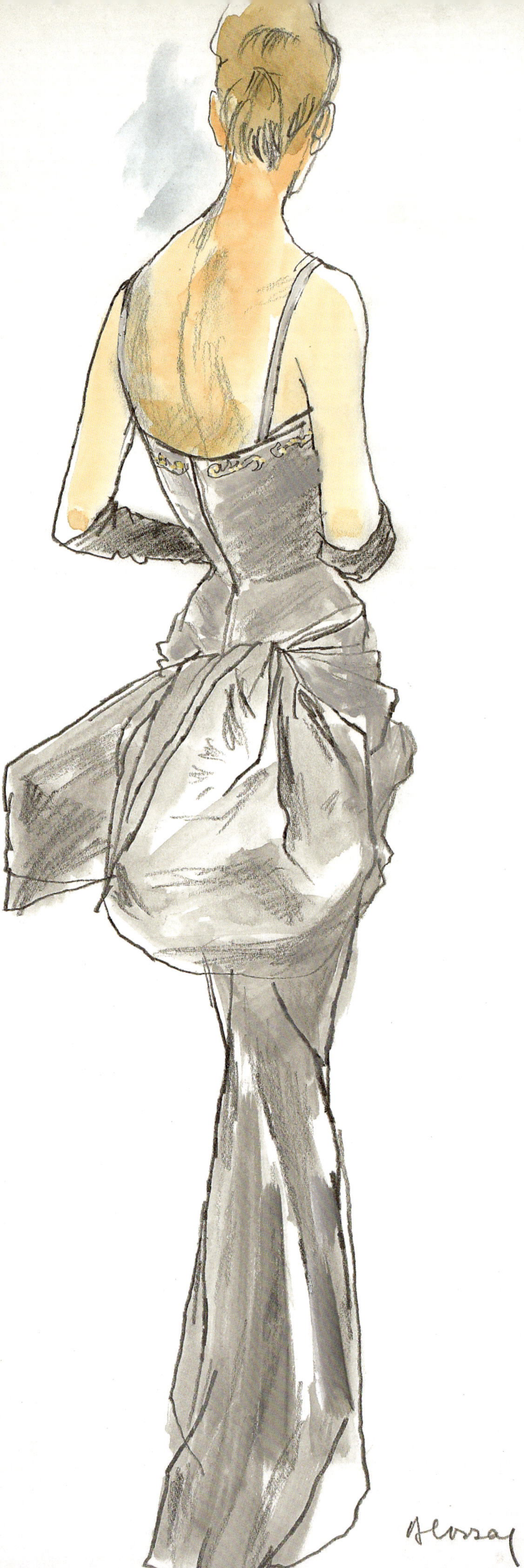

BERNARD BLOSSAC

There was a refinement to Blossac, a graceful pressure to his line. Like Eric and Bouché, he described a world of privilege with enviable ease, but unlike those great *boulevardiers* he retained a discreet distance and cool. And while Gruau distilled everything to its most striking graphic elements, Blossac seduced with his resonant, occasionally hesitant, line and transparent washes of colour. In his own way, he was as daring as any of the great artists of the period; with Blossac it was about things left unsaid. And no one ever painted the curve of a woman's back with such languid grace.

He was born Bernard de la Bourdonnaye-Blossac in Neuilly-sur-Seine in 1917. He studied painting, drawing and design in Paris, first with Maurice Testard and subsequently at La Grande Chaumière and at the atelier of the great poster designer Paul Colin, where he learned theatre set and costume design. A meeting with the couturier Robert Piguet in 1941 led to an introduction to Paul Caldaguès, the president of the Chambre Syndicale, the organization responsible for couture, and from there it was a short step to *Vogue*, *Femina* and *L'Officiel*. Blossac would later admit that in his thirty-year career he never had to seek work.

JACQUES FATH
Blossac demonstrates his peerless draughtsmanship in this 1949 drawing for Jacques Fath. *Courtesy Mr & Mme Alain Matrand de la Bourdonnaye-Blossac/ Galerie Bartsch & Chariau, Munich*

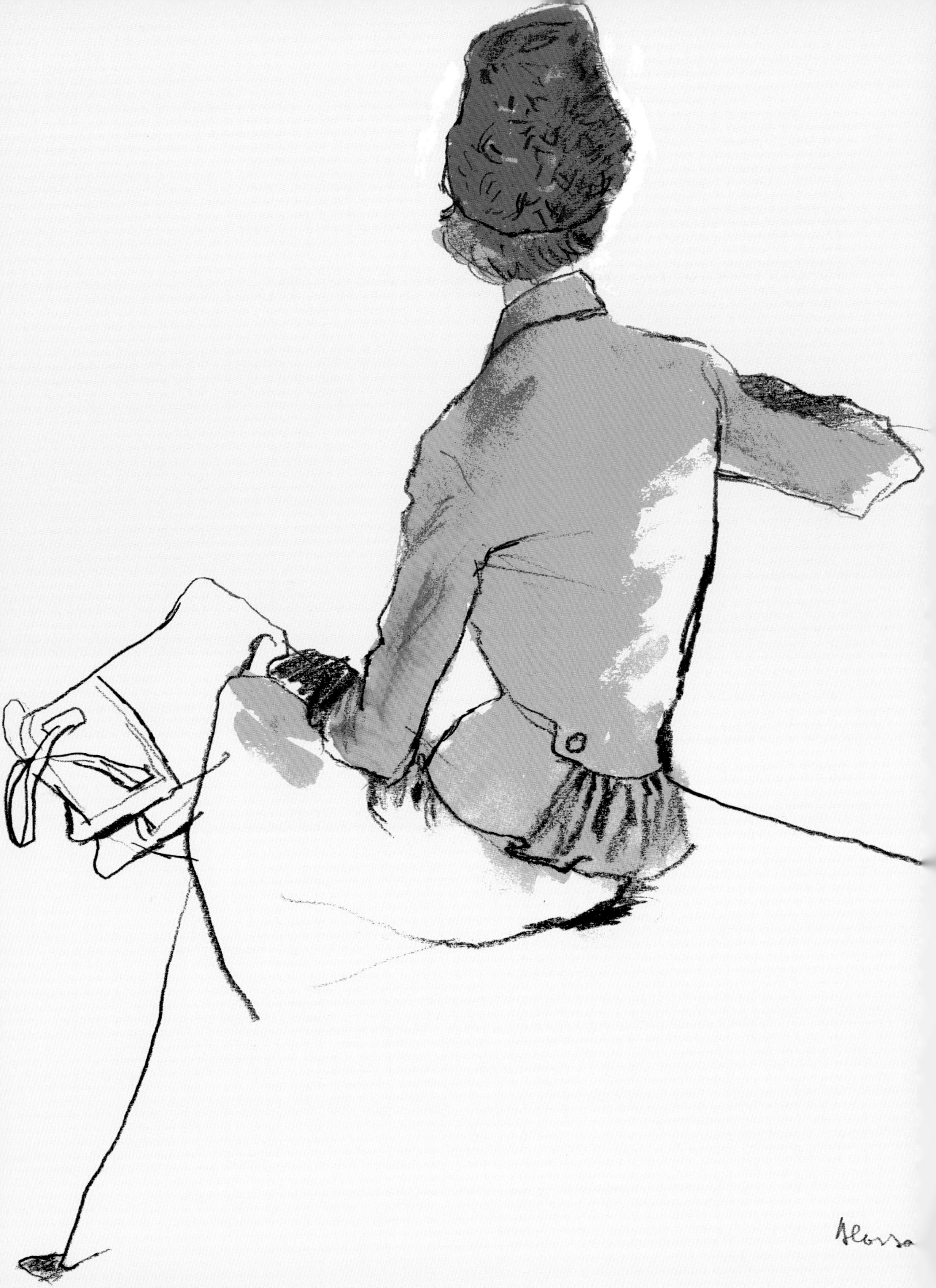

L'AIR DU TEMPS
The opera and the races were Blossac's natural milieu. His elegant drawings focused on the clothes (here Molyneux and Schiaparelli, *left*, and Rosine Paris, *right*, circa 1947), but provided just enough background detail to set the scene. *Courtesy Mr & Mme Alain Matrand de la Bourdonnaye-Blossac/ Private collection*

DIOR
Blossac's subjects were always beautifully observed – note how confidently the leg is drawn with a single line in this illustration for Dior, circa 1952. *Courtesy Mr & Mme Alain Matrand de la Bourdonnaye-Blossac/ Galerie Bartsch & Chariau, Munich*

The Battle for Paris ended the Nazi occupation in August 1944, and in January the following year a special edition of French *Vogue* celebrated a return to something approaching the old order. A patriotic red, white and blue cover by Christian Bérard depicted a galleon sailing triumphantly to victory. Inside, a series of drawings by Blossac (one for every year of the war) showed that despite subtle – and not so subtle – reminders of the occupation (a swastika above the Rue de Rivoli!), fashionable Paris had prevailed. Eric, Vertès and Bouché had all relocated to New York for the duration, and it was fitting that it was Blossac, a Frenchman, who summed up the bittersweet situation. Although the drawings garnered a lot of attention, Blossac worked mainly outside the confines of *Vogue*, principally for *L'Art et la Mode*, *La Femme Chic* and especially for *L'Officiel*.

In the late 1940s and early 1950s, Blossac came into his own. He recorded the elegant world he knew, the comings and goings on the Rue de la Paix, the Faubourg Saint-Honoré and the Avenue Matignon. He stationed himself, sketchbook in hand, in the lobby of the Georges V, or the bar at the Ritz. His acute observational eye also enabled him to record the couture collections with an enviable lightness of touch. Unlike his colleagues at *Vogue*, Blossac was not accorded special treatment and was expected to make what he could of a few tense minutes drawing backstage after the show. He paid particular attention to the models' attitude and expression, claiming to be more interested in making portraits of elegant women than in fashion illustration.

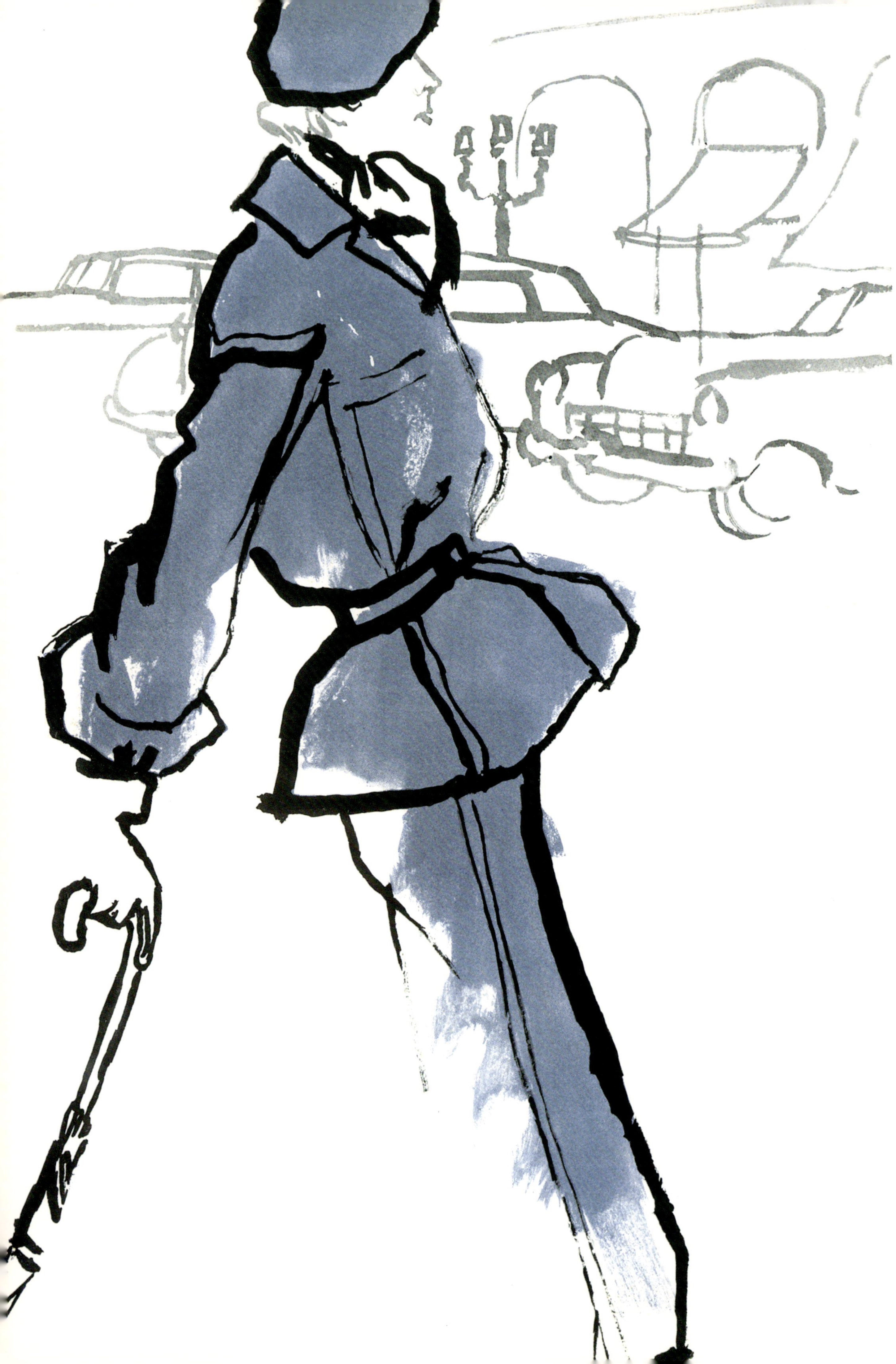

Bernard Blossac 49

PARIS

RUE DE LA PAIX (previous page)
Blossac developed a stronger line and a more graphic approach in the late 1940s. The clothes, from left, are by Dior, Jacques Heim and Marcel Rochas. *Courtesy Mr & Mme Alain Matrand de la Bourdonnaye-Blossac/Private collection*

Blossac's work evolved through the 1950s and 1960s, as he adopted a more emphatic line and blocks of opaque colour. The youthquake of the late 1960s was not to his taste, and he regretted the demise of elegance; 'younger readers have other aspirations,' he observed, ruefully. He worked for L'Oréal and the department store Franck & Fils, and *L'Officiel*, and continued to publish his drawings, in a style unrecognizable from his heyday, until the early 1970s. His last major work was for Harrods in London, a campaign that lasted several years, ending finally in 1974. He was not cut out, he said, like Gruau, for the world of advertising. His retirement was spent in high style as a gentleman of leisure and a collector of eighteenth-century art.

Of all the great fashion artists, Blossac perhaps had the least dramatic career. Independently wealthy, he had no need to pursue the frenetic course of some of his colleagues. It was as an editorial illustrator that he shone. 'My dream was always to be published in fashion magazines,' he once said; 'my dream was realized, I didn't want anything else.' He died in 2001.

CHANGING TIMES
In the 1960s, as fashion illustration began to go out of fashion, Blossac was as confident and dashing as ever. *Above*, a beautifully up-to-the-minute sketch for L'Oréal, circa 1965. *Left*, an illustration for *International Textiles*, 1960. *Courtesy Mr & Mme Alain Matrand de la Bourdonnaye-Blossac/Private collection*

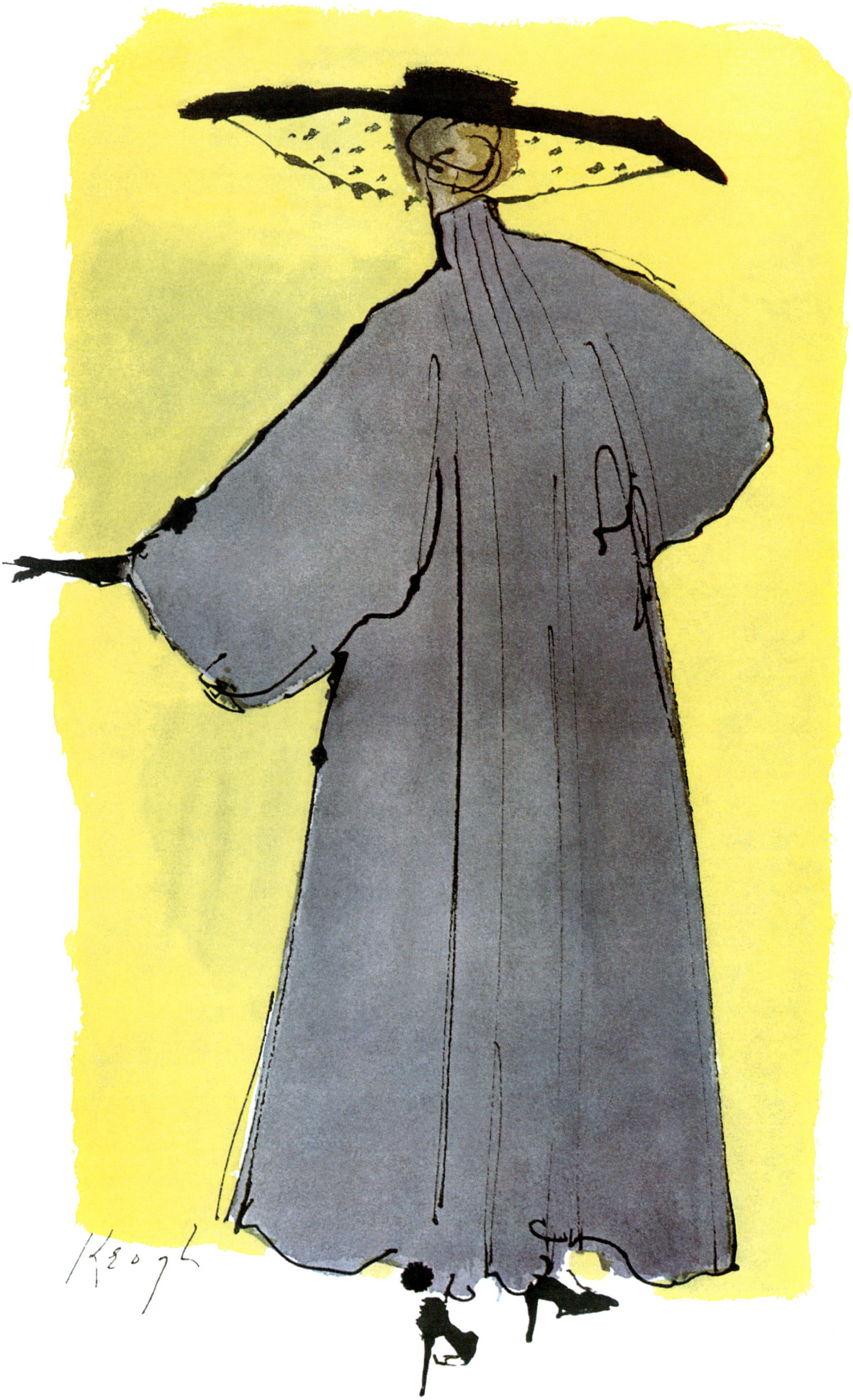
Keogh

KEOGH IN COLOUR

Tom Keogh's appearances in French *Vogue* in the late 1940s and early 1950s were all too brief. Here a zinging cloud of colour and a snappy rendering of a Mad Carpentier coat show what we were missing.
Courtesy French Vogue

TOM KEOGH

Tom Keogh had insouciance and snap. A brilliant colourist, his ravishing palette – citrus yellow, moss green, violet, orange and shocking pink – was underscored by a draughtsman's natural ease; the flick of a brush forever running dry of black ink. In the late 1940s and early 1950s, he breezed through French *Vogue*, as light as air, as fresh and thrilling as newly squeezed paint. For a time it looked as though he would be a natural successor to Bérard or Vertès, but then, all too quickly, he lost momentum, as though the whole thing bored him. Like Vertès, Keogh was extremely versatile; he painted in oils, illustrated book jackets and short stories, designed for the theatre, movies and ballet, and yet there is a frustrating lack of focus to his career.

Keogh was born in San Francisco in 1922 and studied at the Chouinard Art Institute in Los Angeles. There, through a classmate, Willa Kim (who went on to a long and distinguished career as a costume designer), he met the legendary costumier Madame Karinska and in 1944 began working with her on *Kismet*, an MGM Arabian Nights fantasy (Dietrich was in it, wearing gold paint). He continued working with Karinska in New York and in 1948 designed the costumes for Vincent Minnelli's misfire musical, *The Pirate*. By then he had entered into a tempestuous marriage with Theodora Roosevelt, the granddaughter of President 'Teddy' Roosevelt, and the couple had moved to Paris.

COVER STAR
Keogh was never overly concerned with fashion, and *Vogue*, under the editorship of Michel de Brunhoff, was happy enough to run with his delightfully insouciant covers. *Top*, March 1950. *Above*, April 1948. *Right*, December/January 1948. *Courtesy French Vogue*

Keogh was quickly taken up by French *Vogue*, and his splashy, high-profile contributions to the magazine triggered a great demand for his work; advertising for Elizabeth Arden and Jean Desses, Christmas windows at Galeries Lafayette, murals in Arden's *salon des exercises*, costumes and sets for the ballet *Don Quixote*. His private life was no less colourful; though he and Theodora were nominally happy, he began an affair with the fabulously wealthy and eccentric patron Vicomtesse Marie-Laure de Noailles. His wife retaliated by having an affair with the Vicomtesse's chauffeur, complicating an already highly charged situation. There were other affairs and rumours of a suicide attempt, and the couple finally divorced, though they remained on good terms. When Theodora began writing a scandalous series of novels in 1950, it was Tom who illustrated the covers. Long after their divorce (she would remarry twice and outlive him by almost thirty years), she would refer to him as 'my estranged but still beloved Tom.'

In the early 1950s, Keogh turned his attention to ballet, theatre and portraiture. He designed an extended dance sequence for a Fred Astaire musical, *Daddy Long Legs*, in 1955, and another for *Anything Goes* in the following year. On both productions he worked with the choreographer Roland Petit. Keogh reunited with Petit and his wife, Zizi Jeanmaire, for the ballet *Les Belles Damnées*, one of several collaborations in the late 1950s. He illustrated Hemingway short stories for the *Paris Review*, and among several book jackets produced a wonderfully sexy and graphic cover for *Le Repos du Guerrier*.

Back in New York in the late 1960s after twenty years in Paris, Keogh's witty drawings of the catwalk shows for *New York* magazine in 1968 showed that he had lost none of his panache. Nor did he seem aghast at the modish turn fashion had taken. Eric, Bouché, Bérard and Vertès were all gone; of his peer group, only Blossac and Gruau remained and, on the evidence of the New York drawings, Keogh was more at ease than either with the spirit of the times.

Tom Keogh died in 1980, aged just 58. His was an unsatisfying career, crowded with brilliant achievements and missed opportunities. His lifelong friend Willa Kim remembered him fondly. 'He was fun,' she said '…eccentric. He didn't really want to be a costume designer or a fashion illustrator. He wanted to be a serious artist. But he never took it seriously.'

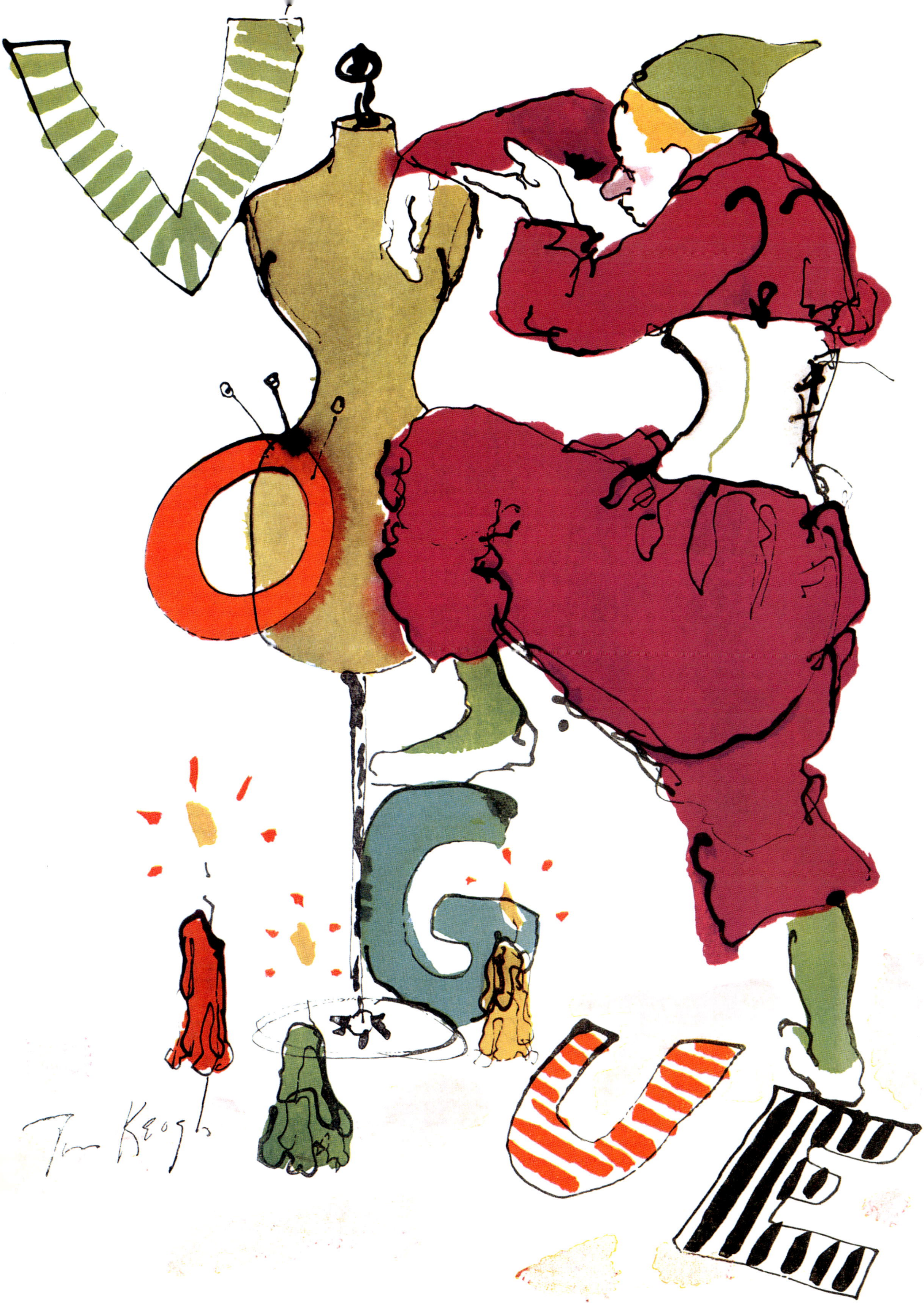
VOGUE

HIGH SOCIETY
Keogh graphically describes two gala attendees in October 1950 *(below)*, and a coat in 'Dumbo grey' by Piguet, in 1948 *(right)*. *Courtesy French Vogue*

101

THE NEW *GRAPHISME*

In the 1940s and 1950s, a brilliant group of photographers – Avedon, Penn and Horst among them – began to dominate the pages of *Vogue* and *Harper's Bazaar.* In response, fashion illustrators adopted a new graphic dynamism as the challenge became 'to do what photography couldn't.'

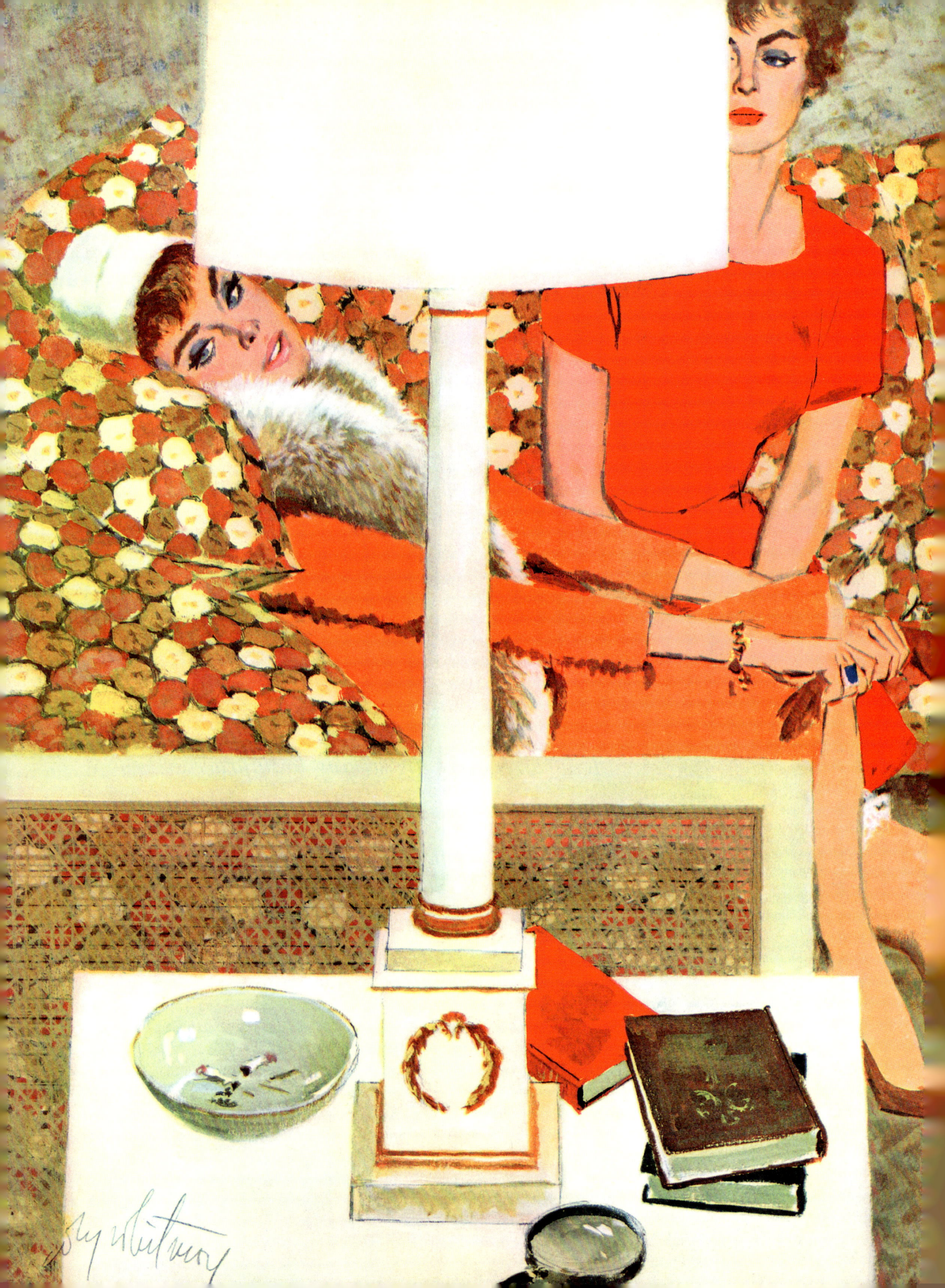

FEMALE TROUBLE

The women's uneasy expressions (and the unorthodox placement of the lamp) underline Whitmore's ability to subvert the clichés of romantic fiction in this 1958 illustration for The Saturday Evening Post. Copyright 1958 SEPS: Licensed by Curtis Publishing, USA

COBY WHITMORE

Coby Whitmore was not a fashion illustrator, though fashion certainly played a part in his work. He was one of mid-century America's great 'romance' artists. Technically brilliant and graphically daring, Whitmore's dazzling cinematic images (Douglas Sirk, anyone?) dominated the pages of women's magazines in the 1940s, 50s and 60s. Along with Al Parker, Joe Bowler, Jon Whitcomb and Joe de Mers (sometimes known as 'clinch,' 'pretty girl' or 'pony tail' artists), Whitmore's subject was America in Love. Or perhaps more accurately, affluent, suburban and white America in Love with its own reflection. And for Whitmore and his peers, the much-derided genre of romantic fiction allowed them a freedom to experiment with design, perspective and *mise en scène* that advertising for Pepsi Cola or Cadillac or American Airlines did not. In a post-Depression, postwar land of plenty, Whitmore was a poet of the radiant, perfect world surface and the anxiety that underpinned it.

He was born M. Coburn Whitmore in Dayton, Ohio, in 1913. After studying at the Dayton Art Institute he moved to Chicago, where he was apprenticed to the commercial studio of the illustrator Haddon Sundblom (although Sundblom is best known today for his iconic Christmas ads for Coca-Cola, he was also a great painter of women, and among the many alumni of the 'Sundblom circle' was the pin-up maestro, Gil Elvgren). Whitmore worked briefly for *The Herald Examiner* and in 1943 he moved to New York, where he signed up with the Charles E. Cooper Studio.

Cooper's was founded in the mid-1930s. By the time Whitmore joined, it was the most prestigious, profitable and highly respected agency in New York. Located on three floors at the corner of Lexington Avenue and 57th Street, the studio boasted a roster of up to sixty top-tier commercial artists. And commerce was certainly at its heart. The core business at the studio was advertising: selling products (and dreams) to an avid and ever-expanding consumer population. Cooper's also provided an unrivalled level of support for its illustrators that included not only studios with north light, but darkrooms, a library, a post room and a handful of sales reps pounding the city beat.

Although advertising was the bedrock of Cooper's business, artists were encouraged to build up a following and garner attention by taking on editorial work. As an added incentive, the studio took no commission on these assignments. Women's magazines, with weekly circulations running into millions, had an insatiable desire for 'boy-girl' art and provided rich pickings for top illustrators (fees for a single image could be as high as $3,000). The market was dominated by seven large-format glossies collectively known as the Seven Sisters: *Cosmopolitan, McCall's, Redbook, Ladies Home Journal, Woman's Day, Woman's Home Companion* and *Good Housekeeping*. With up to half a dozen short stories and serials in each issue, the art of romance was the art of big business.

WIDESCREEN

There is something inescapably cinematic in Whitmore's framing and *mise en scène*, not to mention the glamour of his protagonists (perhaps this is not surprising – both Grace Kelly and Tippi Hedren modelled for Cooper Studio artists before they found stardom). *Above, Courtesy the Collection of the LaRoche-Knight Family. Left, Courtesy the Klompen-LaRoche Family*

107

GOOD HOUSEKEEPING
The pleasures and pitfalls of illustrating romantic fiction included designing spreads with 'blank space' for copy. The results could be intriguing, as in this late 1950s story for *Good Housekeeping*. Courtesy the Collection of the LaRoche-Knight Family

109

AMERICAN EVE
Whitmore once confessed that his primary interest was drawing 'smart clothes on good-looking women.' *Courtesy the Collection of the LaRoche-Knight Family*

Whitmore rose through the ranks. His illustrations appeared in ads for Ivory Snow and Kotex as well as in the leading women's magazines. From 1950 onwards, a series of covers for *The Saturday Evening Post*, snappier and breezier than Rockwell's slices of Americana, signalled a move towards a new stylization in illustration. But it was Al Parker, the don of romance fiction, who led the way in the 1950s, experimenting with a new, modernist approach, utilizing negative space, multiple perspectives and shifts in scale. Parker, perhaps more than any of his peers, shook up the genre and subverted the narrative. His work became both simpler, in that it eliminated extraneous detail, and more complicated in the demands it made of its audience. Whitmore was not far behind. By the mid-1950s, his resplendent, glamorous illustrations had become ever more daring and at times unsettling. His Hollywood blondes (and Technicolor redheads and brunettes) had a vibrant sexiness and an uncompromisingly direct gaze; viewers became voyeurs.

As the decade progressed, television soaked up advertising dollars and photography gained favour, forcing artists to push boundaries, as the imperative became 'to do what photography couldn't'. Like many of the illustrators at Cooper's, Whitmore took painting classes with Reuben Tam at the Brooklyn Museum, which almost certainly had an influence on the looser, more painterly work he began producing from the late 1950s on.

By the early 1960s, the appetite for romance was on the wane, and illustration played a less and less pivotal role in the magazines that had once sustained it. Whitmore was now living with his family (he had three children) in Connecticut, and though things had slowed, he carried on working for commercial clients such as Gallo Wines and magazines such as *The Saturday Evening Post* into the mid-1960s. Always a passionate automobile enthusiast (he once confessed that he 'preferred the scream of a racing engine to the sound of Tchaikovsky'), he also designed and raced sports cars with the celebrated driver John Fitch. In the late 1960s, he moved to Hilton Head Island, South Carolina, where he established himself as a successful portrait painter.

Ten years before his death in 1988, Coby Whitmore was inducted into the Society of Illustrators' Hall of Fame. 'Coby lived well, loved well and drove well and showed untold others how to do it too,' his nephew said recently; 'all done unselfishly and with great humility… just an old-fashioned nice guy.'

STORYVILLE
Two characteristically graphic spreads from *Good Housekeeping* in the late 1950s. Whitmore's avant-garde compositions fascinated readers and delighted his peers. *Private collection/Hearst Corporation*

When a woman wishes to go back in time, it is for a man she seeks to meet again. May we now present Lydia Paget?

AFTER THE INTERVAL

■ Who has never wished to go back and begin again? As far as the minor human errors are concerned, this is often possible—embroidery can be unpicked, flower beds replanted, even quarrels made up—by dint of nothing more than patience and good temper. Sadly different is the case of those unfortunates who would retrace not mere days or months but years, perhaps decades, perhaps half a lifetime. For them, as a rule, there is no hope.

Every rule, however, has its exceptions. The case of Lydia Paget, who wished with all her heart, at the age of thirty-three, to go back to a precise midsummer 12 years past, was remarkable in that she was offered the chance to do so.

Driving a hired, slightly ramshackle small car down to her godmother's home in the country, Miss Paget examined this extraordinary circumstance with equal astonishment and gratitude. She was a good driver and knew the way. Also, while driving, she was accustomed to meditating, usually upon whatever assignment lay ahead of her in her work as a professional director of amateur dramatics. She handled local pageants, Greek pastorals, modern farce—come one, come all—with equal skill, although it wasn't what she had set out to do. Now, subconsciously turning left or right in accordance with an invisible map, subconsciously obeying every rule of the road, Lydia safely let her mind range back, to recapitulate and re-examine, before she allowed herself to hope.

Once she stopped and got out to look at herself. The mirror from her purse was fair-sized and almost cruelly clear; nor does sunshine flatter. It was a fair test and not too dismaying. Obviously I don't look twenty-one, thought Lydia Paget, but neither will Roger, I suppose, look thirty.

Not uncommonly, when *(Continued on page 149)*

BY MARGERY SHARP
ILLUSTRATED BY COBY WHITMORE

He's away. She's at home. Who's with him tonight—man or woman? She's at home—wondering—

LIFE OF A SALESMAN

BY ADELA ROGERS ST. JOHNS

This was, Cherry realized bitterly, the eighth dinner in a row—if you could call it dinner—she had eaten alone. Considering the whole five weeks, this particular five weeks since Tip had left on his fall trip, she had probably eaten twenty-five dinners by herself. It was too many.

The first four weeks she'd gone out a few times. The Haldanes, next door, had been short a fourth for bridge, and to bridge fiends like the Haldanes even Cherry Blakesley was better than no fourth at all. Once Norma Crosby had got a baby sitter, and she and Cherry had gone to dinner at the Tail o' the Cock and then to a movie. A couple of times Cherry had gone over to take potluck with Renee Dolan, whose husband was a newsreel cameraman on an assignment somewhere in the Pacific.

Of course she only went out when Tip had already called, early. If he hadn't, she stayed home, waiting.

The fifth and sixth weeks were the toughest. For eight nights now she'd eaten alone. The point was, how many times more was she prepared to do it while Tip was gallivanting around with some of his pals—or gals, for all she knew—on the road? The chances were pretty good that a convivial soul like Tip wasn't eating alone. He might be having dinner with almost anybody. All right, so maybe it was business. Or maybe it wasn't.

With one of the graceful silver forks that were part of her wedding silver, new just three years ago, Cherry poked at her pineapple-and-cottage-cheese salad and decided that, healthful or not, one more bite of it would choke her, the way she felt.

Every time Tip left on a trip she promised him she'd cook herself a real meal, a hot meal, once a day.

"You *eat*, you hear me?" Tip said, pretending to give her a sock on the chin with his closed fist and just missing. "I like you thin, but not *that* thin."

"Sure, sure, I'll eat," Cherry said, her face pressed against his sweater, right under his chin. "I'll stuff myself like a goose. Don't you worry about *me*."

"You don't worry about me either and it's a deal," Tip said, opening the car door, ready to take off for six endless weeks.

Cherry always watched him roar around the corner on two wheels, always waited to catch his last frantic, excited wave, always went into the empty house filled to the brim with good *(Continued on page 224)*

ILLUSTRATED BY COBY WHITMORE

THE GOOD LIFE
Whitmore seldom painted scenes as lyrical and straightforwardly romantic as this *(above)*. This slightly surreal scene *(right)* was almost certainly more to his taste. *Courtesy the Collection of the LaRoche-Knight Family*

112

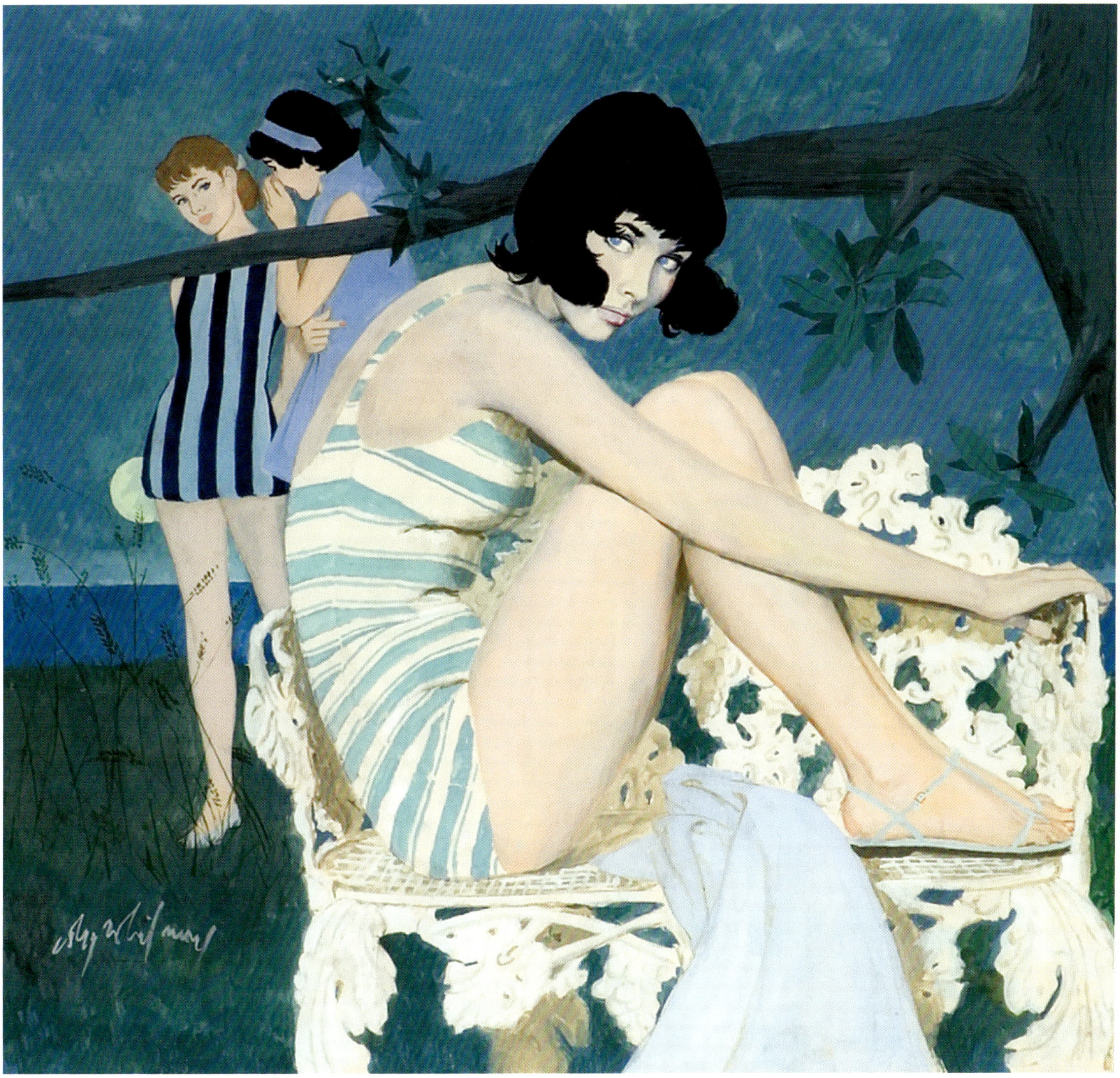

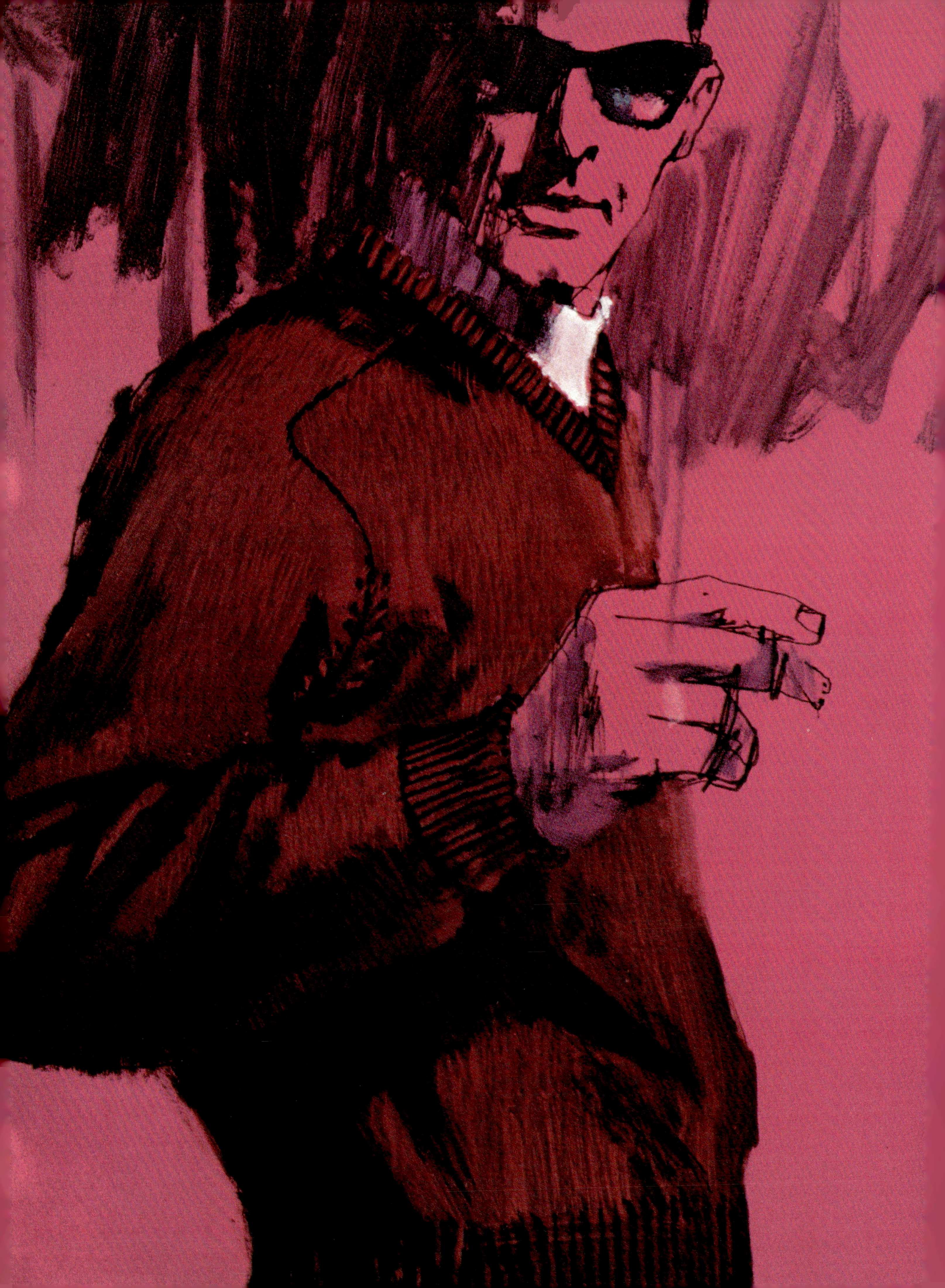

PURITAN SPORTSWEAR
A typically sexy and assured ad for, Puritan Sportswear, circa 1965. Copyright Bob Peak Estate

BOB PEAK

Bob Peak was once asked how he felt about being labelled a 'commercial illustrator'. 'I love it!' he said; 'I AM a commercial illustrator. That's all I ever wanted to be, even as a little kid.' In the late 1950s and early 1960s, Peak produced works of art for mass consumption that became part of America's visual landscape. There were times during his forty-year career (he died in 1992) when Peak's work was, quite literally, everywhere: on newsstands and advertising hoardings; in magazines and galleries; on stamps and – most strikingly – on movie posters. Indeed, it is as a poster artist that he is best remembered today. Peak's fashion illustrations, though less well known, utilize the key elements of his signature style: authoritative draughtsmanship, dazzling technique and dramatic compositional flair. Bridging the Eisenhower and Kennedy eras, his illustrations of men's fashion are the last word in laid-back, masculine glamour. Try looking at them today without hearing the swooping chords of a Burt Bacharach melody, or feeling the kick of a third martini.

MAD MEN
In the late 1950s and early 1960s, Bob Peak was Madison Avenue's illustrator of choice when a laid-back, Rat Pack glamour was called for. The drawings on these pages are for Diners Club, 1965 (*above*), Dobbs Hats, 1957 and Monsieur Lanvin, 1963.
Copyright Bob Peak Estate

Peak was born in Colorado in 1927. He studied geology at Wichita State University, and following a brief tour of duty with the navy, he enrolled in the Art Center College of Design, Los Angeles, in 1950. Graduating three years later, he headed for New York, with his wife (also an art school graduate) and young family in tow.

In New York, Peak signed up at Fredman-Chaite Studios on West 47th Street. Like its rival, the Cooper Studios, Fredman-Chaite ran a stable of top-tier commercial artists, specializing in advertising and editorial work. Initially, Peak's bravura style baffled art buyers: 'you're going to have to pull in your horns,' he was told; 'there's no market for your flamboyant work.' Then, in 1958, Peak landed an advertising campaign for Old Hickory Whisky (beating his idol, René Bouché to the job), which changed everything. 'I went from making nothing, to thirty or forty thousand a year,' he recalled some time later, still bemused. In this 'Mad Men' era, art directors and account executives saw both the creative and commercial imperative of illustration, and before long Peak had notched up campaigns for TWA, 7-Up and Columbia records. At the same time, his work was appearing in the defining magazines of the period: *Time, Esquire, Sports Illustrated* (who sent him on a seventeen-day hunting trip with the Shah of Iran that resulted in a bout of dysentery), *Redbook* and *Cosmopolitan*. In 1961 he was voted 'Artist of the Year' by the Artists Guild of New York.

Peak's two principal fashion accounts were for Puritan Sportswear and Dobbs hats. In the Dobbs ads, a Madison Avenue executive, tightly framed in a cinematic landscape, elicits admiring glances from a string of Social Register beauties. For Puritan, an account that would eventually see Peak producing twenty-five to thirty ads a year, he opened out his canvas, depicting sophisticated men of the world (fashionably attired and with a *de rigeur* cigarette – smoking went with everything) at their ease in the great outdoors.

FIGARO

the beginning of a new
international *gift* habit

FIGARO
    VETYVER
        LAVANDE

Cologne	3.75	Talc	2.00
After Shave	3.00	Soap	2.00

PLUS TAX

COPYRIGHT 1963, LANVIN-PARFUMS, INC.

MONSIEUR LANVIN

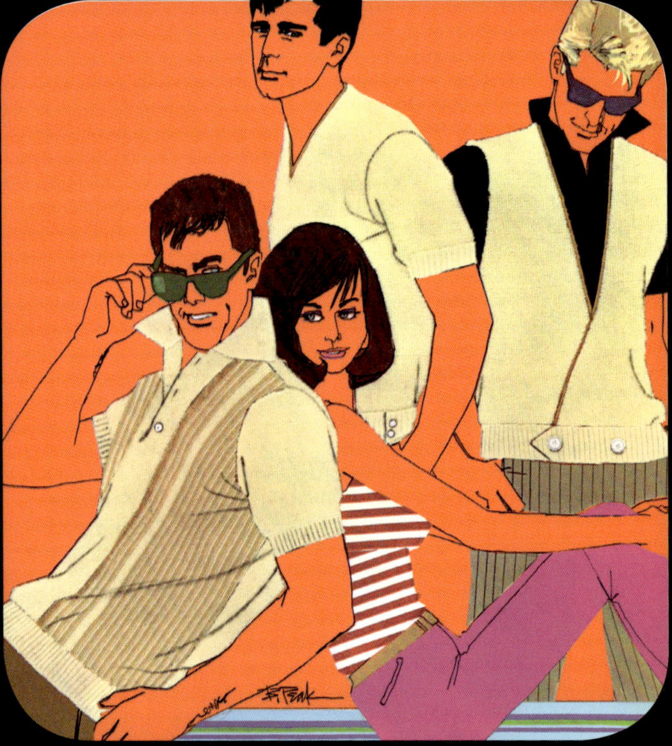

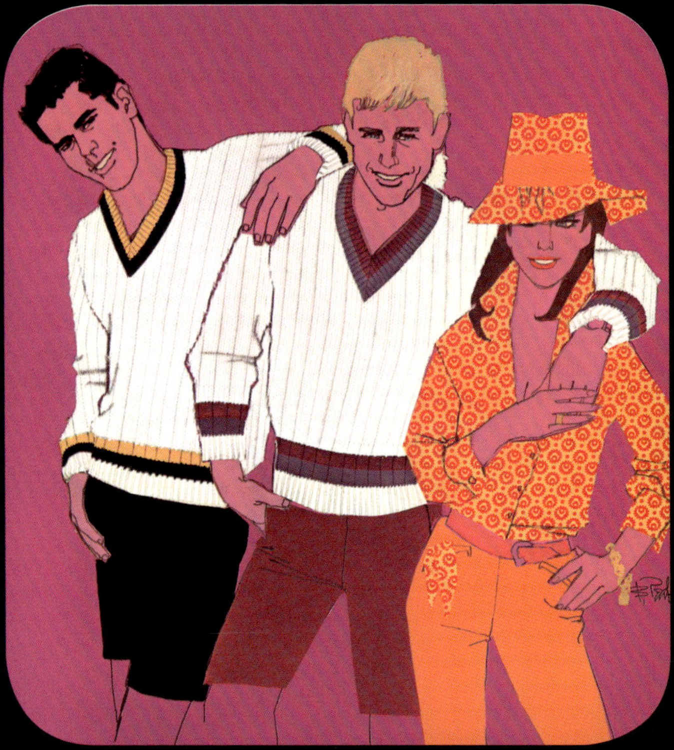

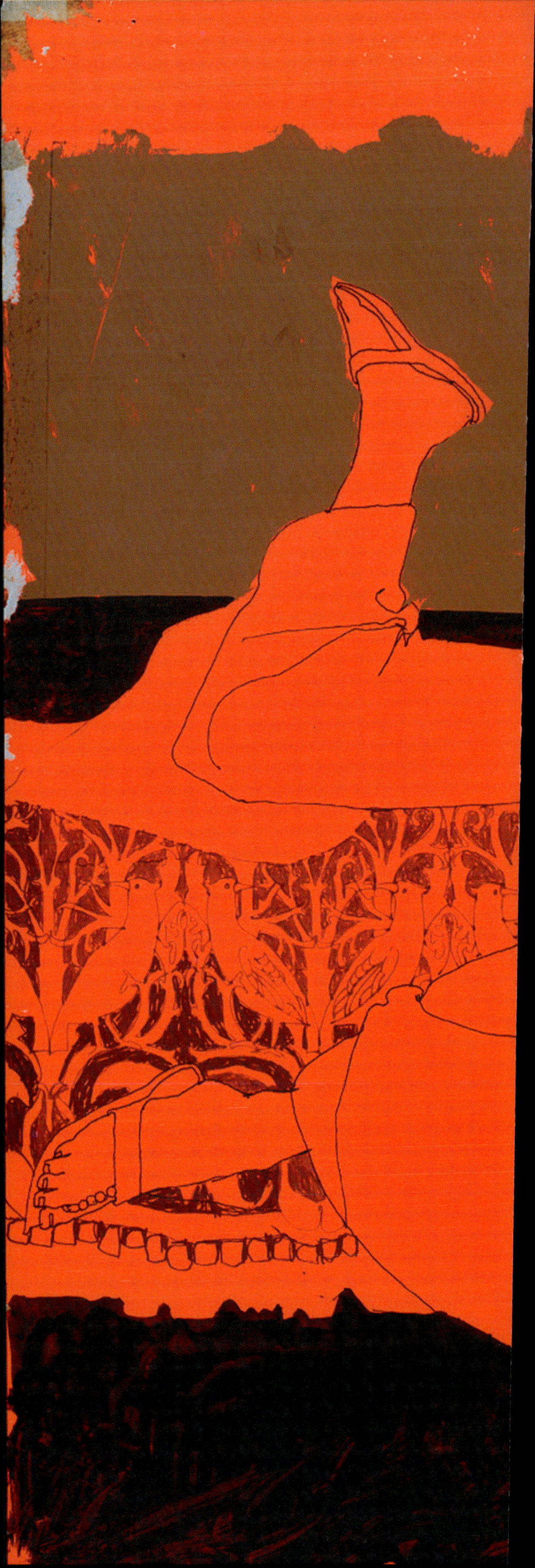

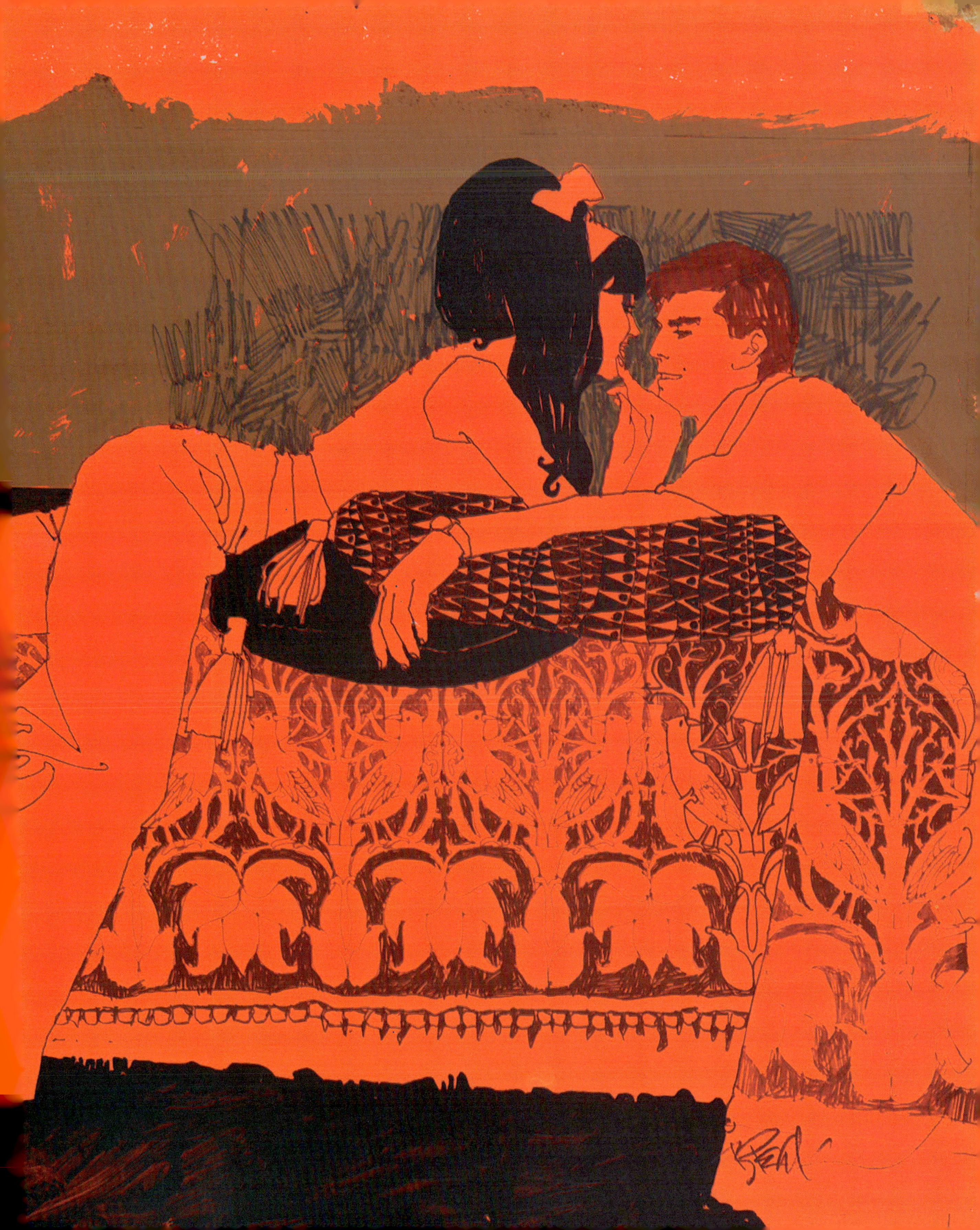

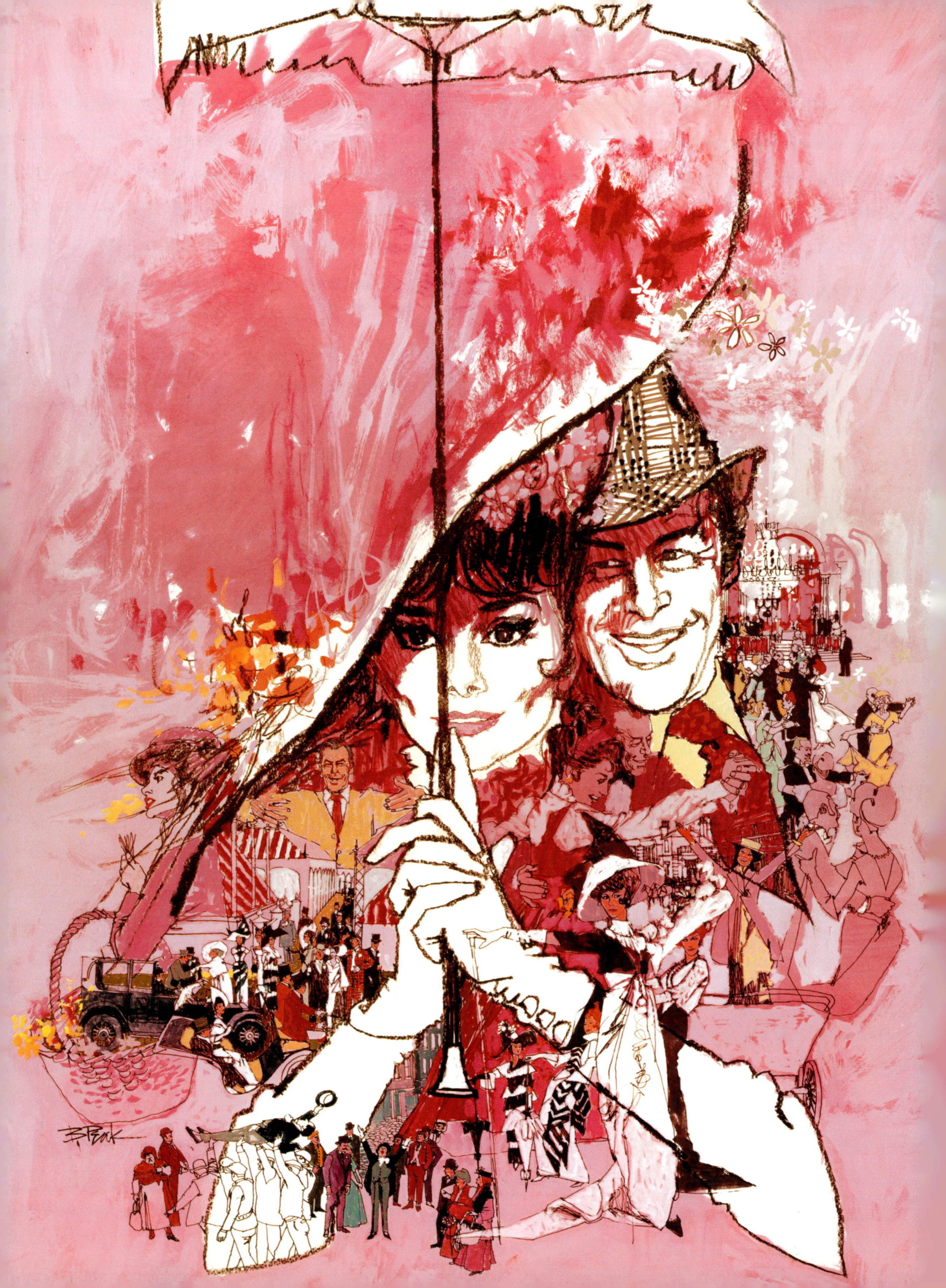
B. Peak

YEAH, BABY! *(previous spread)*
Peak used cut paper collage and an eye-popping colour palette to great graphic effect in the mid-1960s. *Left*, two 1965 advertisements for Puritan Sportswear. *Right*, a short story illustration for *Redbook* magazine, 1966. *Copyright Bob Peak Estate*

The 1960s had a galvanizing effect on Peak. His palette flared into a kaleidoscope of scarlet, fuchsia, orange and chartreuse. The archetypal Peak Man, a Cary Grant/Gregory Peck hybrid, got hip, and his companion morphed into a seminal swinging chick with a Bardot pout and hellcat hair. Op Art and Pop Art patterns swirled across the surface of his drawings, taking them to the brink of abstraction. From the late 1960s on, Peak concentrated on movie-poster work, describing it as the 'most democratic advertising art' (lucrative too – he was able to command $100,000 for a campaign), and gradually he left fashion behind. It's our loss. Still, there were memorable posters from the period, including *Camelot* reimagined as a medieval summer of love in 1967, and über-cool artwork for two silly spy movies, *Modesty Blaise* and *In Like Flint*, which could never live up to Peak's vision of them.

By the 1970s, with musicals and spy movies out of fashion, Peak, ever the pragmatist and always ahead of the curve, explored new techniques. He took up the airbrush and turned his attention to science fiction and fantasy, designing posters for *Star Trek*, *Superman* and *Excalibur*, among others. By the time of his death in 1992, Peak was the acknowledged master of the genre, and had completed more than 100 designs.

MOVIE MAESTRO
Peak's 1964 poster for the musical *My Fair Lady* (*opposite*), with its elegantly reductive portraits of Audrey Hepburn and Rex Harrison, swirling set pieces and dramatic shifts in scale, was the first movie poster to win an award from the Society of Illustrators. *Above*, charcoal study of Marlon Brando for Schaefer Award Theatre, 1962. *Copyright Bob Peak Estate*

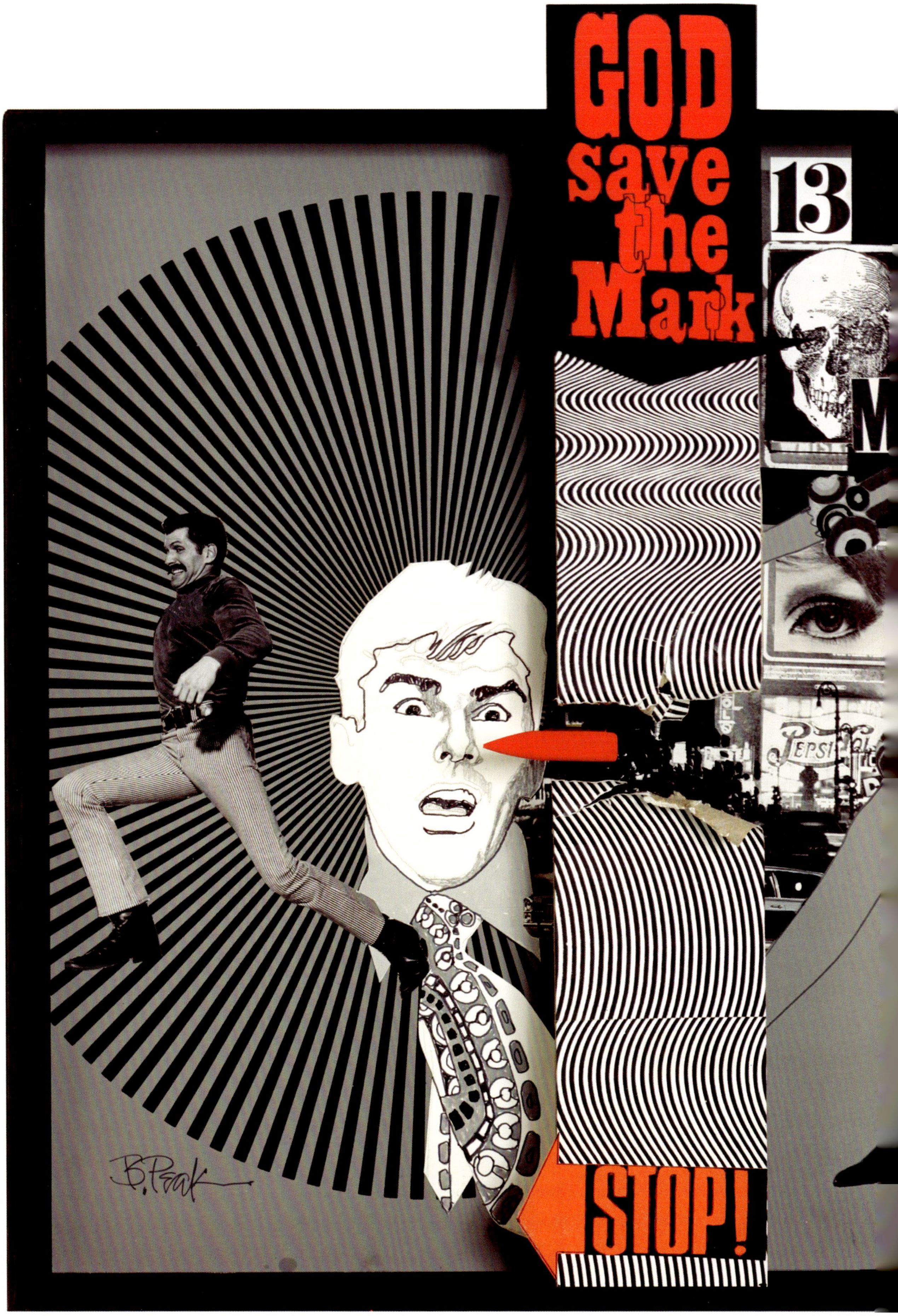
GOD save the Mark
13
STOP!
B. Peak

TO THE LIMIT

A dizzying composition of girls, guns, Op Art and 3D elements features in this exhilarating editorial illustration from 1970. *Copyright Bob Peak Estate*

123

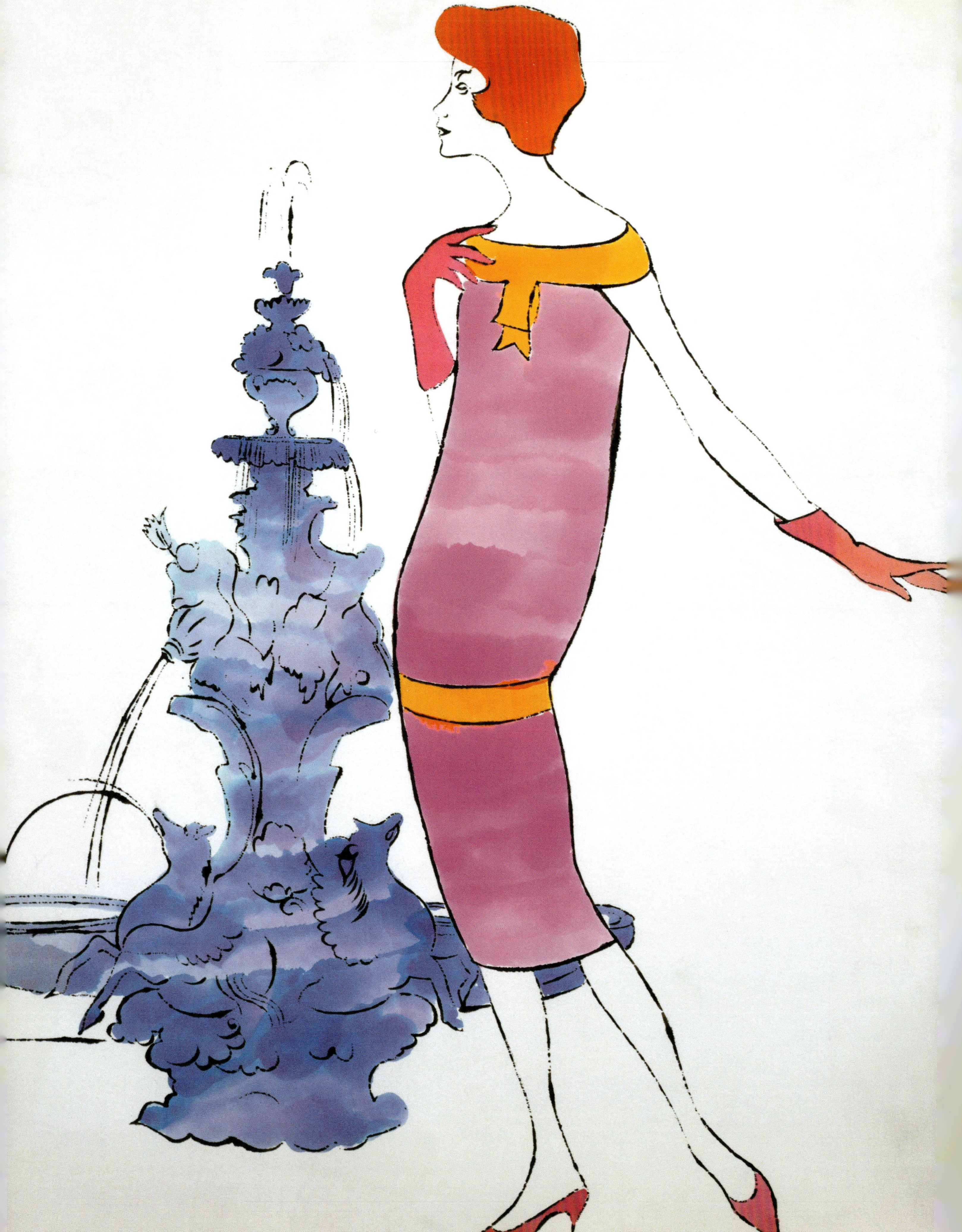

ANDY WARHOL

Andy Warhol [signature]

BLUE PERIOD
Fifty years after they were created, Warhol's fashion illustrations remain irresistibly modern. *Female Fashion Figure*, circa 1960. Courtesy Corbis

Andy Warhola (that second 'a' would quickly be dropped) arrived in Manhattan in the summer of 1949, a graduate of the Carnegie Institute in Pittsburgh. He was not quite 21. Within months he had landed his first job as a commercial artist, for *Glamour* magazine. That assignment, drawing shoes for the fashion pages and illustrating an article entitled *Success is a Job in New York*, was certainly prescient. For wouldn't success and glamour (and shoes) be among Warhol's most sustained and sustaining *leitmotifs*?

By the early 1960s, when Warhol gave up taking commercial assignments to concentrate on his career as a Pop artist, he was successful by any measure. From his first, barely there, line drawings in the margins of *Esquire* and *Bazaar* to full-blown advertising campaigns for I. Miller and windows for Bonwit Teller, Warhol had become one of the most sought-after illustrators in America. On the way he had accumulated a slew of awards, set up Andy Warhol Enterprises Inc. to handle his business interests, and moved to a stylish townhouse on Lexington Avenue. In fact, by the late 1950s Andy Warhol was 'almost famous'.

Happy butterfly day

Andy Warhol

Warhol achieved all this by dint of ambition, application, an extraordinary capacity for work, and timing. He was a hypersensitive and slightly unnerving presence – 'a sphinx without a riddle,' as Truman Capote later dubbed him, but he was certainly memorable. Tina S. Fredericks, the art editor who gave Warhol his break at *Glamour*, remembered him as 'diffident almost to the point of disappearance but somehow immediately and immensely appealing.' Warhol apparently knew how to foster the cult of his own personality from the beginning. Shy he may have been, but he insisted on making connections and contacts himself (even after he had taken on an agent) and he usually came bearing gifts; a brown paper bag might contain a hand-drawn flyer or a limited-edition book interleaved with brightly coloured flags. He was deft, eager to please and relished direction. For art directors in that long-ago era of superstar illustrators, their agents and egos, he was an answered prayer.

Warhol quickly realized that the most efficient way of making money (and we shouldn't underestimate the financial imperative for the son of Czech immigrants, brought up in the Depression) was not by inflating his prices – magazines and agencies, then as now, had a fairly inflexible pay structure – but by taking on more work, by doing everything that was asked of him. To that end he developed a way of working that suited both his love of imagery that 'looked printed' and his need for speed – the blotted-line technique. Essentially this involved tracing an original master drawing using a fountain pen and blotting it, little by little, line by line, onto a sheet of Strathmore paper, creating a third-generation image. Up to ten 'prints' could be made from an original and then inked up in any number of colour combinations. As time went on and his workload increased, this hand-colouring, and sometimes the drawing itself, would be given over to assistants. In 1952, when Warhol's mother joined him from Pittsburgh, she too was co-opted into service, producing the distinctive, decorative calligraphy that adorned much of his work. (She would receive an Art Directors Club certificate for her endeavours in 1958.)

NATURE, PERFECTED
Warhol frequently used flora and fauna motifs in his illustrations, as here in *Happy Butterfly Day*, 1955, *left*, and *Female Head*, circa 1958, *right*. Courtesy Corbis

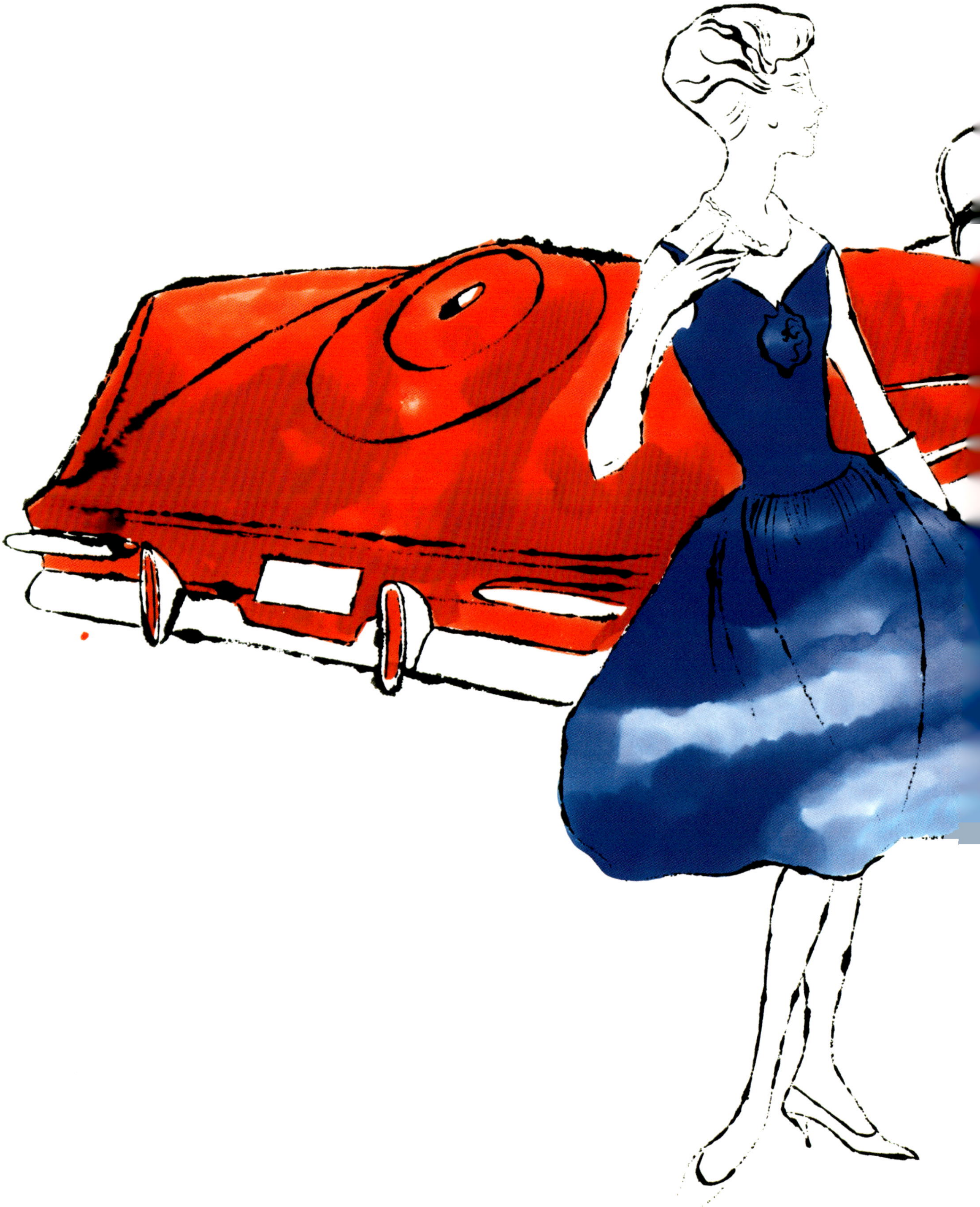

AMERICAN DREAM
Warhol took on late 1950s' consumerism with his customary flair in *Female Fashion Figure*, circa 1959.
Courtesy Corbis

In later years, Warhol seldom discussed his pre-Pop career and much of the original work was destroyed. Yet these early drawings, with their sly humour and acidic, eye-popping colour, have a graphic sophistication and lightness of touch that still resonates today. Half a century on, Warhol remains inescapably modern. His influences included Cocteau and Matisse, the American illustrator Ben Shahn, whose broken, blotted line many felt he had appropriated, and Paul Klee. Having found a technique that suited his needs, he saw little reason to deviate from it. Warhol's fashion drawings were executed in the same way as any other, and his style could seemingly be adapted to any subject matter: cherubs, butterflies, boys, even the dangers of drug abuse. Somehow, like everything he did, it worked.

Andy Warhol turned his back on commercial art to become a 'business artist', a cultural icon and a global celebrity. He made movies, presided over his infamous Factory, and taught the world to see Marilyn and Elvis and Liz his way. But was he ever so exuberant or charming again?

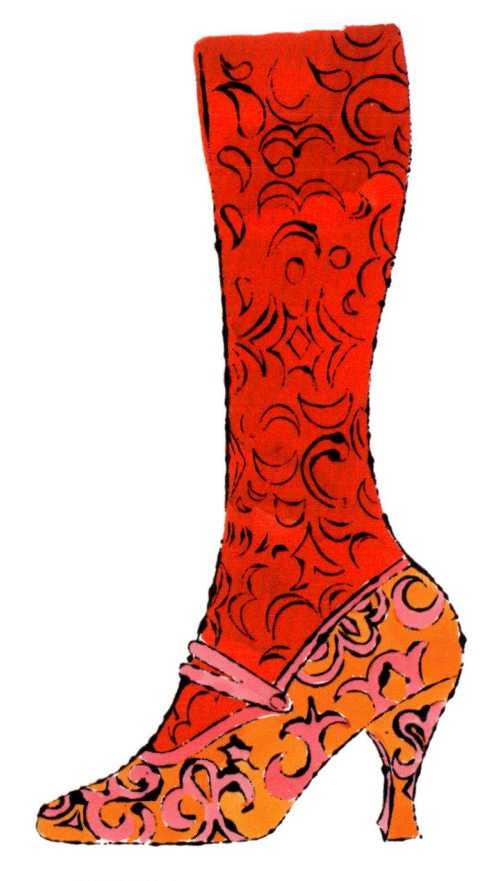

LEG ART
Shoes were never far from Warhol's mind during his years as a commercial illustrator. Here, Dr. Martin's inks give 1955's *Shoe and Leg* its characteristically vibrant look. *Courtesy Corbis*

EXHIBITIONIST
Multiple Fashion Accessories, circa 1960, catalogue from Timothy Taylor Gallery, London, 2007. *Courtesy Timothy Taylor Gallery*

SCHIAPARELLI
Warhol's unicorn (in a suitably shocking shade of pink) enlivens this 1957 advertising illustration for Schiaparelli gloves. *Private collection*

Schiaparelli

* *a division of* FOWNES GLOVES

FROM THE SALON TO THE STREET

The death of René Bouché in 1963 marked the end of the era of classical fashion illustration. Inspired by the youthquake of the 1960s and the street fashions of the 1980s, a new generation of artists set about revitalizing the art form, stirring a palpable energy and unapologetic sensuality into the mix.

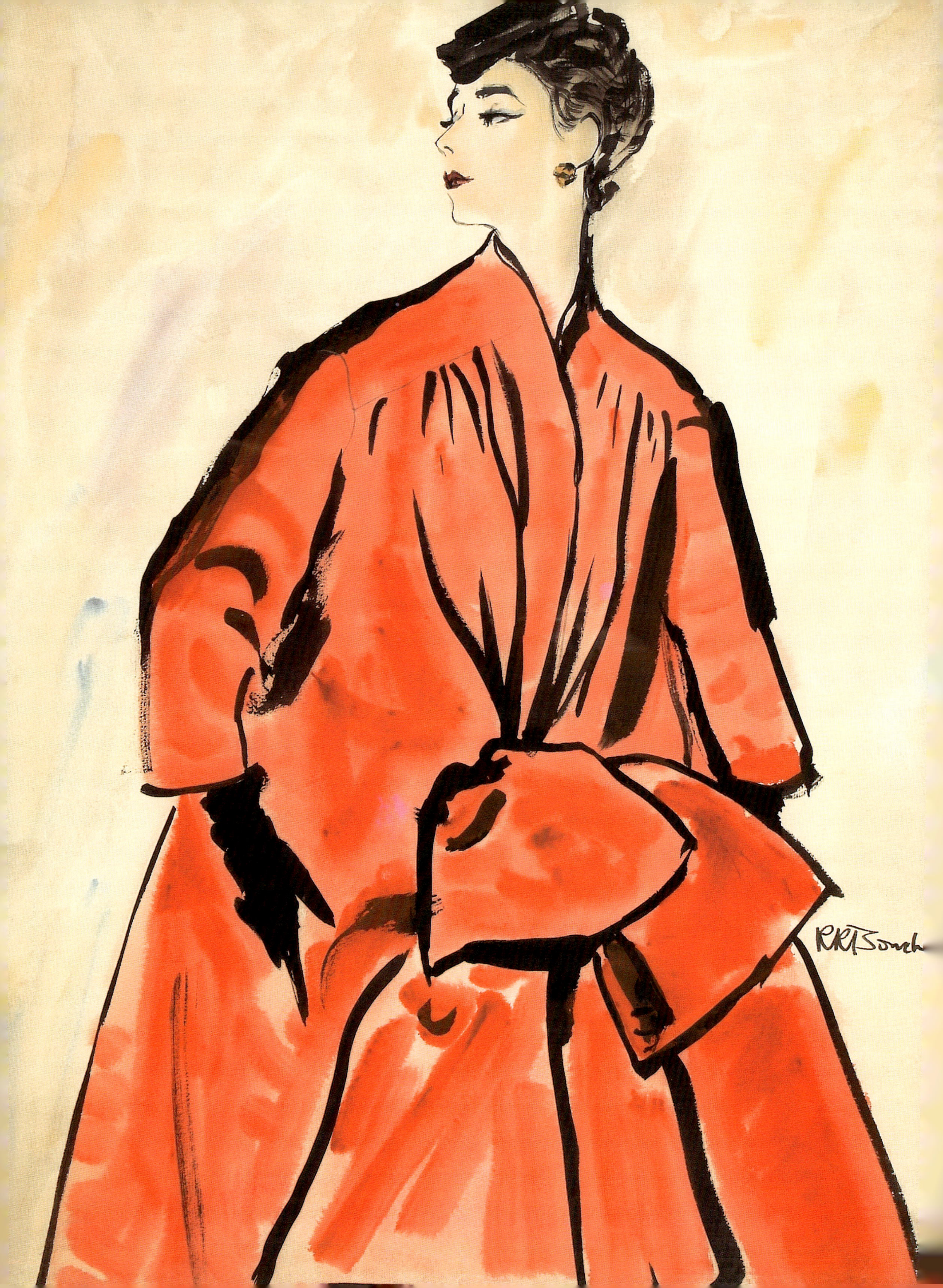

BALENCIAGA
A variation of this characteristically confident study of a Balenciaga coat was used on the cover of American *Vogue* in 1953. *Courtesy Estate of René Bouché*

RENÉ BOUCHÉ

Like all the great fashion artists who forged long careers, René Bouché was versatile. He could handle editorial, advertising, reportage and travel assignments with equal aplomb, but his lasting legacy will undoubtedly be as a social portraitist. No other artist (with the exception of Warhol, a few years later) so successfully blurred the line between fashion, art, celebrity and portraiture, and his list of subjects reads like a roll call of bold-face mid-century names. *Time* magazine, reviewing an exhibition in 1959, noted that 'he was not one to portray the bellhop or the country maid' and ranked him alongside Boldini and Sargent. Bouché no doubt would have enjoyed the comparison: 'I consider myself the avant garde,' he said, 'because nobody sings the song of the upper level of society. Nobody speaks of the exceptional human being.'

FASHION CORRESPONDENT
Bouché lived in New York, but travelled regularly to Paris to cover the couture collections. Shown here, from 1953, a Dior cover for French *Vogue (above)* and a design by Madame Grés *(right)*. Courtesy French *Vogue*

He was born René August Buchstein, in Prague, in 1905. His mother died when he was 9 years old and by the time he was in his mid-teens he had moved to Munich, where he studied art history, supporting himself by illustrating children's books. After a period in Berlin, during which he married the German artist Margo 'Pony' Schoenlank, he moved with his wife to Paris in 1934, where their son, Michel, was born. There, Bouché (he had adopted the surname while in Germany) studied at the Académie Ozenfant and worked for commercial clients including Nestlé, Ascott Shoes and Peugeot. His drawings began to appear in the lifestyle magazine *Plaisirs de France* and, from 1938, in *Vogue*. His early work for the magazine had an easy, throwaway assurance and was undoubtedly influenced by *Vogue's* leading artist of the time, Eric.

The war separated Bouché from his family. He joined the army, was captured and spent a period in a detention camp, from which he escaped and made his way via Lisbon to the United States. In America he joined up once more, but was given an honourable discharge a short time later after sustaining serious injuries. In 1941 he presented himself at the *Vogue* offices in New York to an underwhelming response. He was given six weeks to come up to scratch. When he duly presented a new portfolio, he was hired and, although he was never officially under contract, he remained at *Vogue* until his death in 1963.

Bouché's style began to evolve, more flamboyant than Eric's; his line was a little more trenchant and his eye a little sharper. Soon he was working steadily for *Vogue*. When the *Queen Elizabeth* was relaunched in 1946, he was on board as the magazine's eyes and ears. He also sent back drawings from postwar Madrid, Lisbon, Frankfurt and Paris. In the late 1940s he briefly became involved with the Abstract Expressionist movement in New York, although he maintained his commercial clients: Elizabeth Arden, Charles of the Ritz and Saks Fifth Avenue.

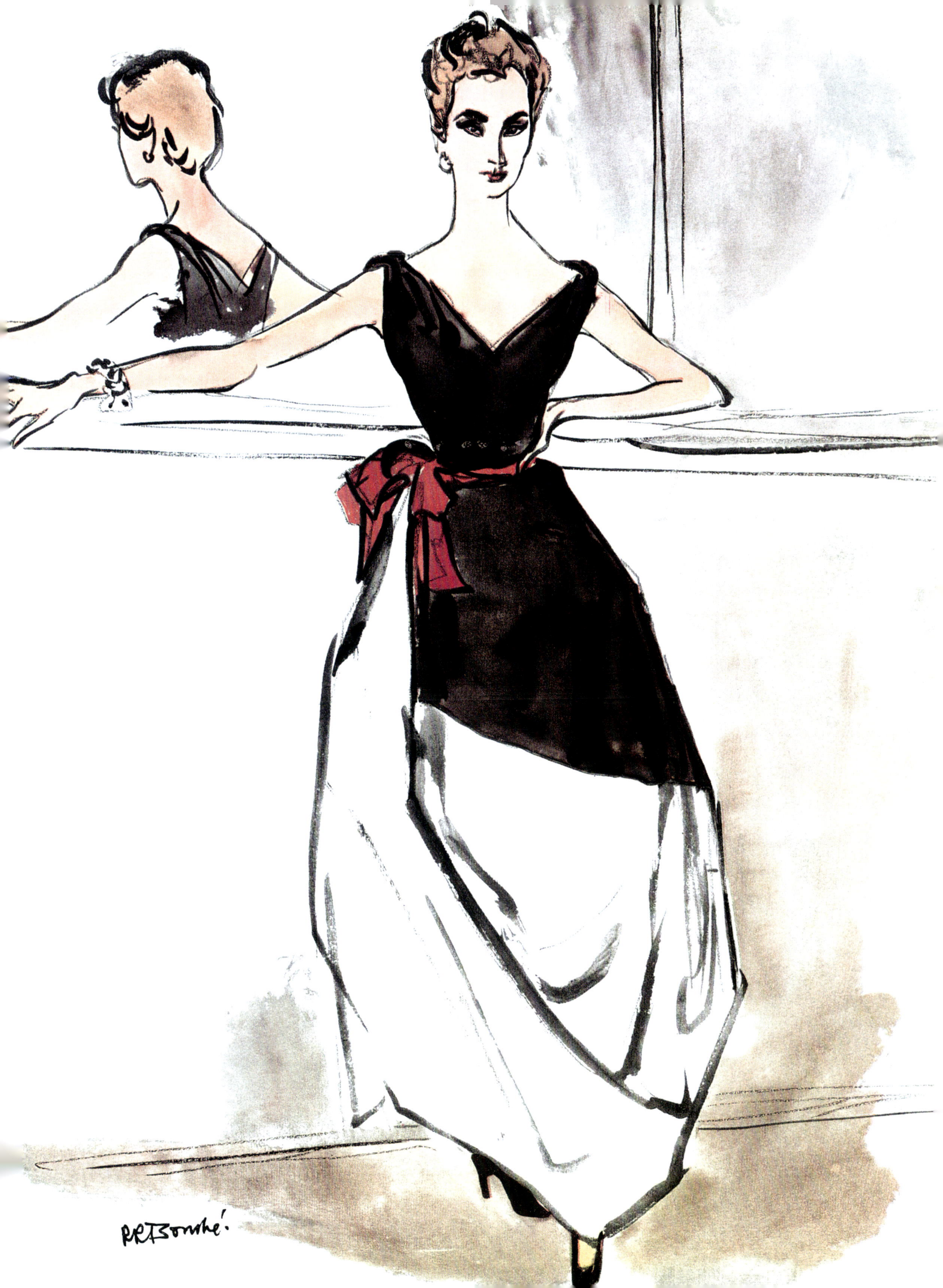
RRBouché.

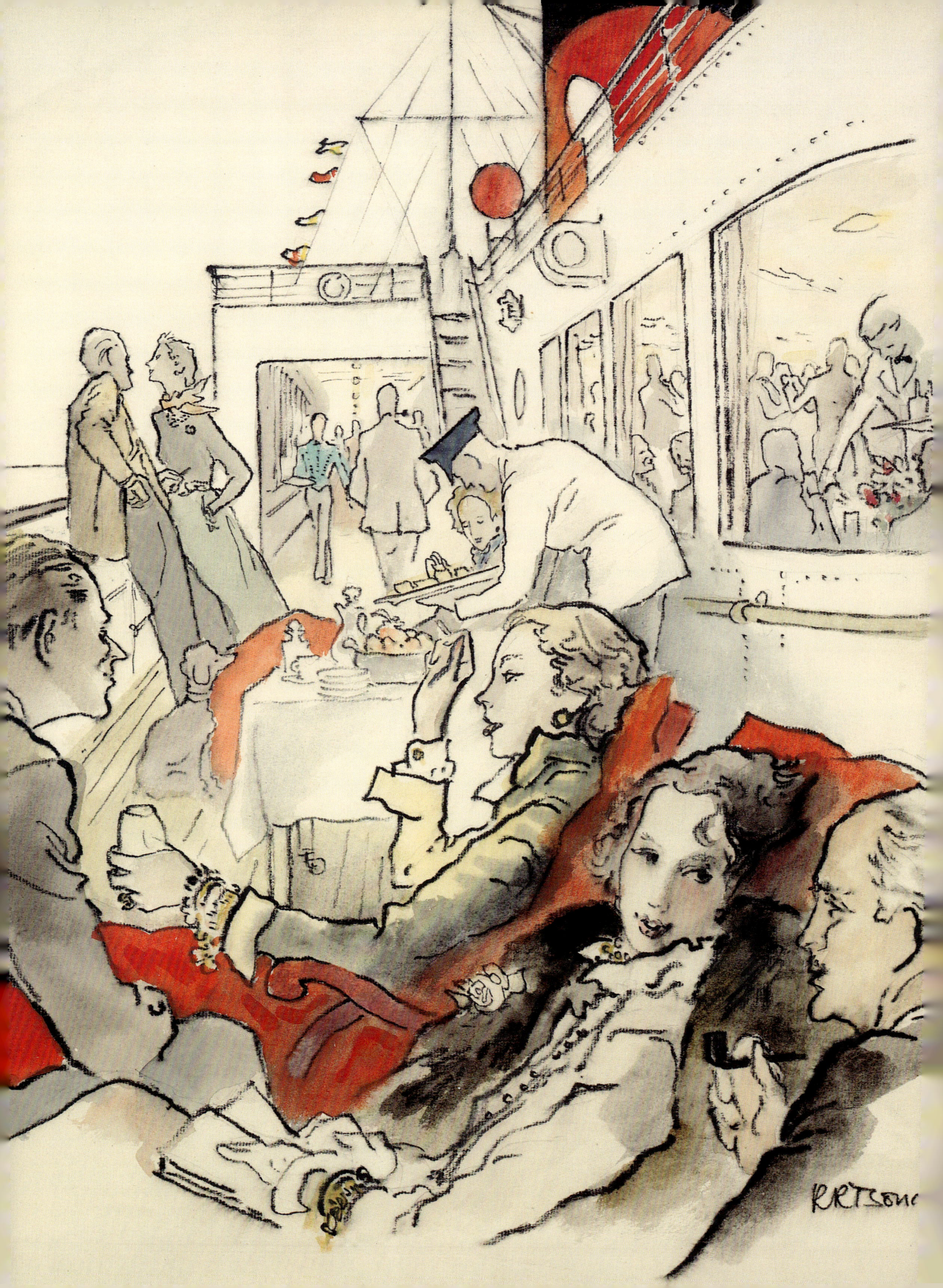

CONDÉ NAST TRAVELLER
A trip to Japan in 1957 produced some exquisite drawings of geisha life. *Courtesy Estate of René Bouché (above)*. Bouché conjures up the relaxed luxury of travel by ocean liner, circa 1955 *(left)*. *Courtesy The Bridgeman Art Library*

Throughout the 1950s, a series of travel pieces showed how brilliant Bouché could be when engaged; he went to Japan to study the rituals of geishas, to Dublin for the horse races and to the French Riviera, where a lyrical set of drawings captured the European aristocracy at play. And there was always Paris couture; although Bouché sometimes seemed bored by fashion, Dior, Givenchy and Balenciaga inspired him to create some of his most memorable images. And, as a highly valued contributor at *Vogue*, he was certainly accorded star treatment. After the show, a model and a selection of clothes would be rushed over to his penthouse suite at the Crillon – Garbo was a frequent next-door neighbour – and work, however pressing, could always be halted for a civilized lunch on the terrace, with its views of the Place de la Concorde.

Bouché had great intensity and charm. 'He got on with everybody,' according to his widow, Denise Bouché Fitch, whom he met at *Vogue* in 1956, and married in 1962 (although he reunited with Margo after the war, they divorced in 1954). The 1950s also saw Bouché's emergence as a portraitist. His charcoal sketches of 'significant contemporaries', as *Life* magazine dubbed them, were linear, perceptive and had a lightening veracity. They could flatter, or not. Bouché described them as a kind of 'loving criticism'.

MARELLA AGNELLI
Bouché spent a week on the Riviera in July 1957,
recording the jet set at work and at play for *Vogue*.
He drew the style icon and wife of Fiat magnate
Gianni Agnelli at their fabled villa, La Leopolda.
Courtesy Condé Nast Archive

JACQUELINE KENNEDY
Bouché first drew Jackie Kennedy's sister, Lee, in 1958. Later he made several drawings of the future First Lady, including this seldom-seen study. Later still, he painted both President Kennedy and his brother, Edward, for the cover of *Life* magazine. So familiar did he become to the Kennedy clan that he was known simply as 'Paintbrush'. *Courtesy Estate of René Bouché*

MARLENE DIETRICH

Dietrich was a great friend of Bouché's, and he made several drawings of her. This portrait from the late 1950s would be used to advertise her concert appearances until her retirement. *Courtesy Deutsche Kinemathek – Marlene Dietrich Collection, Berlin*

Bouché also painted a series of large-scale oils of notable figures for the cover of *Time* magazine and undertook several private commissions a year (for fees of up to $10,000). Among the artists who sat for him were Braque, De Kooning, Calder and Motherwell; writers included Capote, Auden, Huxley and Isak Dinesen; entertainers Sinatra, Dietrich and Judy Garland; society swans Babe Paley, C.Z. Guest and Marella Agnelli; musicians Stravinsky, Bernstein and Lenny Goodman; and, in the white heat of their glamour, President and Mrs Kennedy.

Bouché never gave up his commercial commissions. He designed costumes and sets for *Offenbach in the Underworld* for the American Ballet Theater, murals for the New York Hilton, and he continued working for *Vogue*. His last, unfulfilled, commission, which he received on the day of his death in England, was to paint the Archbishop of Canterbury.

In *Vogue's* September 1963 obituary, William S. Lieberman, Chairman of Twentieth Century Art at the Metropolitan Museum looked back: 'One evening not so long ago, René Bouché spoke to me about his work. He said that he believed that warmth, dignity, elegance and sophistication, even charm, are positive values for the painter, not to be effaced but rather to be nourished and kept beautiful. Although he admired the vanguard of American artists, his personal friends, he decided not to keep in step with them. He made a decision and quite deliberately set out to make his work and life one. He succeeded.'

JUDY GARLAND
One of Bouché's last commercial assignments was to sketch Judy Garland rehearsing her debut television series in 1963. The drawings appeared posthumously with a brief obituary in *TV Guide* in October that year. *Courtesy TV Guide Magazine, LLC, copyright 1963*

SAMMY DAVIS, JR.
'A meagre, sharp fellow, crammed with talent' is brilliantly conjoured in deft brushstrokes for *Vogue* in 1956. *Courtesy Condé Nast Archive*

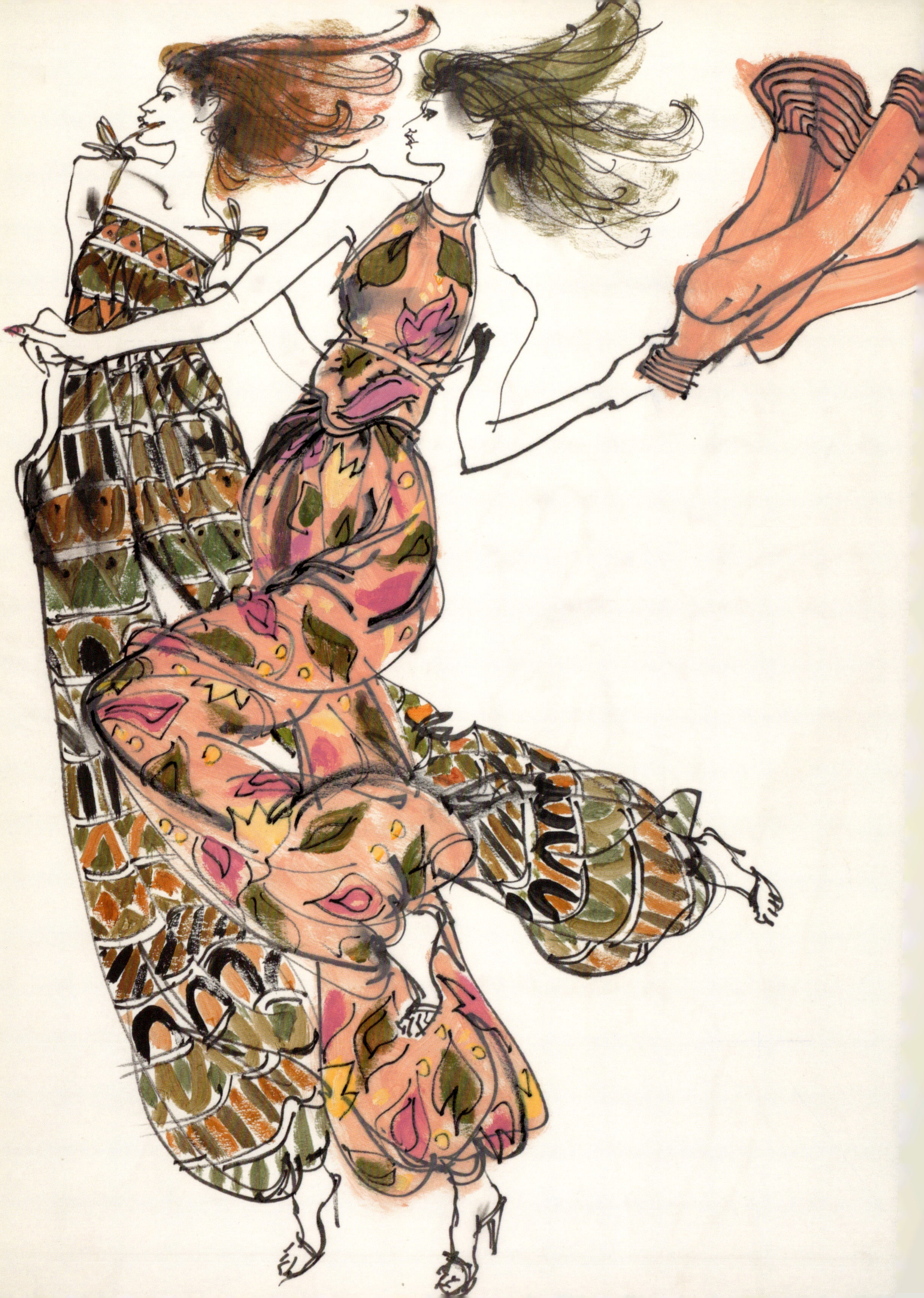

SWINGING CHIC

Block's mastery of composition and movement (as well as his eye for pattern) are beautifully realized in this 1981 drawing for *Women's Wear Daily*. The jumpsuits are by Bill Tice. *Courtesy Condé Nast Archive/Courtesy Pointed Leaf Press*

KENNETH PAUL BLOCK

Kenneth Paul Block was fashion illustration's ace reporter. A forty-year veteran of the trenches at *Women's Wear Daily* (the US fashion industry's trade paper) and later its glossier sister publication *W*, Block never failed to paint the picture, to give you the story. He was a master of movement and his models, poised to turn on a dime, are as snappy and sinuous as showgirls. Compare Block's gestural, dynamic view of fashion shows in Paris or New York with the pedestrian catwalk photography of the time and the difference is telling. The photographs give you the detail; Block puts you in the front row.

Block was born into a comfortable middle-class family in Larchmont, New York, in 1924. Drawing 'glamorous women in beautiful clothes' was, he later said, all he ever wanted to do. Fortunately, inspiration was near at hand in the form of his stylish aunt, Elsie Dick, who was an editor at *Harper's Bazaar*. The family later moved to Manhattan and Block began his training at Parsons School of Design. From there, his first professional job was for McCall's Patterns. The extraordinary level of detail required by that discipline proved to be invaluable. However stylized and spontaneous his drawings would become in later years, Block never forgot that showing the clothes (and how they worked) was central to the illustrator's art. In the mid-1950s he joined the staff at *Women's Wear Daily*, where he would remain until the illustration department was closed down in 1992.

PIERRE CARDIN
Block's expressive and inimitable line effortlessly conjours up a mid-1960s design by Pierre Cardin. *Courtesy Condé Nast Archive/Courtesy Pointed Leaf Press*

DIANA VREELAND
Vreeland was drawn by Bouché, Bérard and Cecil Beaton, among many others. Although she never sat officially for Kenneth Paul Block, the two were friends and worked together during Vreeland's tenure at the Metropolitan Museum. *Courtesy Morton Ribyat/Dean Rhys Morgan Collection*

BLOCK IN BLACK AND WHITE
A brilliantly observed drawing from the mid-1960s shows Block at his most pared-down and confident. *Courtesy Morton Ribyat/Dean Rhys Morgan Collection*

Women's Wear Daily, a family-owned and run newspaper, was founded in 1910. By the time Block joined it, it was well established as the 'bible of fashion'. Aimed at industry professionals, Seventh Avenue seers, *WWD* predicted trends and reported on the business of fashion from an unapologetically American standpoint. As drawing slipped quietly from the pages of *Vogue* and *Bazaar*, *WWD*'s staff artists battled relentless deadlines and the notoriously hit-and-miss quality of newsprint to bring its audience their daily fashion fix.

Taking over the reins in 1960 after a stint as the paper's European bureau chief, John Fairchild was in expansive mood. As the world looked to America and the youthful dazzle of the Kennedys, pondered the Space Race and witnessed the gradual loosening of Paris' stranglehold on high fashion, Fairchild oversaw *WWD*'s evolution from trade paper to lively, design-conscious and upbeat daily. 'This paper doesn't have to be boring,' he decreed; '…it should be colorful and visual and conversational and amusing.' He hired a new art director, Rudy Millendorf, gave more space to visual content and introduced a byline for the previously anonymous artists. At any one time, half a dozen or so illustrators worked full-time for the paper, a unique set-up, then and now. In the 1960s, these included talents such as Steven Stipelman, Pedro Barrios and, briefly, Antonio Lopez. But, as his style matured, it was Block who became first among equals. Working in charcoal (a medium enhanced, if anything, by the rudimentary print quality), he refined his craft and cut to the chase. His beat included the New York social scene and he could frequently be spotted, cigarette holder in one hand, sketching in Manhattan's swankiest watering holes. His ambition to draw beautiful women in beautiful clothes was realized in his elegant portraits of the style icons of the day. Babe Paley, the Duchess of Windsor, Gloria Guinness et al. were never more gloriously themselves than in a drawing by Kenneth Paul Block.

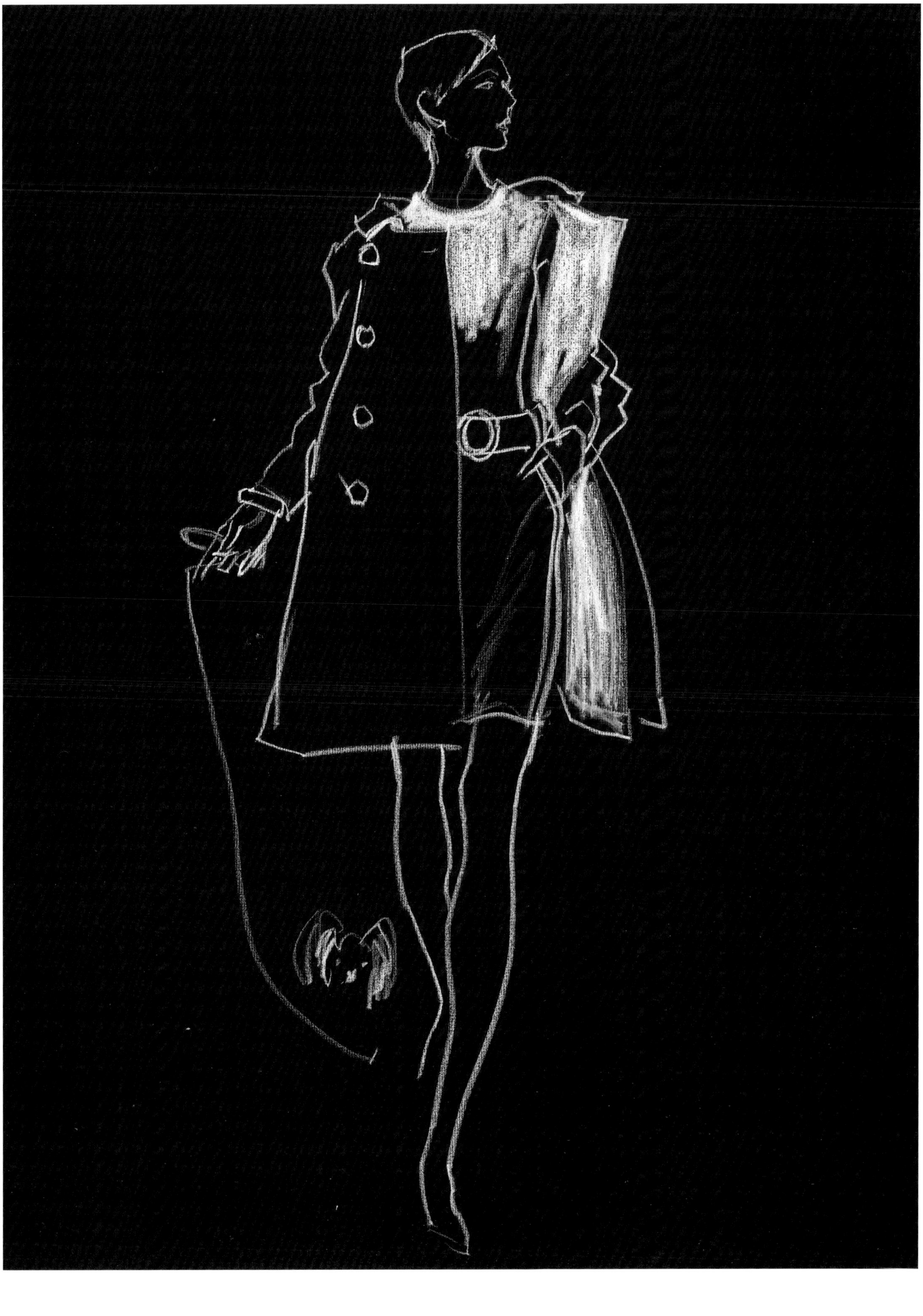

THE FASHIONS

Paris

AT HOME VELVET FOP ... beige ... long with full blown sleeves, limp wrist lace, high ecru lace ruff to eyelashes.

NAUGHTY LADY BLACK DRESS ... demure top in clingy silk velvet with black chiffon floating sleeves ... hem in three layers of chiffon — see-through to mid-calf. Mother of pearl stockings.

PORTRAIT DRESS in orange peau d'ange ... simple, tight and high waisted ... wide wide cape with high muffler of orange and ecru feathers.

TURN - ME - AROUND DRESS in electric blue chiffon ... naughty low back with matching blue ostrich feathers. Garbo nape frizzed hair.

BLACK VELVET FOP ... high lace neck ruff ... full blown sleeves with lace to fingertips. Black sheer naughty stockings and ankle-strap shoes. Hair brushed back and Garbo-curled.

THE FASHIONS

Dior

LEADING LADY DRESS in white silk satin . . . very fitted just-below-waist belt with 30s round buckle . . . noodle fringe.

LITTLE MISS PRIM in black velvet . . . white satin collar and cuffs. Poupée makeup and black sheer stockings.

SMOCK DRESS in apricot, pepper and salt Donegal tweed . . . brown corduroy collar, brown chiffon foppy bow, brown felt hat.

LITTLE SCHOOLGIRL pleated tablier in bright innocent plaid . . . under gold suede dufflecoat lined in sheepskin. Black velvet jockey cap and black crochet stockings.

THE LITTLE BLACK CREPE DRESS . . . with intricate seaming to create trompe l'oeil high waist . . . orange suede belt, black patent jockey cap, black sheer stockings and vamp shoes.

Drawings by Kenneth Paul Block by Wireless Fairchild News Service

HALSTON
ORIGINALS

Block travelled regularly to Paris to report on the couture shows from the early 1960s onwards. He never knew what kind of reception he might receive, since *WWD* was often feuding with designers. Sometimes he found himself 'off the list' and had to work 'from dictation.' At other times there was special treatment and access. It is a tribute to Block's skill that it is impossible to tell his real and imagined images apart.

Like all the great fashion artists, Block was responsive to the cross-pollination within the arts. In the 1960s this meant Pop art and a newly graphic and youthful silhouette giving way to the influences of Art Nouveau and the brief potency of flower power. Block adapted his style, turning to pen and marker, giving a new urgency to his drawings.

In 1972, Fairchild began publishing *W*, an upmarket consumer publication. Block kept pace; his drawings of designs by Zandra Rhodes, Halston and Michael Vollbracht, seminal names of the era, are among his most authoritative. By now he had negotiated a three-day week with *WWD*, leaving him time to work for clients such as Bonwit Teller, Bergdorf Goodman and Lord & Taylor from the Riverside Drive apartment he shared with his partner, Morton Ribyat.

In 1992, Fairchild closed the department without notice, dismissing the illustrators, starting, we are told, with Block. 'We were lemmings,' he said later, with what may have been a tinge of regret; 'everyone else did it, so we did.' Block was almost 70, and although he did not want for work, he was now deprived of the job that had come to define him. If he was bitter, he never said so publicly.

Shortly before his death in 2009, Block bequeathed more than 2,000 drawings to the Museum of Fine Arts in Boston and collaborated with Susan Mulcahy on a dazzling monograph, *Drawing Fashion*. Lengthy obituaries showed the esteem in which he was held and several of the old guard, including Hubert de Givenchy, Pierre Bergé and Oscar de la Renta, were quick to pay tribute. 'Kenneth helped to turn *Women's Wear* into a huge success,' Fairchild told Susan Mulcahy. 'People opened doors. Every designer wanted their clothes sketched by Kenneth.'

For almost four decades, Kenneth Paul Block's work defined the look of *WWD* and the aspirations of its readers. For many, he was quite simply the Man Who Drew New York.

HALSTON
Was ever a designer more indelibly associated with New York in the 1970s and 1980s than Halston? Between them, Block and Joe Eula (perhaps his only rival as an illustrator in that period) produced some of the designer's most evocative advertising imagery. This drawing is from 1980. *Courtesy Morton Ribyat*

DIOR (previous spread)
Block adapted to the poor print quality of *WWD* by frequently eliminating halftone from his drawings, as in this July 1967 Dior sketchbook. *Courtesy Condé Nast Archive/Courtesy Pointed Leaf Press*

FASHION SHOW
A variation of this drawing appeared on the cover of James Brady's 1992 novel *Fashion Show*. *Courtesy Pointed Leaf Press*

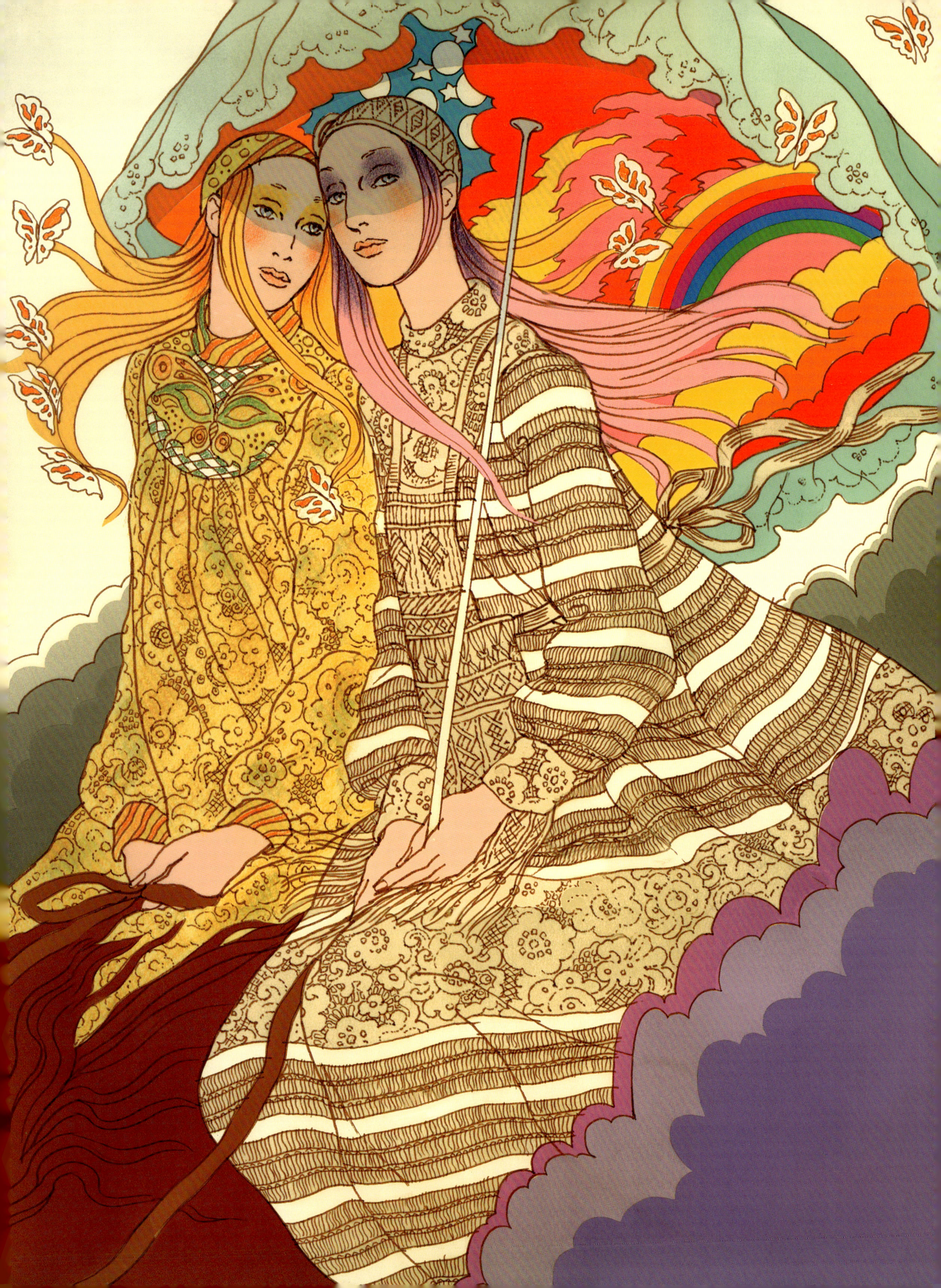

BACK TO THE DRAWING BOARD
This complex and beautifully observed illustration was one of a series that appeared in British *Vogue* in July 1970. *Copyright Estate of Antonio Lopez and Juan Ramos/Courtesy Jason Brooks Collection*

ANTONIO LOPEZ

More than twenty years after his death, Antonio's legend refuses to fade. As a fashion artist, innovator and provocateur he had no equal. Redefining fashion illustration when it was at its least fashionable (in the 1960s), Antonio championed a new beauty ideal which was neither exclusively white nor Western. His were the girls who counted – Jerry! Grace! Paloma! Pat! – and the boys who mattered. Like Warhol (with whom he was friends), Antonio's life and art were one. To many he was the ultimate fashion illustrator: exuberant, mercurial, shape-shifting and good-naturedly narcissistic, with a beauty and clarity to his line that could break your heart.

Antonio was born in Utuado, Puerto Rico, in 1943. The story goes that at the age of 2 he was already making fashion drawings of his mother, a seamstress and dressmaker. He experienced an early fame of sorts, tap dancing on Puerto Rican TV before his family moved to Spanish Harlem in 1950. Young, precociously gifted and gay, Antonio taught himself to be tough: 'you had to be a member of a gang for self-preservation,' he said; 'so I ended up as "war counsellor" to the Comanches.'

As a student in the early 1960s at Fashion Institute of Technology (FIT) in New York, Antonio met Juan Ramos, who became his life-long partner, collaborator and alter ego. It was a symbiotic relationship; Antonio the artist, Ramos the art director and creative sounding-board. Neither took a passive role, according to the artist Paul Caranicas, who lived in the pair's orbit for many years: 'Their teamwork was a unique creative process. It was not a smooth or a tranquil path, but the fights that erupted, and the ensuing tension, only heightened the synergy between them.'

When *Women's Wear Daily* offered him a job, Antonio dropped out of FIT. 'I wanted to illustrate fashion and *WWD* was the place to be,' he recalled. He was 19. His early drawings for the paper had an elegant smoky assurance and were somewhat in the style of Bouché and Kenneth Paul Block, but by the time he left *WWD* for the *New York Times* in 1963, he was ready to cut loose. Antonio always worked from life, but now his drawings incorporated collage, lettering – whatever graphic device caught his eye. Rather than looking to past masters of fashion illustration, he channelled pop culture – Warhol, Lichtenstein, the Beatles' *Yellow Submarine* and artists as diverse as Goya, Boldini and Léger. Kinetic, irrepressibly youthful and startlingly sexy, Antonio's work captured the mood of the times as surely as Gruau had defined the elegant Paris of the New Look almost twenty years before.

Antonio was soon freelancing for *Harper's Bazaar*, British *Vogue* and French *Elle*, staying ahead of the curve by jettisoning a style even as he mastered it. In 1969, after several trips to Europe, he and Ramos settled in Paris, where they moved into a St. Germain apartment owned by Karl Lagerfeld. 'The Paris years were party years,' said Paul Caranicas, who joined the group in 1972; 'that is not to say that we did not work hard, but we played extra hard.' Antonio experimented with new techniques: meticulously detailed tonal studies in pencil, Fauvist portraits in oil pastel, and collages of Instamatic pictures, his latest obsession. He worked for French and Italian *Vogue*, for *GQ*, *Elle* and *Bazaar*. In 1975, he contributed several pages of drawings to the *April in Paris* issue of Andy Warhol's *Interview* magazine, affectionately sending up the denizens of his favourite haunts, La Coupole and Le Club Sept. Anna Piaggi of Italian *Vogue* remembered the dreamlike trips south for the summer; 'the Train Bleu, the arrivals in St. Tropez, the Rolls Royce awaiting him and all his troupe. Hats, umbrellas, trunks, Polaroids, the colourful suitcases and the girls in their most outrageous hotpants.'

OP & POP
A ground-breaking sequence of drawings embracing the then-current vogue for Op and Pop art appeared in *The Fashion of the Times* in March 1965. They included 'French Export' (*left*) and 'Speed Demons' (*right*). Copyright Estate of Antonio Lopez and Juan Ramos/Courtesy Galerie Bartsch & Chariau, Munich

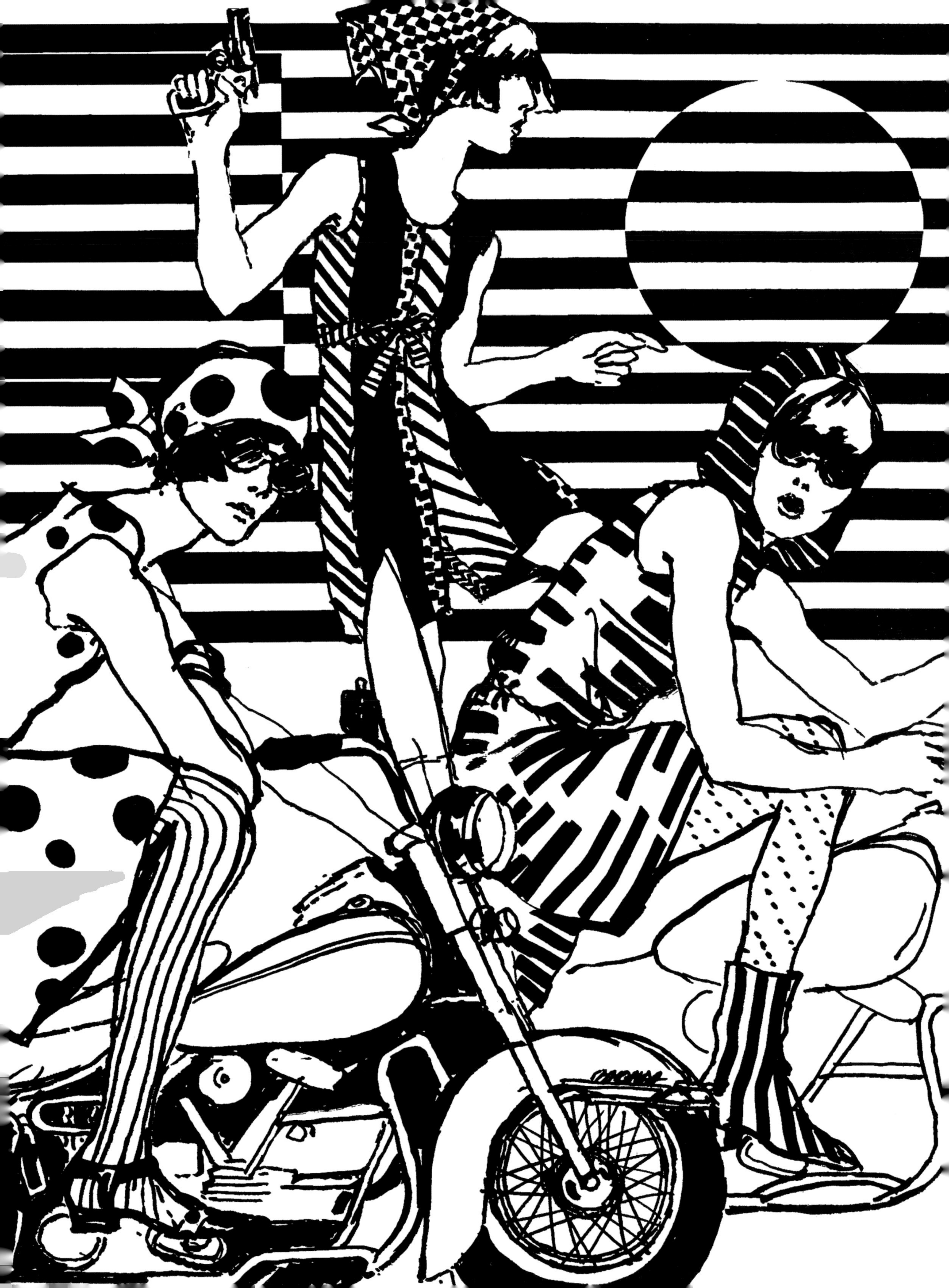

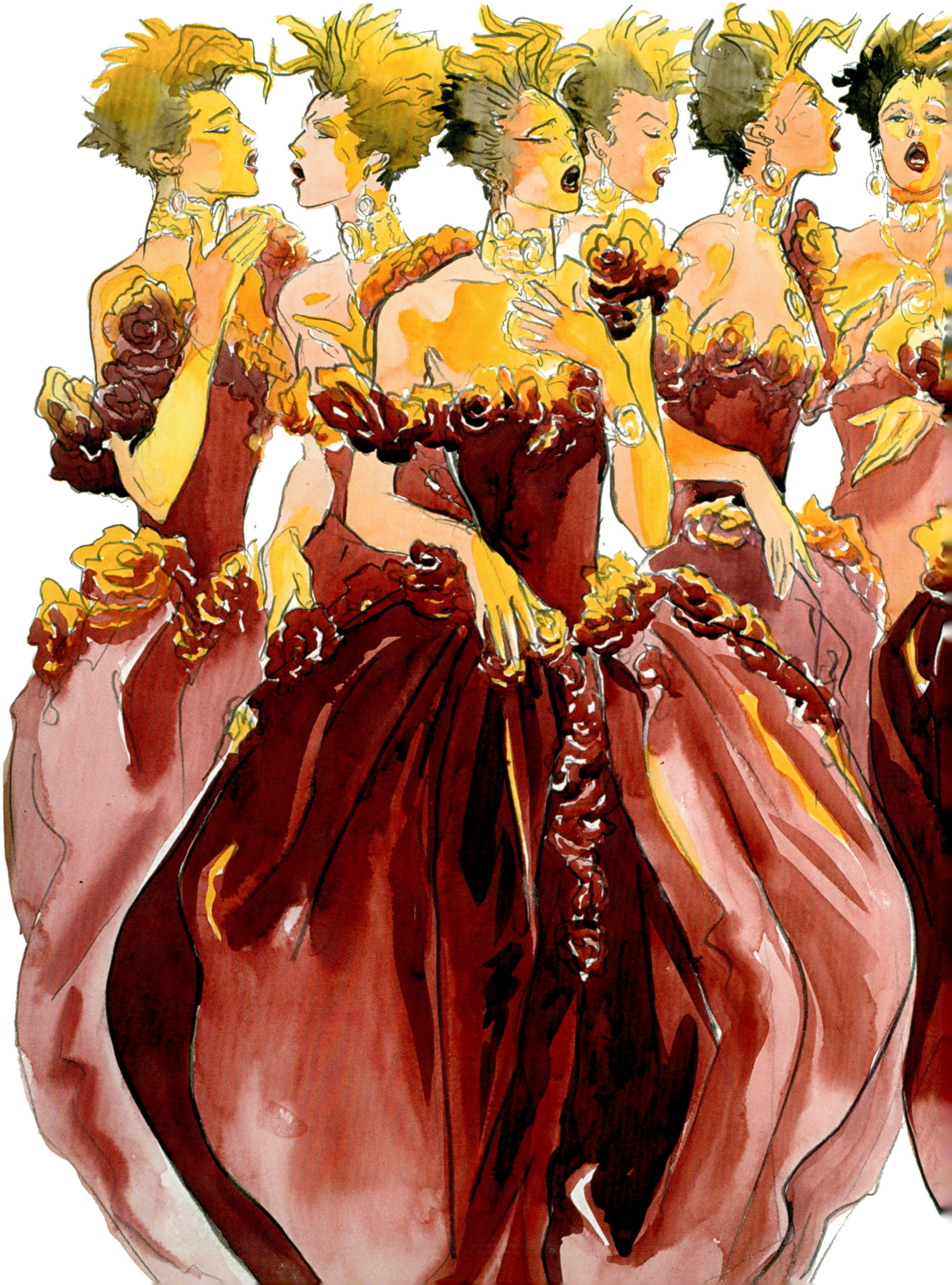

CAPUCCI
A dress by Capucci, seen from multiple angles, appeared as a fold out in *Vanity* magazine, April 1983. *Copyright Estate of Antonio Lopez and Juan Ramos/Courtesy Galerie Bartsch & Chariau, Munich*

Vanity

fashion

48 PAGINE DI PRET-A-PORTER ITALIANO ILLUSTRATE DA ANTONIO LOPEZ

In 1975, Antonio and Ramos returned to New York, setting up a studio at 876 Broadway. Three years later, they moved into a cavernous space on Union Square West that would prove every bit as chaotic and creative as Warhol's infamous Factory. Antonio was as restless as ever: 'My inspiration changes daily,' he said; 'Today it was Leonardo da Vinci. Yesterday it was Elizabethan costume, and the day before what some guy was wearing in the gym. My use of period ideas has nothing to do with adapting a certain style or look. Instead it forces modernism to go somewhere else. To be more than it is.'

He published two books, *Antonio's Girls* and *Antonio's Tales of 1001 Nights*, and became increasingly inspired by street fashion (while simultaneously working on campaigns for Yves Saint Laurent and Oscar de la Renta – he was a pioneer of the hi-low concept). He exhibited, travelled and worked at a frenetic pace, relishing his role as the most famous fashion artist in the world. In Milan in 1981 he began collaborating with Anna Piaggi on the magazine *Vanity*, giving free rein to his eclectic impulses.

At the time of his death (from AIDS) in Los Angeles in 1987, Antonio was attempting to establish a reputation as an artist beyond the sphere of fashion. But of course he was already an artist, perhaps *the* fashion artist of the modern era, whose influence, not least in his colourful and quixotic life, continues to resonate.

VANITY

Launched in September 1981, *Vanity* hinged on the creative partnership between Antonio and fashion editor Anna Piaggi. *Left*, Antonio's self-portrait on the cover of the first issue. *Above right*, 'Cinzia Ruggeri', *Vanity* No 8, October 1983; *below right*, Cecil Beaton, 'My Fair Lady', *Vanity* No 4, October 1982. *Copyright Estate of Antonio Lopez and Juan Ramos/Tony Glenville Collection*

YVES SAINT LAURENT
Despite his burgeoning interest in street culture, this 1983 drawing for YSL shows that high fashion was still very much Antonio's métier. *Copyright Estate of Antonio Lopez and Juan Ramos/Courtesy Galerie Bartsch & Chariau, Munich*

DOZE
One of the members of the seminal hip-hop band, Rock Steady Crew, Doze posed several times for Antonio. This pencil drawing is from 1985.
Copyright Estate of Antonio Lopez and Juan Ramos/ Courtesy Galerie Bartsch & Chariau, Munich

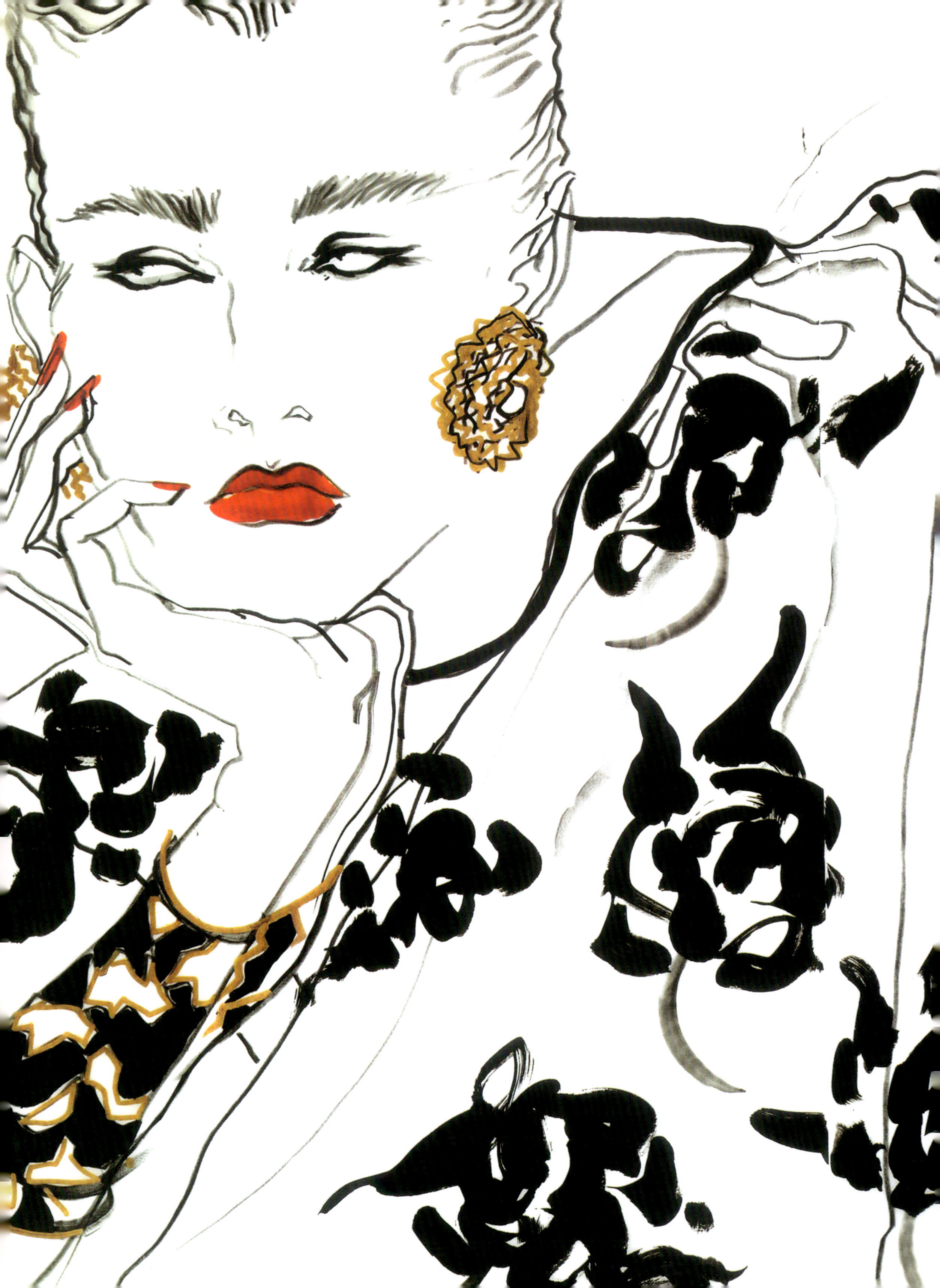

GLAMSLAM

Unapologetically glamorous and self-confident, the 'Viramontes Woman' was every bit as emblematic of her time as the 'Gruau Woman' forty years before. *Courtesy Estate of Tony Viramontes*

TONY VIRAMONTES

Tony Viramontes died in 1988, aged just 31. His career lasted barely five years, but in that time he produced a body of work – literally thousands of drawings – of extraordinary energy and attack. For Viramontes, a sheet of white paper held no fear; every drawing was a leap of faith and a fight to the death. There was nothing faint-hearted or apologetic in his approach or in his use of materials. His scowling models, with their flashing eyes and scarlet mouths, were forever in motion, their fluid movement curtailed only by the paper's edge or the juddering snap of charcoal. Although he shared a certain 'street' sensibility with Antonio Lopez, there was something defiantly high fashion too in his aesthetic, while his album covers for seminal artists of the period – Duran Duran, Donna Summer and Janet Jackson – caught the *glitzkrieg* mood of the 1980s.

Viramontes was born in West Los Angeles in 1956, to Mexican parents. A brilliant draughtsman and already fascinated by fashion, as a teenager, he co-opted high school students into modelling for him. Later, he engineered a meeting with his favourite model Rene Russo, who would become a friend, mentor and muse. After high school, he studied at the Art Center College of Design in Los Angeles, before moving to New York in the late 1970s, where he studied first at FIT and subsequently at Parsons.

In Manhattan Viramontes met Antonio Lopez, who was at the height of his career. If Lopez felt threatened by the handsome and dynamic young pretender, he didn't show it; instead he acted as mentor, recommending him to art directors and passing on the occasional job he was too busy to do.

In 1983, Viramontes, like so many fashion illustrators before him, left for Paris. He didn't look back. His first illustrations appeared in *Lei, Per Lui* and in British *Vogue*. The great milliner Stephen Jones, at the beginning of his own career, sat in on a drawing session for *Vogue* and remembers the highly charged environment (not to mention the chic Avenue de Saxe address) and a pile of drawings getting ever higher. Viramontes, who cited Cocteau, Schiele and Man Ray as his inspirations, would later admit, 'of the hundreds of sketches I might make for one drawing, it's almost always the first which states the essential.' Like all the great fashion artists, he was a man of his time. His sweeping, hedonistic images reflected the New Wave energy of the decade. He favoured androgyny – men in eyeliner, women on the prowl – and conventional beauty was anathema to him.

VALENTINO
Few fashion artists could command the page with the confidence Viramontes brings to this sketch for Valentino, circa 1983 *(right)*. *Courtesy Estate of Tony Viramontes*

IN BLACK AND WHITE *(this page)*
Two typically dynamic charcoal drawings from 1984. Study of Teri Toy *(top)* and fashion by Azzedine Alaïa *(right)*. *Courtesy Estate of Tony Viramontes*

FASHION FORWARD *(overleaf)*
A marching army of models in Halston knitwear remains one of Viramontes' strongest and most evocative images. *Courtesy Estate of Tony Viramontes*

165

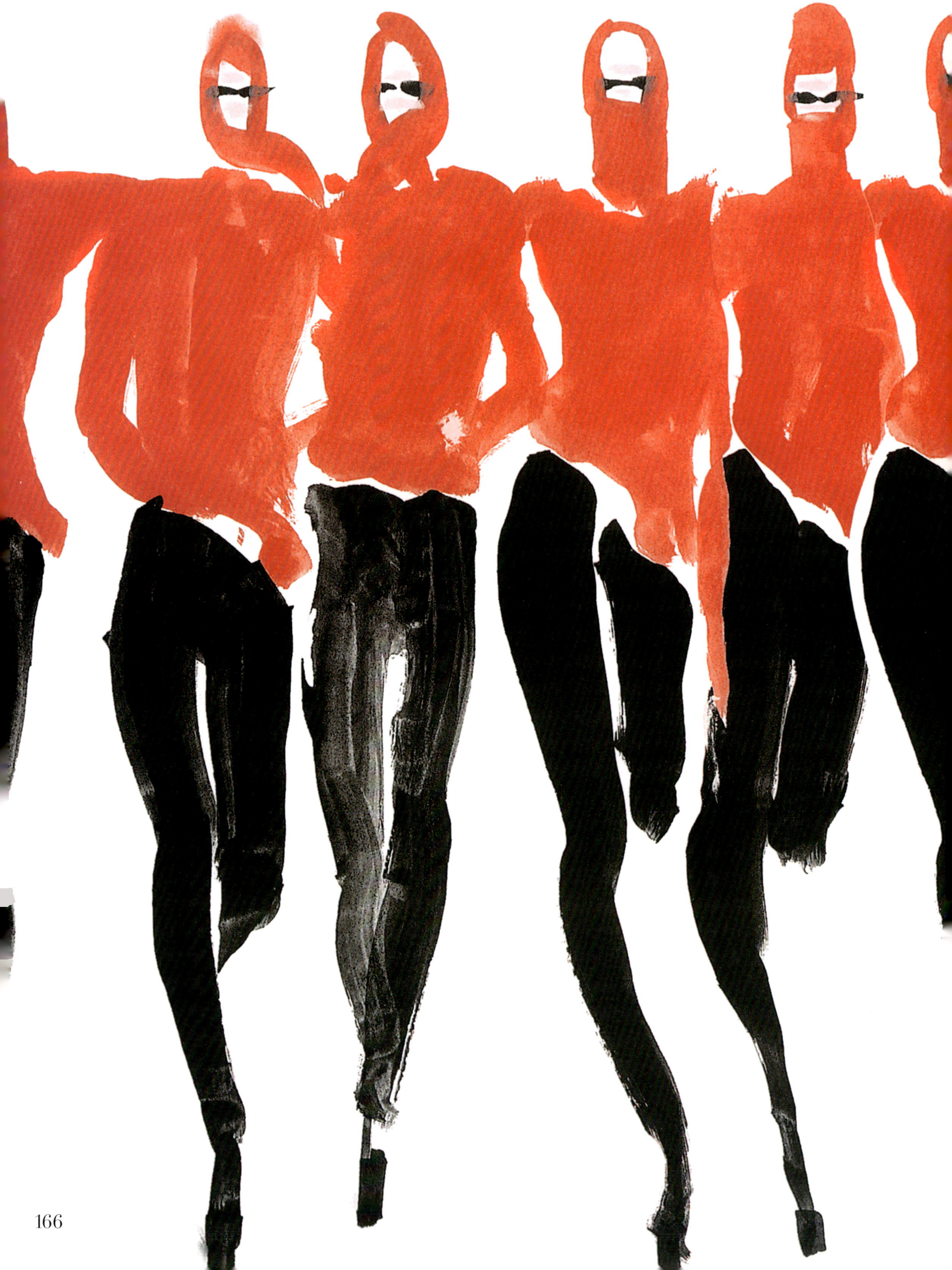

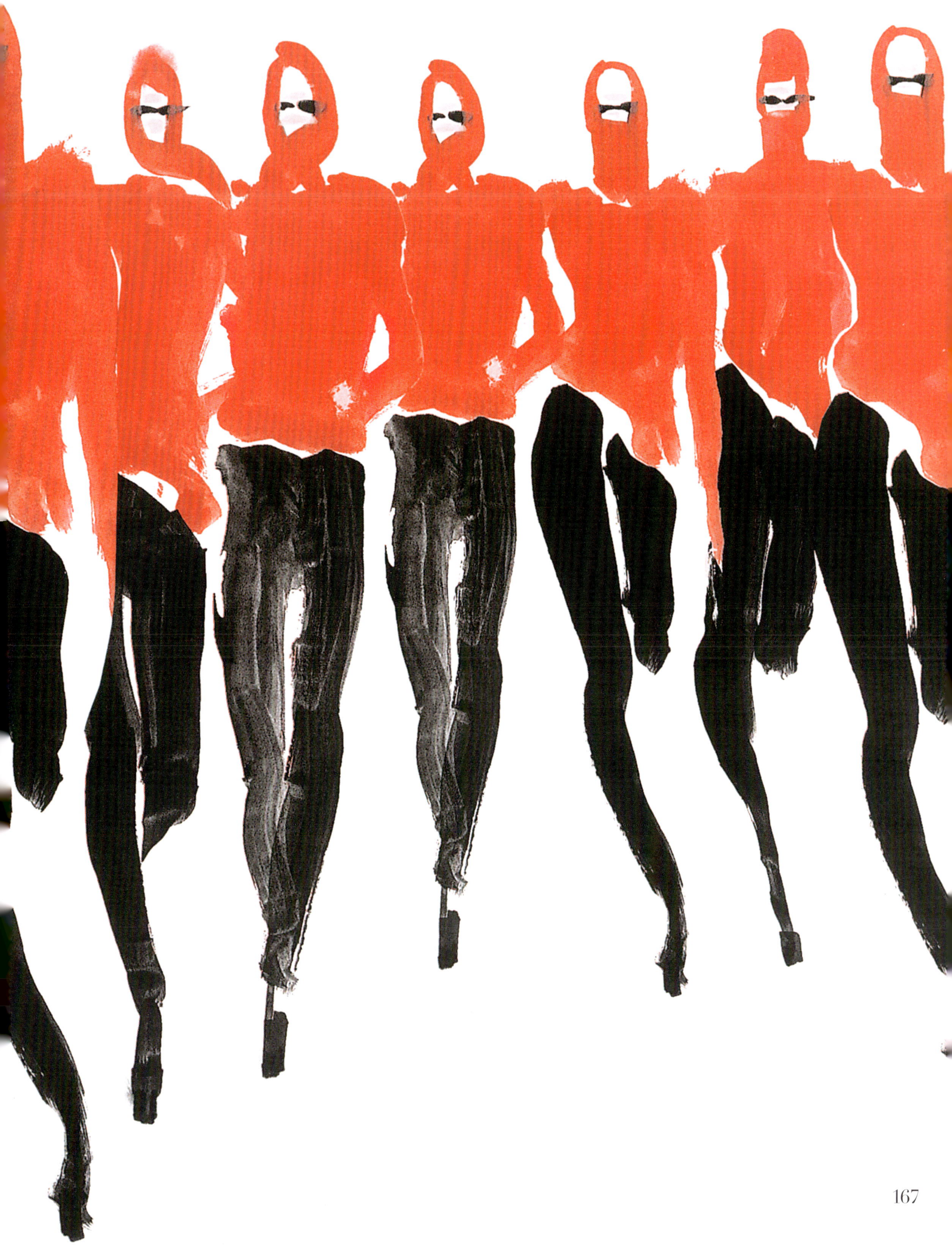

The fashion world quickly caught on: Viramontes did campaigns for Valentino, Saint Laurent and Claude Montana, portraits of Paloma Picasso and Diana Ross, and pages of editorial in the pioneering (and entirely illustrated) fashion magazine *La Mode en Peinture*. At the same time, his international reputation was growing; he worked extensively in Tokyo, in Germany and in London. He could handle more conventional assignments too, such as a beauty campaign for Rochas, though even that was a little rich for the American market. The Japanese designer Hanae Mori, who had been a supporter since the New York days, was surprised to be asked by an American journalist where she had 'found' Viramontes; 'In your own backyard,' she replied.

In Paris, Viramontes lived as he worked: at full tilt. Nights were spent at the Le Club Sept or Le Palace. No one remembered much about the dawns. Stephen Jones recalls him 'always working, always on the lookout for models who would inspire him; he would have four or five girls in fur coats out in the sunshine, holding poses… he was a ringmaster.' He also needed constant stimulus: 'I look for new ideas because I always want to be in a state of creative anxiety and insecurity. If I feel sure of myself I cannot be creative. I try to renew myself.' To that end, Viramontes took up photography, using collage and large-scale Polaroids. His cover for Janet Jackson's 1985 album *Control* indicated a bold new phase.

But by 1985 Viramontes was already ill, an early victim of the AIDS epidemic. After completing the Jackson album cover and an assignment for German *Vogue*, he supervized the galleys of a book dedicated to his work before returning to his family home in Los Angeles, where he died in 1988. Tony Viramontes was a supernova. Two decades after his death, his work still shimmers with a sensuality and a power that remain undimmed.

GALLEYS
Xerox pages from a mock-up of the book *Viramontes*, which was published in Japan in 1988, the year of the artist's death. The designer Hanae Mori assisted with the publication. *Courtesy Estate of Tony Viramontes*

CHANEL
A 1984 drawing of Chanel haute couture, originally made for *La Mode en Peinture*, the short-lived but highly influential magazine founded by Prosper Assouline. *Courtesy Estate of Tony Viramontes*

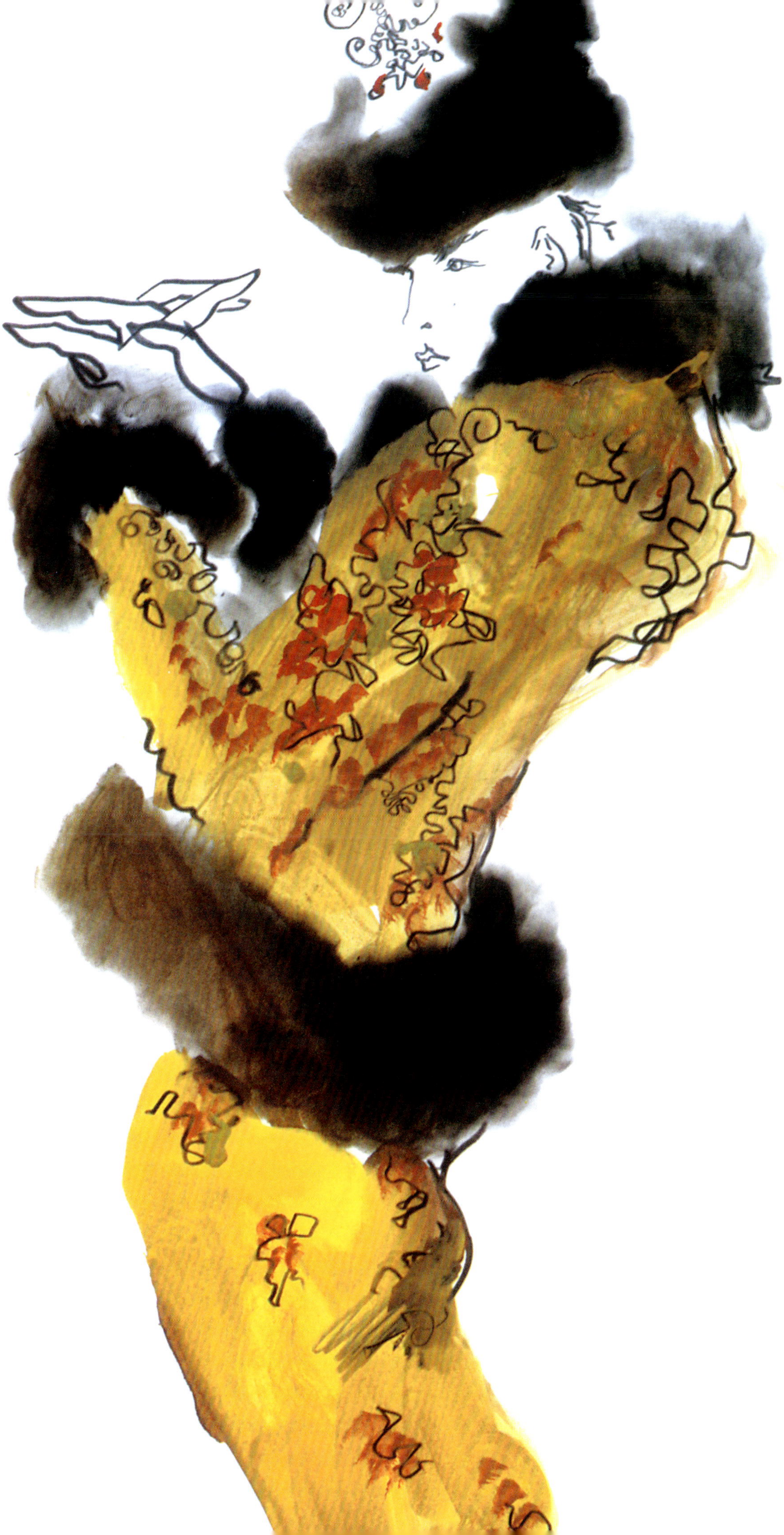

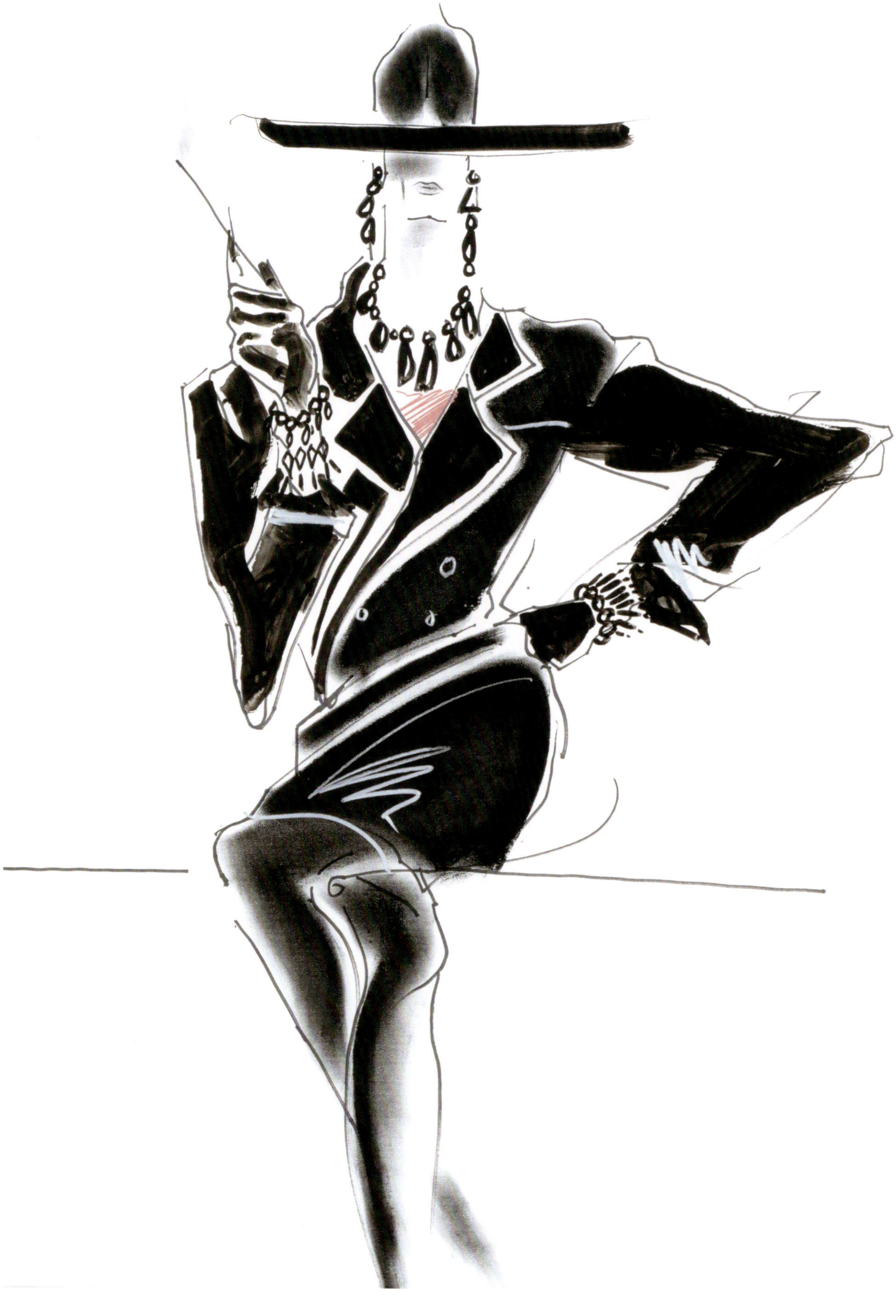

GLAMORAMA
Viramontes' high-fashion drawings for Valentino Couture (*this page*) and Yves Saint Laurent (*opposite*) in 1984 showcase his dynamic signature style. *Courtesy Estate of Tony Viramontes*

DAVID DOWNTON
IN CONVERSATION

DAVID DOWNTON INTERVIEWED BY TONY GLENVILLE

Tony Glenville is a fashion journalist and historian. He is Creative Director of the London College of Fashion.

TG: How did *Masters of Fashion Illustration* come about?

DD: In 2007, I published a journal, *Pourquoi Pas?*, celebrating the work of great fashion illustrators. The following year we did a second issue. I really enjoyed the process, and was thinking about doing a third one when I was approached to do a book on my own work. *Masters of Fashion Illustration* was a way of combining both things.

TG: Did you find it easy to select artists to go in the book?

DD: Yes, these are the artists I most admire and whose work I have always loved. Erté was something of an exception; I have to admit I was never a great fan of his. All those staircases and feathers… But then I looked at his work again and realized how I'd underestimated him as a graphic artist. I think his *Harper's Bazaar* covers from the 1930s are extraordinary.

TG: What about the structure of the book?

DD: Well, I knew I wanted to begin at the turn of the twentieth century and finish in the late 1980s with the deaths of Antonio and Viramontes. I also knew it should run chronologically, so that there would be a sense of the times, and fashion, and the fashion in drawing changing. In a way the structure (though not the design!) took care of itself.

TG: Did the list change much from your initial thoughts?

DD: Not too much. As I say, I was able to make it a personal list, so I brought in artists like Bob Peak and Coby Whitmore, who were not strictly speaking fashion illustrators, but who do seem to me to be relevant.

TG: What has been the biggest surprise in researching the work in detail?

DD: I think the sheer scale and variety of the projects they took on. Working for *Vogue* and *Harper's Bazaar* was just the beginning; Vertès won two Oscars, Bouché painted portraits of everyone, including President Kennedy, Bob Peak was known as the 'Father of the Modern Movie Poster'. And almost everyone seemed to design for the opera, or the theatre, or the ballet. I suppose what I mean is that they were true commercial artists, and they accepted few limitations.

TG: Do you think there was a Golden Age of fashion illustration?

DD: The first Golden Age was undoubtedly at the turn of the twentieth century. Before the rise of photography it was artists who interpreted the work of the great designers. Essentially they invented fashion illustration as an art form. Then, from the 1930s through until the early 1960s, another generation took things further and became part of the fabric of the great magazines of the day. They were very well treated too… suites at the Crillon or the Ritz, first class travel. All that has pretty much vanished now.

TG: Are there any survivors from the postwar generation left to talk about those days?

DD: Very few. Alfredo Bouret, who worked in Paris for Balenciaga, lives in Sydney. Kenneth Paul Block died only recently, in 2009. One of the best things about doing the book for me was the chance to talk to René Bouché's widow, Denise Bouché Fitch, to the costume designer Willa Kim, a friend of Tom Keogh's from his college days in the 1940s, and to the illustrator Murray Tinkleman, who worked at the Cooper Studios with Coby Whitmore.

TG: If you could interview one artist from the past, who would it be?

DD: I think Tom Keogh. He is the hardest to pin down. He had a brilliant career, but it often seemed to bore him. His work in French *Vogue* in the 1940s and 1950s is exhilarating, but he drifted away just as he was becoming established. He worked in the movies, as a portrait artist, he designed for the ballet, but never seemed engaged for long with anything. He had a fairly colourful private life too.

TG: You mentioned earlier that you knew early on that you wanted to finish the book with Antonio and Viramontes; I was wondering why?

DD: I think their deaths in the 1980s brought an era of fashion illustration to a close. The modern era, essentially the last twenty years, has been fascinating but much more difficult to define. And the mid-century illustrators are the ones I most admire, so I suppose I was being indulgent.

TG: I'm sure you have favourites, though, among the illustrators working today.

DD: Of course. I think Mats Gustafson and François Berthoud are great fashion illustrators of the last twenty years. In very different ways, they reinvented the art form. They didn't look back, they didn't refer to each other, but both were revolutionary. I also really admire Jason Brooks, Gladys Perint Palmer, Michael Roberts, Richard Gray, Jean Phillipe Delhomme, all great artists.

TG: I suppose what's interesting is that all those you mention are such individual talents, no one replicates or even resembles another.

DD: Precisely, and that is a very big difference today. In the past, Willaumez, for example, fairly closely resembled Eric and the two enjoyed parallel and very high-profile careers at *Vogue*. And whole 'schools' grew up around Gruau and Kenneth Paul Block.

TG: You mention René Gruau and I am surprised to see that he's not included. Not only because he was undoubtedly a master of fashion illustration, but I know you really admire him.

DD: I very much wanted to include him. And you are right, for me he was the greatest, certainly in his golden period from the mid-1940s to the mid-1960s. The chapter was written and designed but, in the end, it became a question of economics. Those ten pages would have taken up a substantial slice of the picture budget for the entire book and the publishers felt that the cost just couldn't be justified. We were lucky that many of the artists and their estates were extremely gracious and helpful. But Gruau is a genius, whether or not he is in my book, and fortunately there are a number of beautiful monographs on him, which I have listed on page 217.

TG: Do you think there are many unsung heroes or heroines of fashion illustration who have yet to be celebrated?

DD: There are certainly a great many unsung heroines. Too many. I would love to see a book on the work of Dorothy Hood, Constance Wibout, Jane Bixby, Barbara Pearlman, Elizabeth Suter and Betty Brader Ashley, to name just a few. Many of them had very interesting and highly successful careers without ever quite breaking into the top rank. But then, of how many professions is that not true in the early and mid-twentieth century?

TG: And again, things are radically different today, there are just as many, if not more, very strong female fashion illustrators coming through.

DD: Absolutely. Of the current generation, I think Stina Persson, Cecilia Carlstedt and Autumn Whitehurst really stand out.

TG: You've often said that you didn't intend to become a fashion illustrator, that it happened more or less by chance.

DD: Well, as a child I wanted to be Bob Peak (the movie poster artist), although I wouldn't have been able to name him. I used to sit and laboriously copy film posters from the *Evening Standard* in HB pencil. *When Dinosaurs Ruled The Earth*, I remember, and *Shalako* and *Carry on Doctor*. Unfortunately being a film poster artist requires a very specific set of skills that I don't have. On the other hand, perhaps it's just as well, as no one does illustrated film posters today. As an art form it's almost completely dead. A tragedy, as far as I'm concerned.

TG: I know that your first trip to couture in 1996 really made you re-evaluate what you were doing and what you would like to do in the future. Was it really as defining a moment as that?

DD: I think it was. In some ways everything was going along very nicely, the work was coming in and my phone was ringing, but I was also getting very bored. Going to Paris on someone else's money sounded good to me. I knew something about fashion, although I had never been to a show, and the whole idea was certainly fascinating to me.

TG: So, you went to Paris as a jobbing illustrator, 'wagging your tail when the phone rang,' as you put it, and came back as a fashion illustrator?

DD: More or less. At least in my head. It wasn't as simple or straightforward as that of course, but Paris and couture gave me something to think about, to focus on. One of the many revelations of that trip was that I rediscovered my ambition. After that everything changed, not overnight, but gradually.

TG: What do you try and convey in your fashion illustrations?

DD: I am after a kind of controlled spontaneity. My mantra is always to 'keep working until it looks effortless.' My ideal drawing is one that looks as though it just happened without too much intervention from me. Of course it's all an illusion. I do dozens of drawings, sometimes more, before I get to *the* one.

TG: Do you have a preferred work method?

DD: Not really. It depends on the job, my mood, the circumstances in which I'm working.

TG: But you don't work digitally?

DD: No, I deliberately never learned to. I find it very frustrating and confining to work sitting at a desk in front of a screen. That said, I have nothing against the computer. I use mine every day, just not creatively.

TG: Do you think fashion illustration has altered radically, in terms of technique and practice?

DD: Undeniably. There are no rules today, no restrictions. There is no prescribed way of working, no prevailing style. Hand-drawn and digitally made imagery are equally valid. In fact, I don't think there has ever been a better or more confusing time to be a fashion illustrator. Drawing may have all but disappeared from the high-end glossy magazines, but it proliferates elsewhere; in galleries and on club flyers, in books and newspapers and on CD covers. Occasionally there are advertising campaigns, more and more there are collaborations between artists and designers. Very few illustrators work week after week, or month after month, for the same publication. I don't think we will ever again see a situation like the one Kenneth Paul Block had at *Women's Wear Daily* (he worked for the paper on an almost daily basis for nearly forty years).

TG: You have become well known for your 'fashion portraits' of some of the world's most beautiful women. Tell me about that.

DD: Again it was chance. In 1998, I had an exhibition of fashion drawings and through a complicated series of circumstances Marie Helvin came to the opening. I asked if I could draw her and that's what started it all, and I must say, I've loved every minute of it. Of course, sitting across the drawing board from Erin O'Connor or Carmen or Amanda Harlech or Dita Von Teese is no bad place to be.

TG: You did some covers for Australian *Vogue* last year, with Cate Blanchett.

DD: Yes. It was very exciting. I was absolutely amazed that *Vogue* wanted to use drawing on the cover after all these years. We actually did four different covers for their fiftieth anniversary issue. And, in a way, it was like going back to the era we've been discussing. I drew Cate at the Dorchester in London, we had brilliant hair and make-up and styling, the whole thing was unhurried and beautifully handled. In fact, it was like being a 'master of fashion illustration' for a whole day.

TG: I was going to ask you whether you think of yourself as a 'master of fashion illustration'?

DD: Well, no, but I am hopeful. Quite a few fashion illustrators worked into their eighties, their nineties even, so there is time.

FASHION

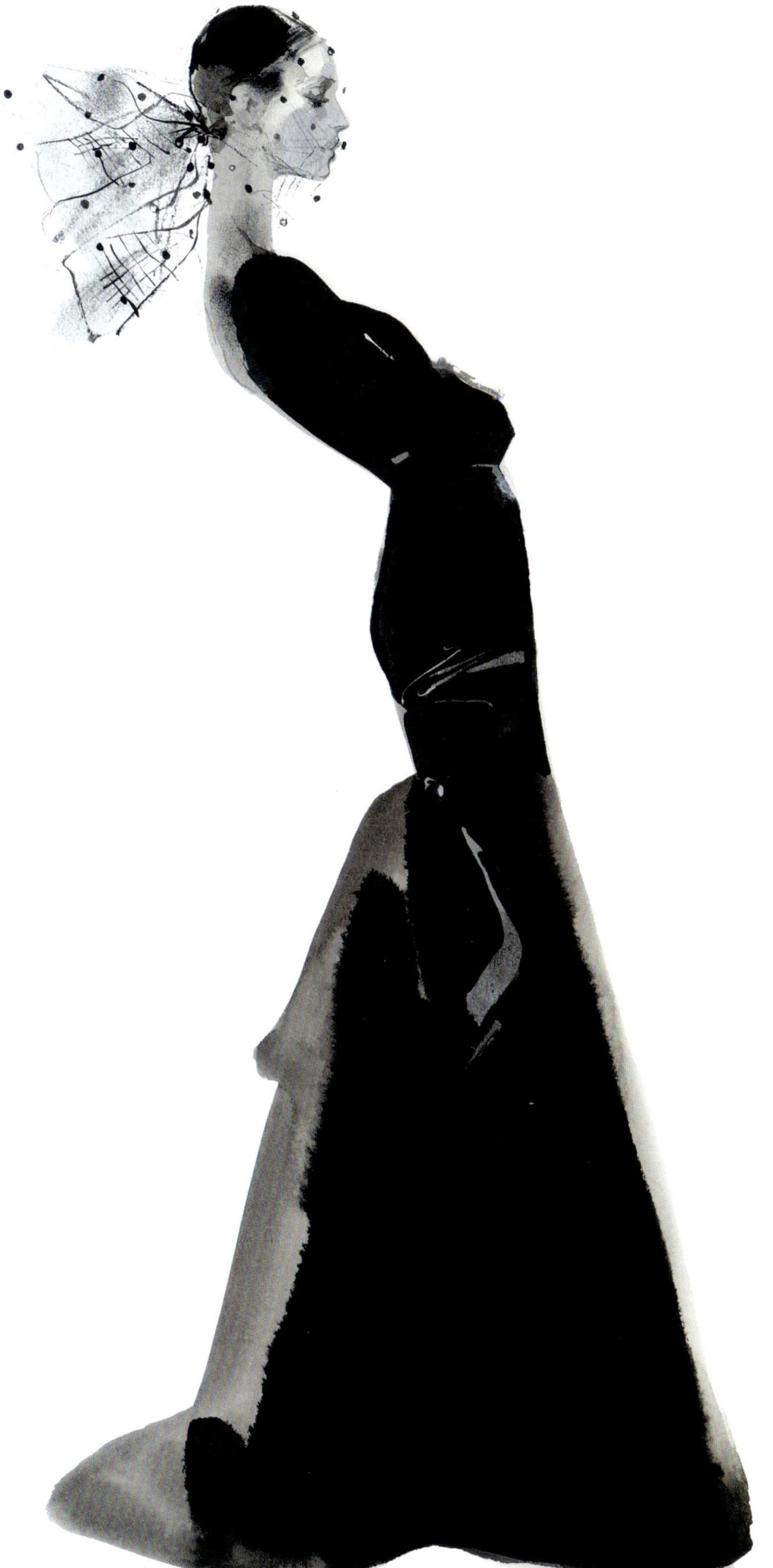

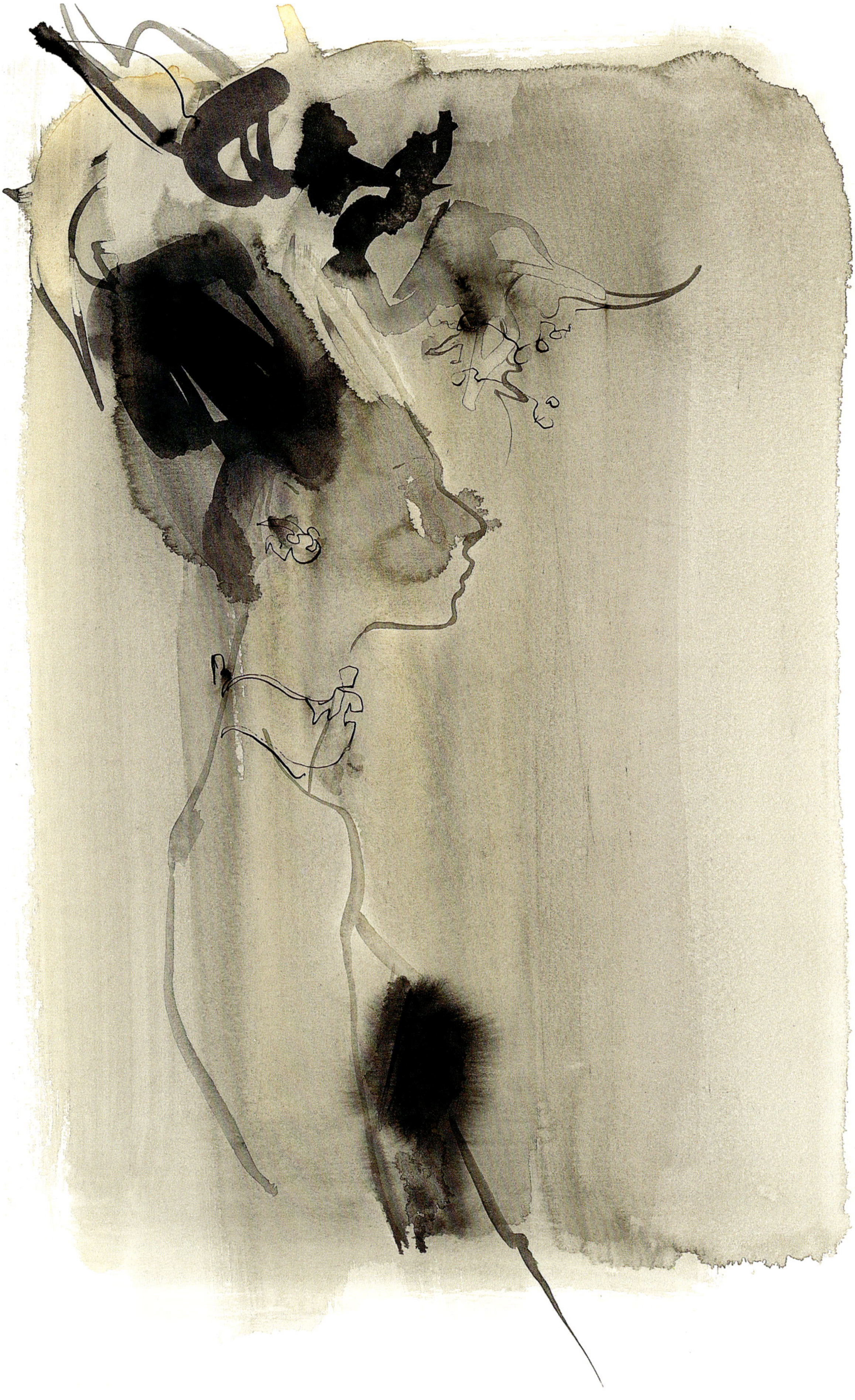

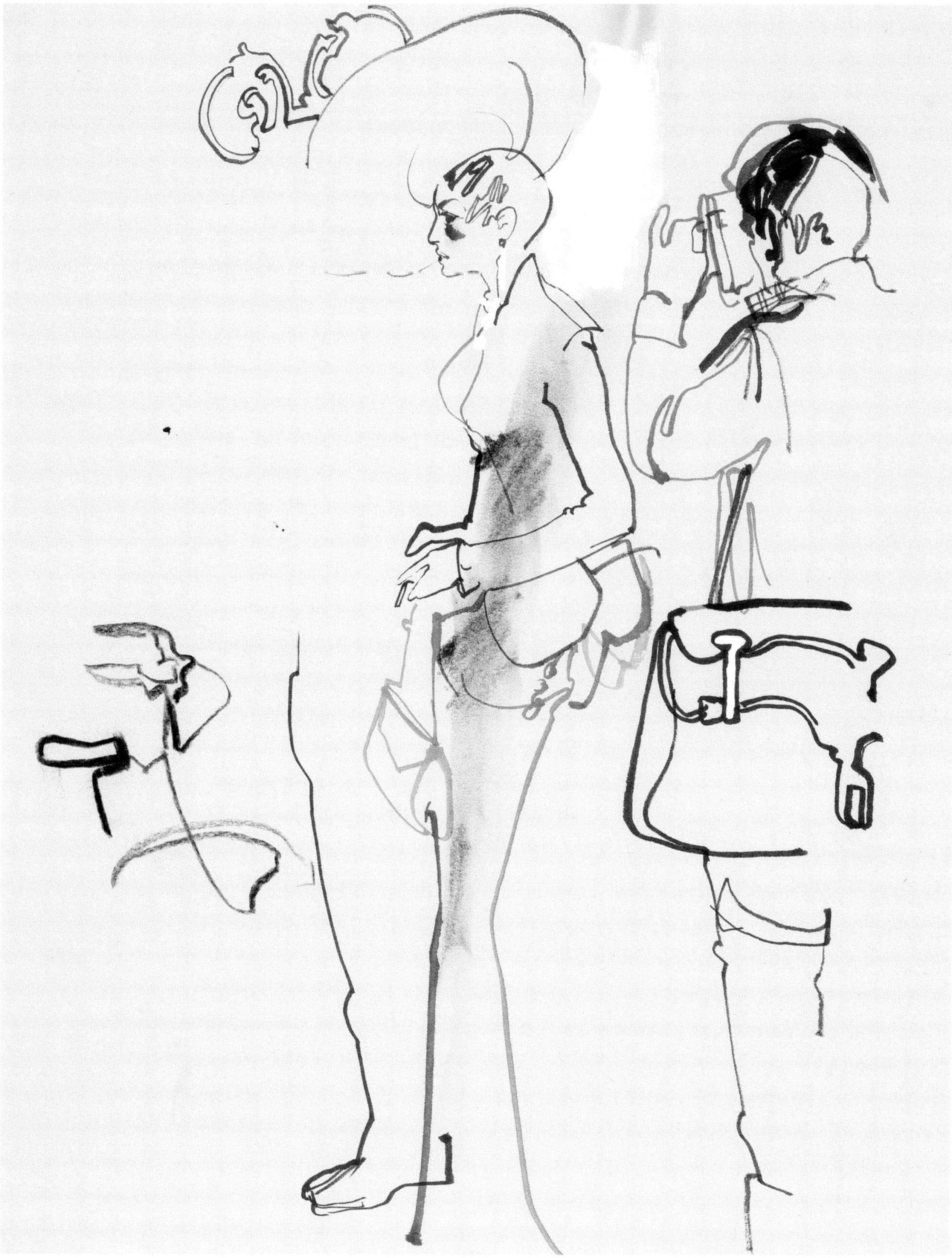

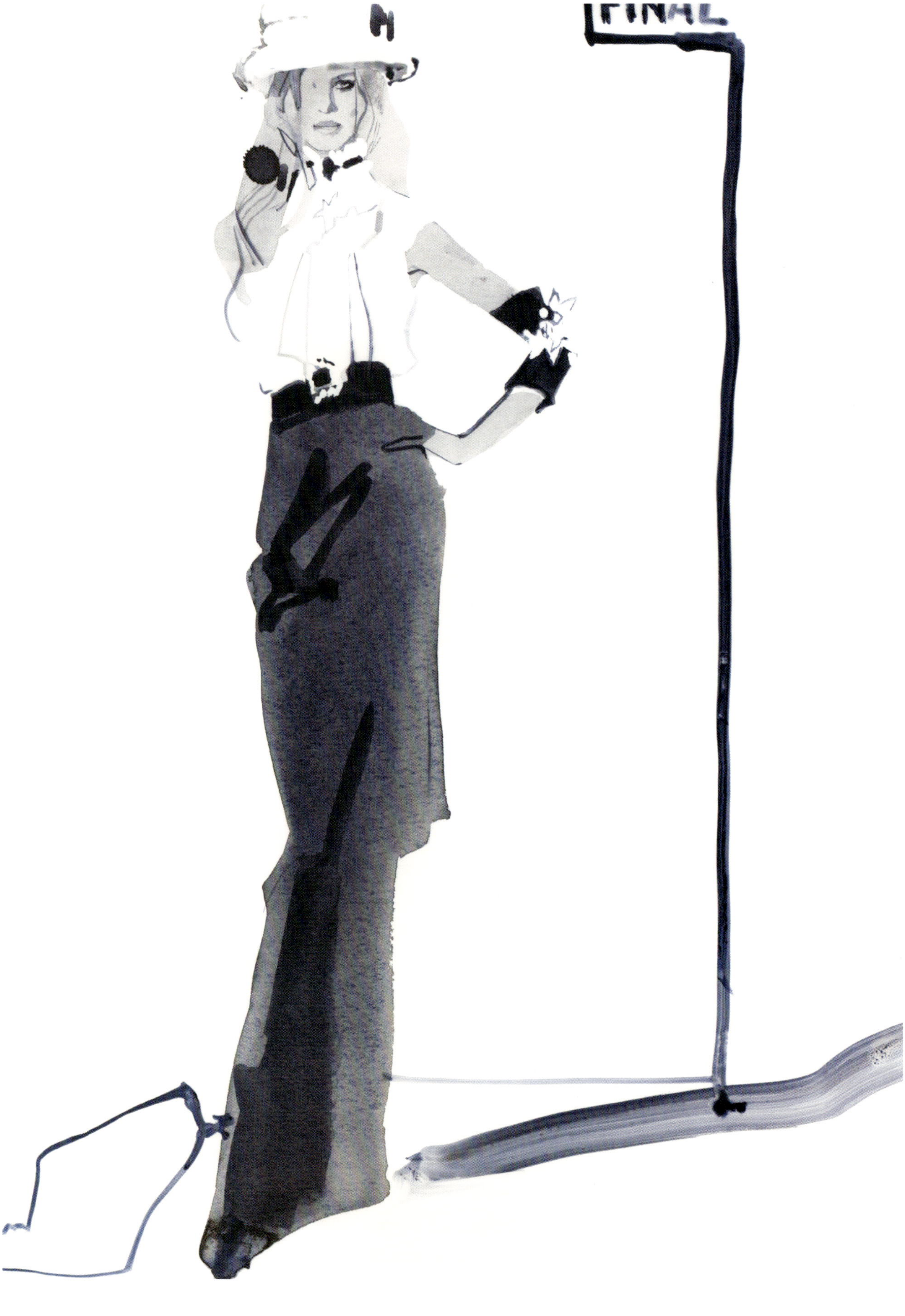
FINAL

PARIS-LONDRES

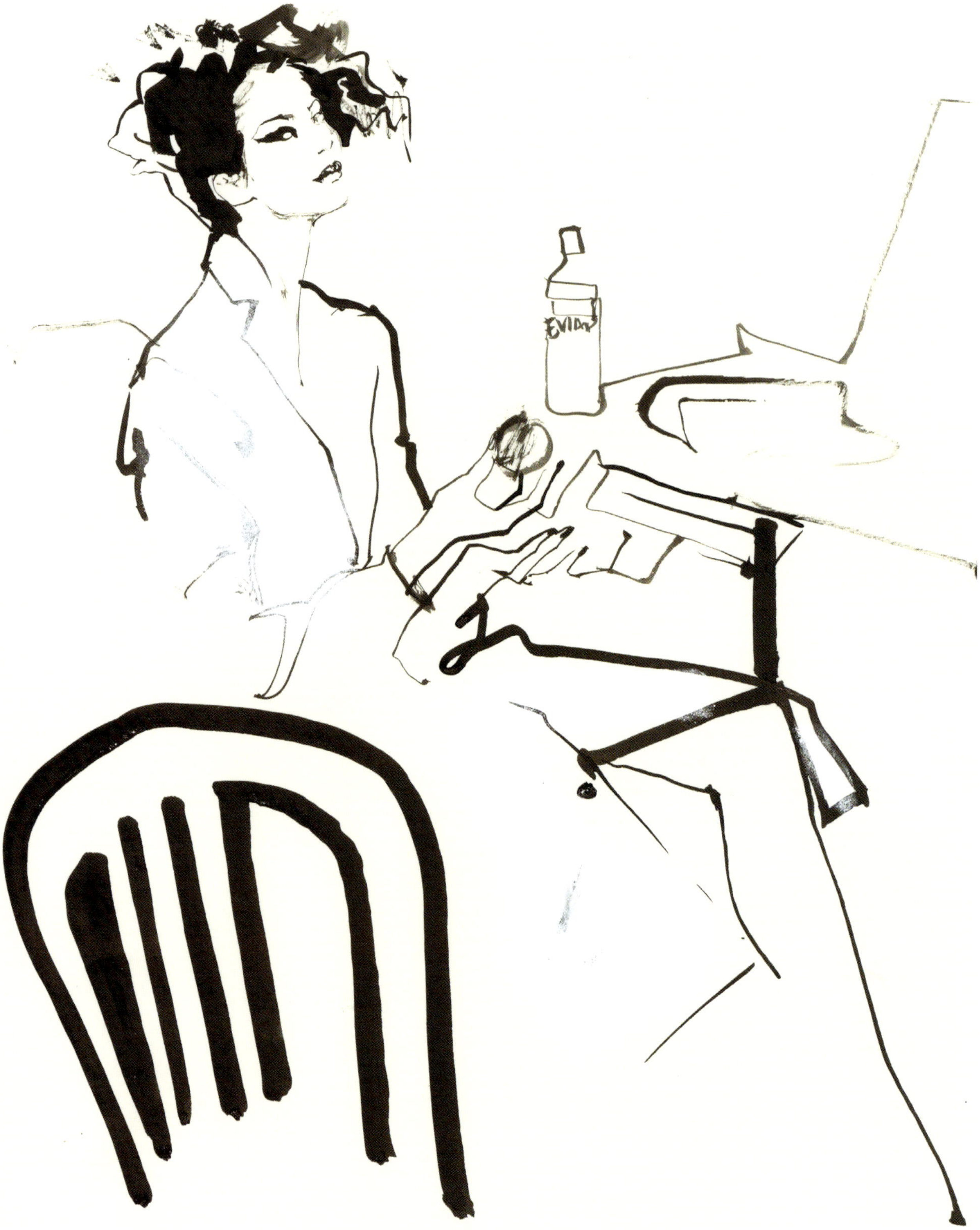

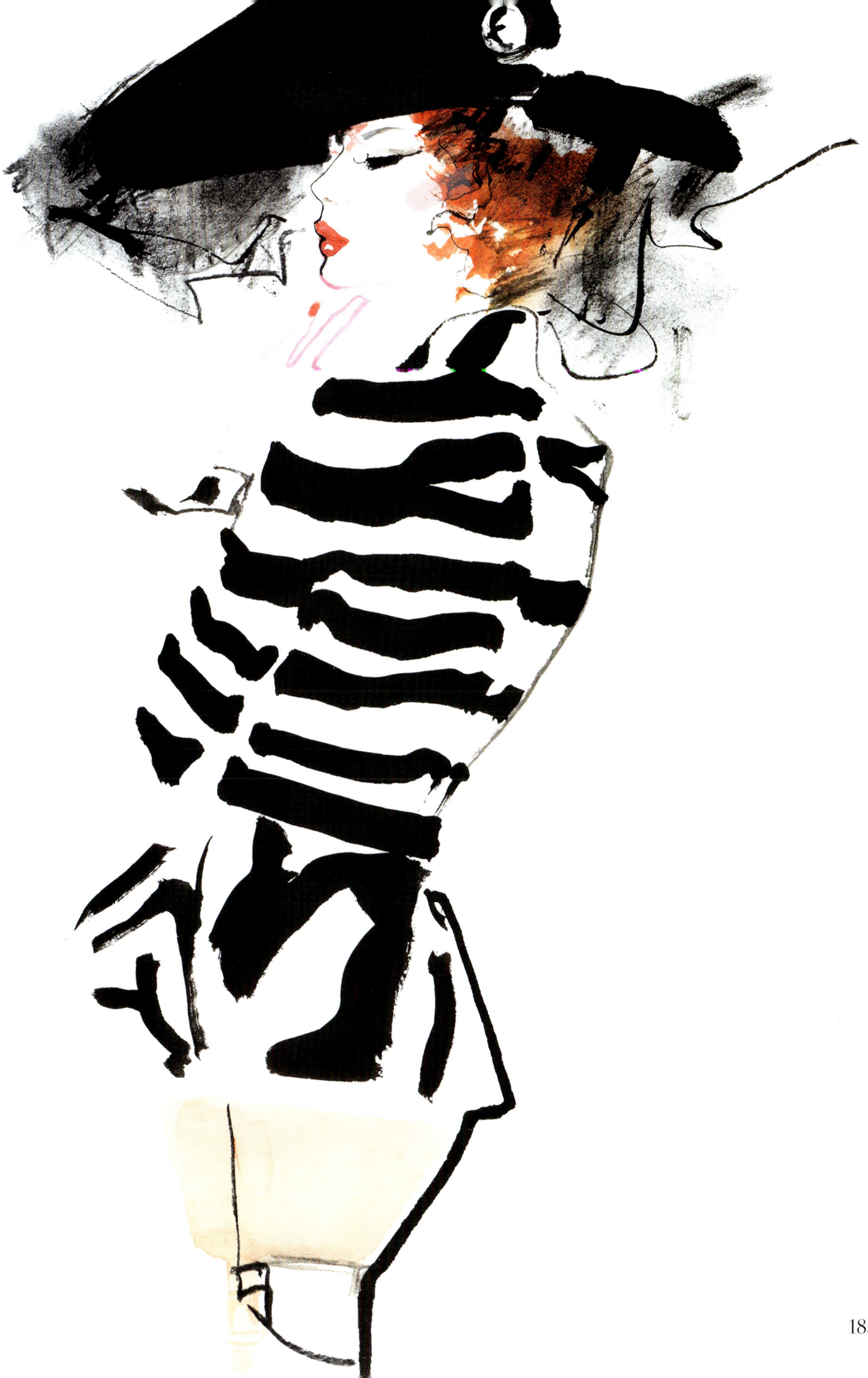

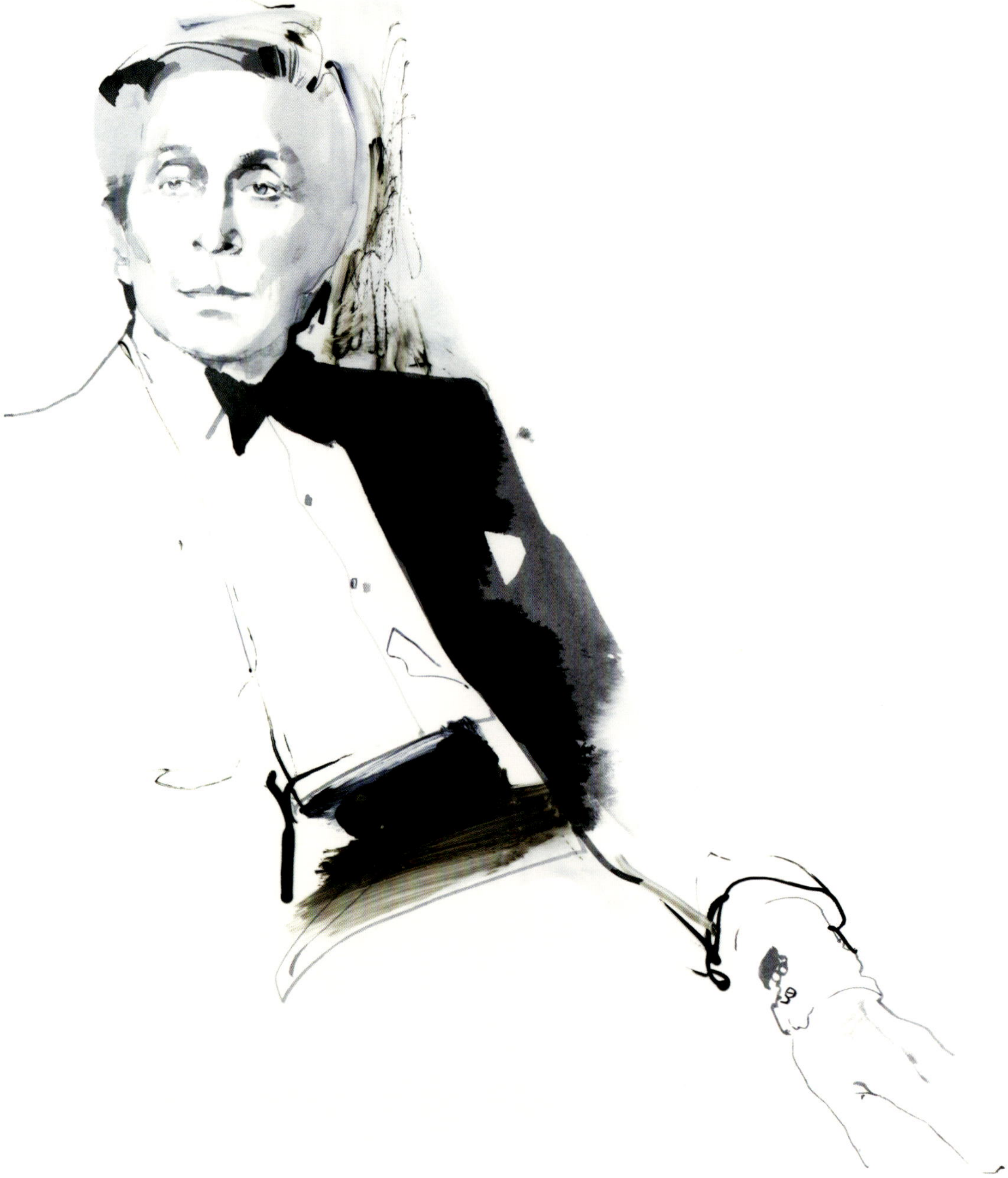

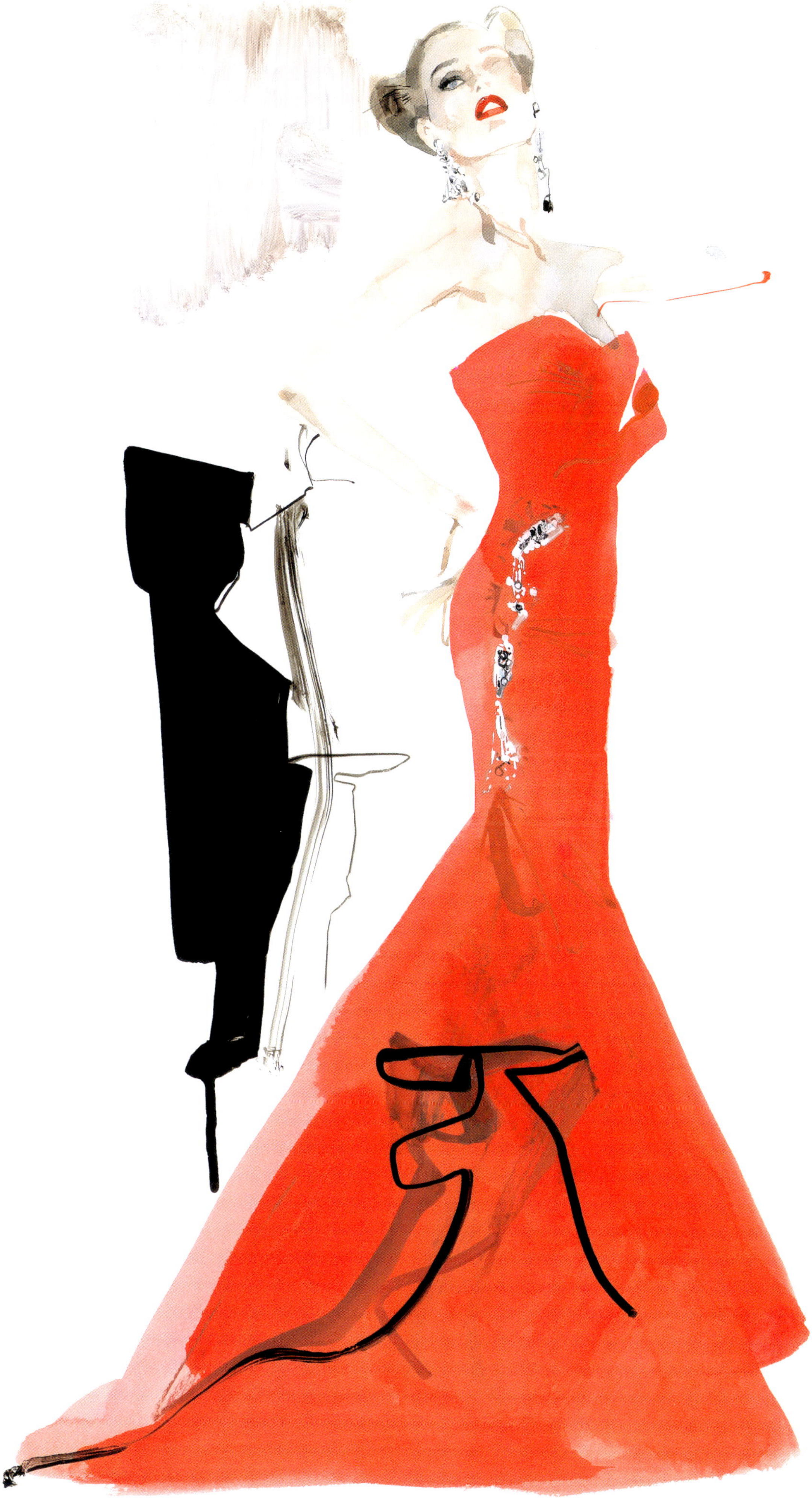

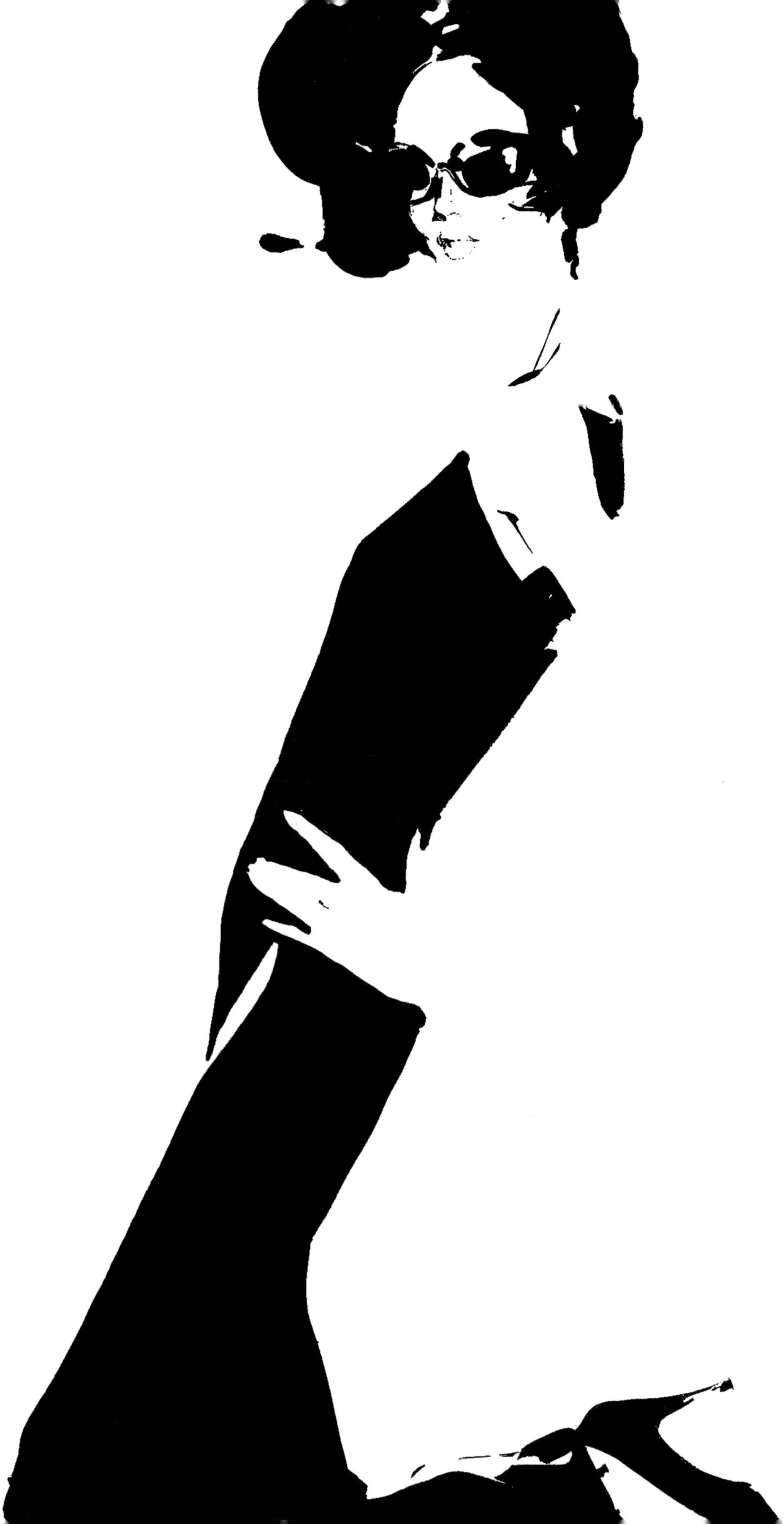

Salon Violet
Paris

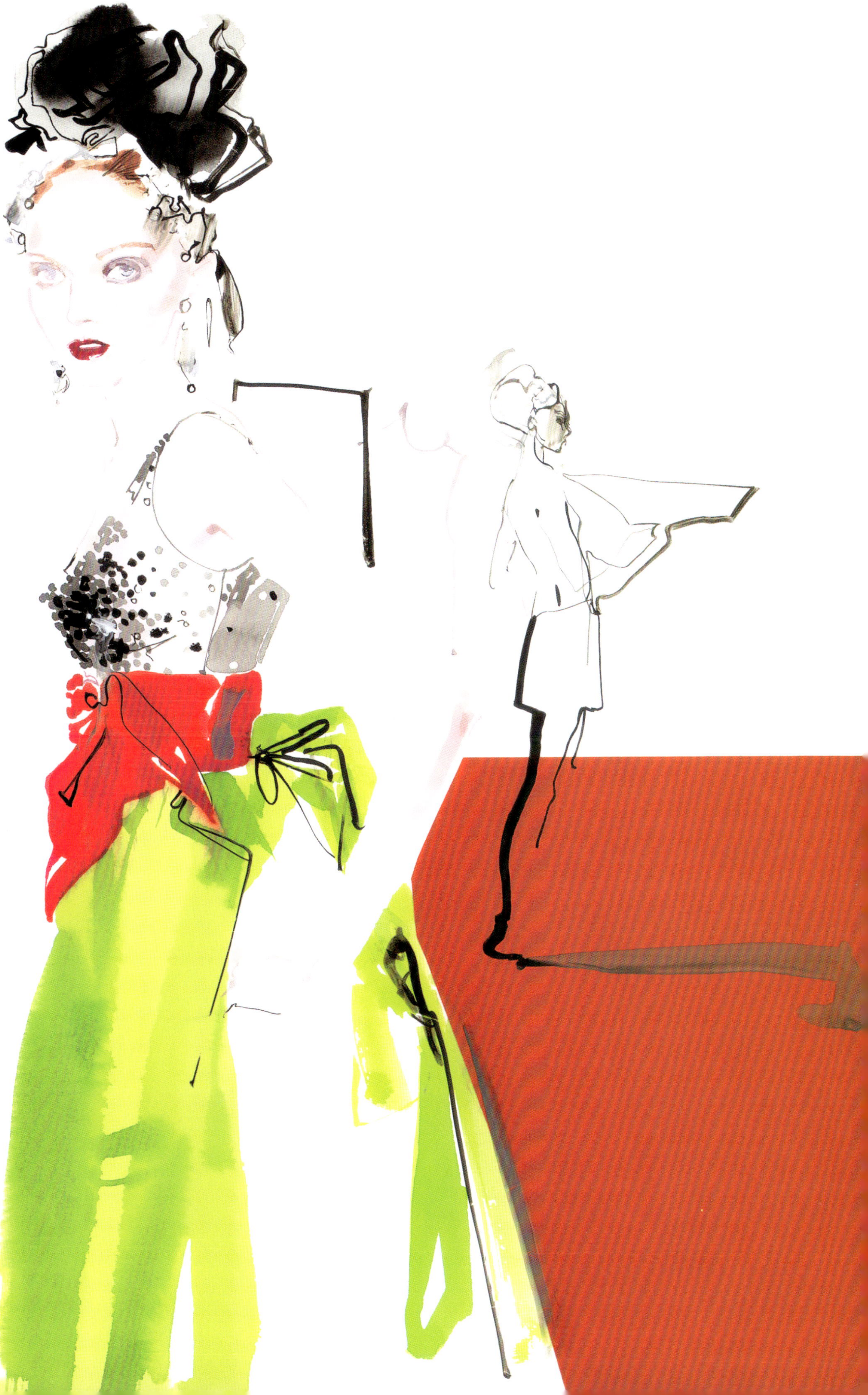

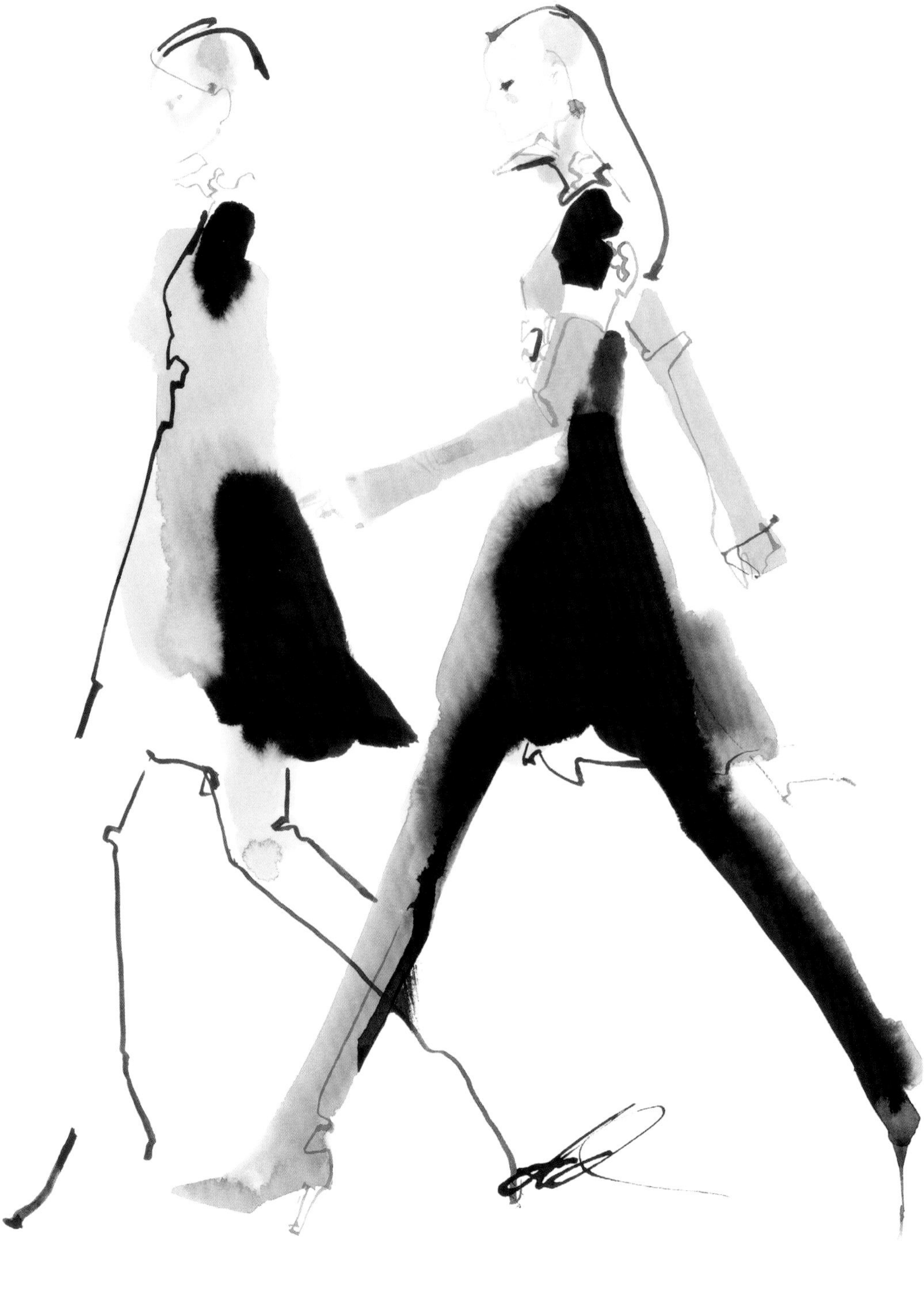

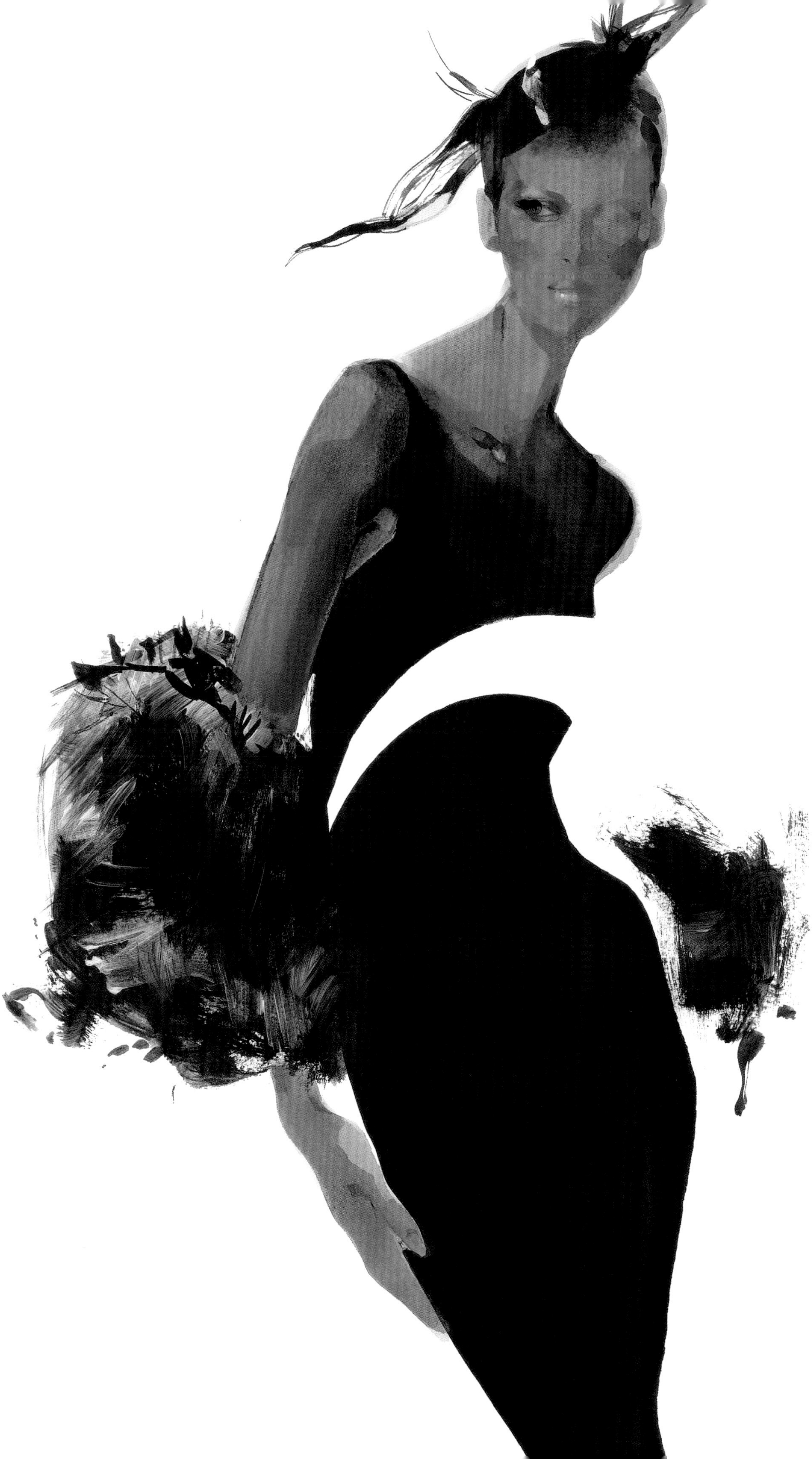

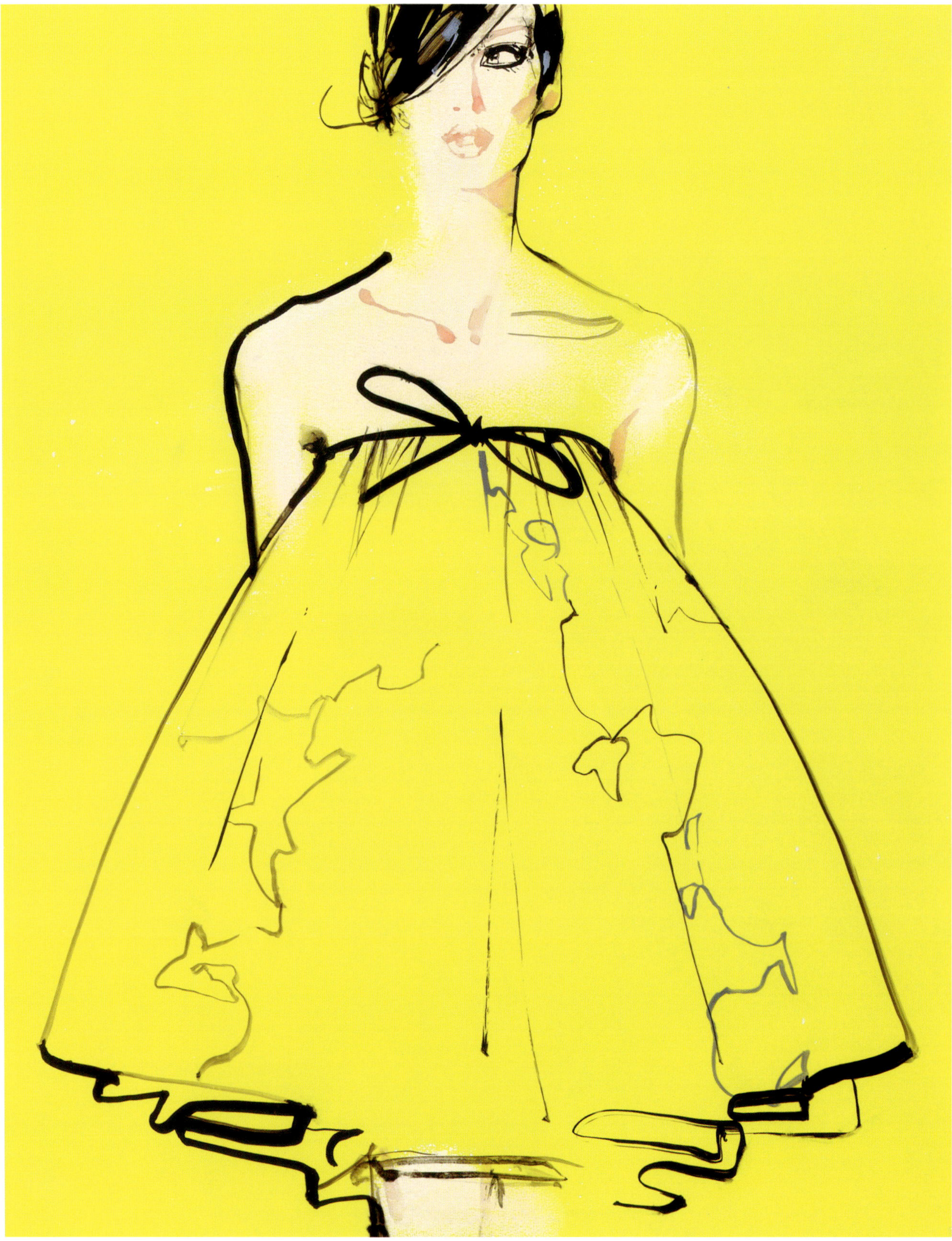

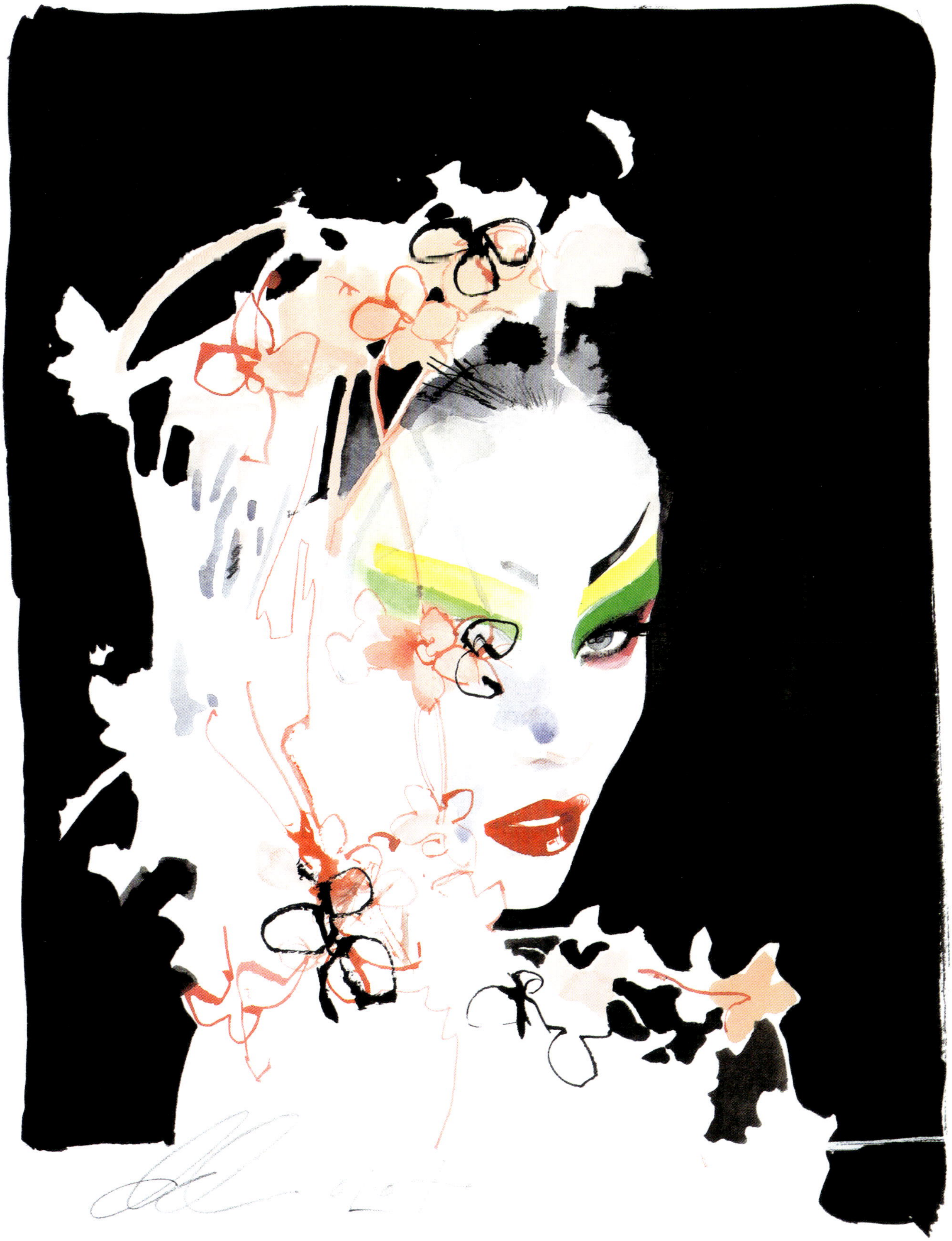

Backstage

— Pierre Bergé

PORTRAITS

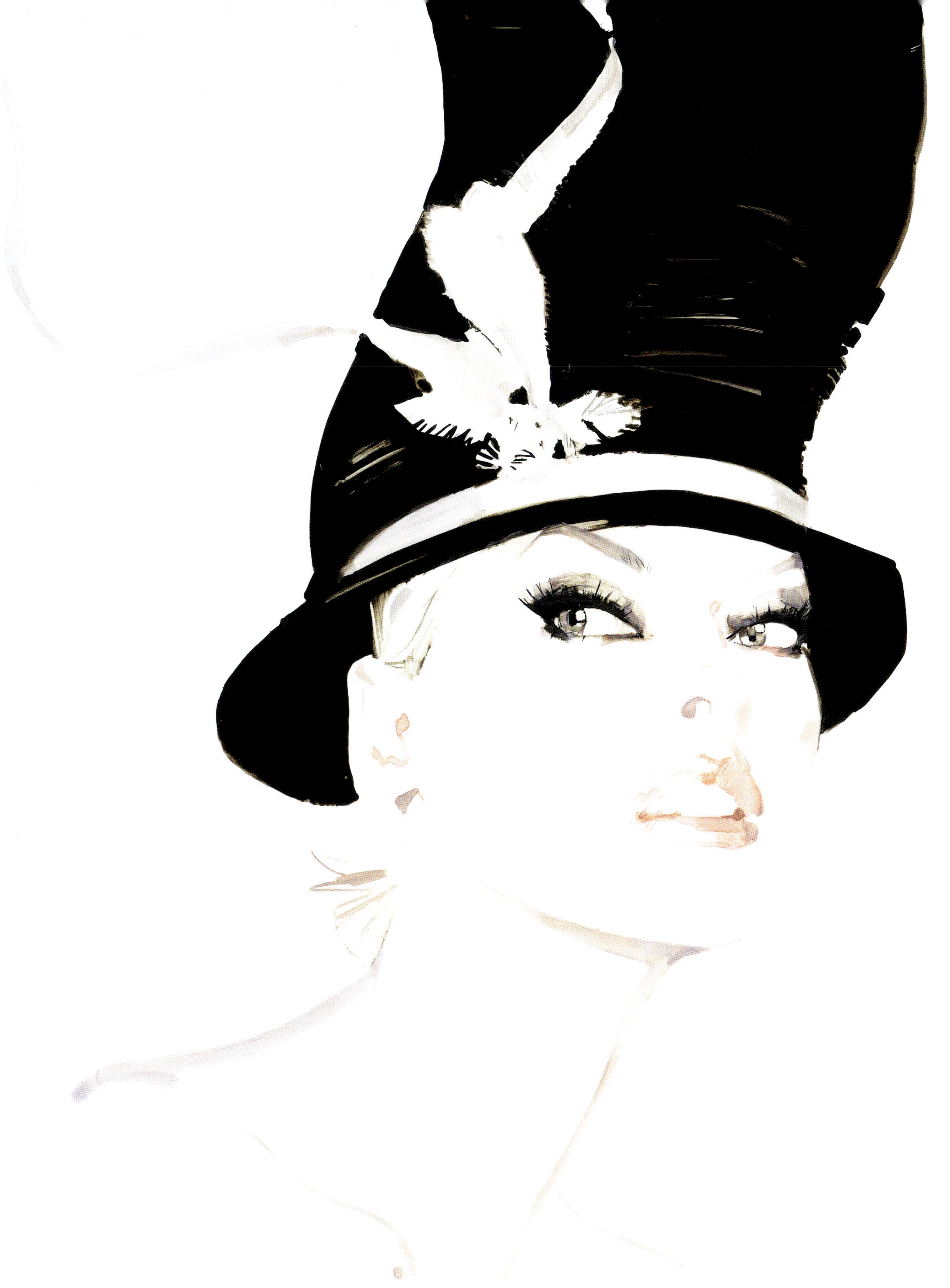

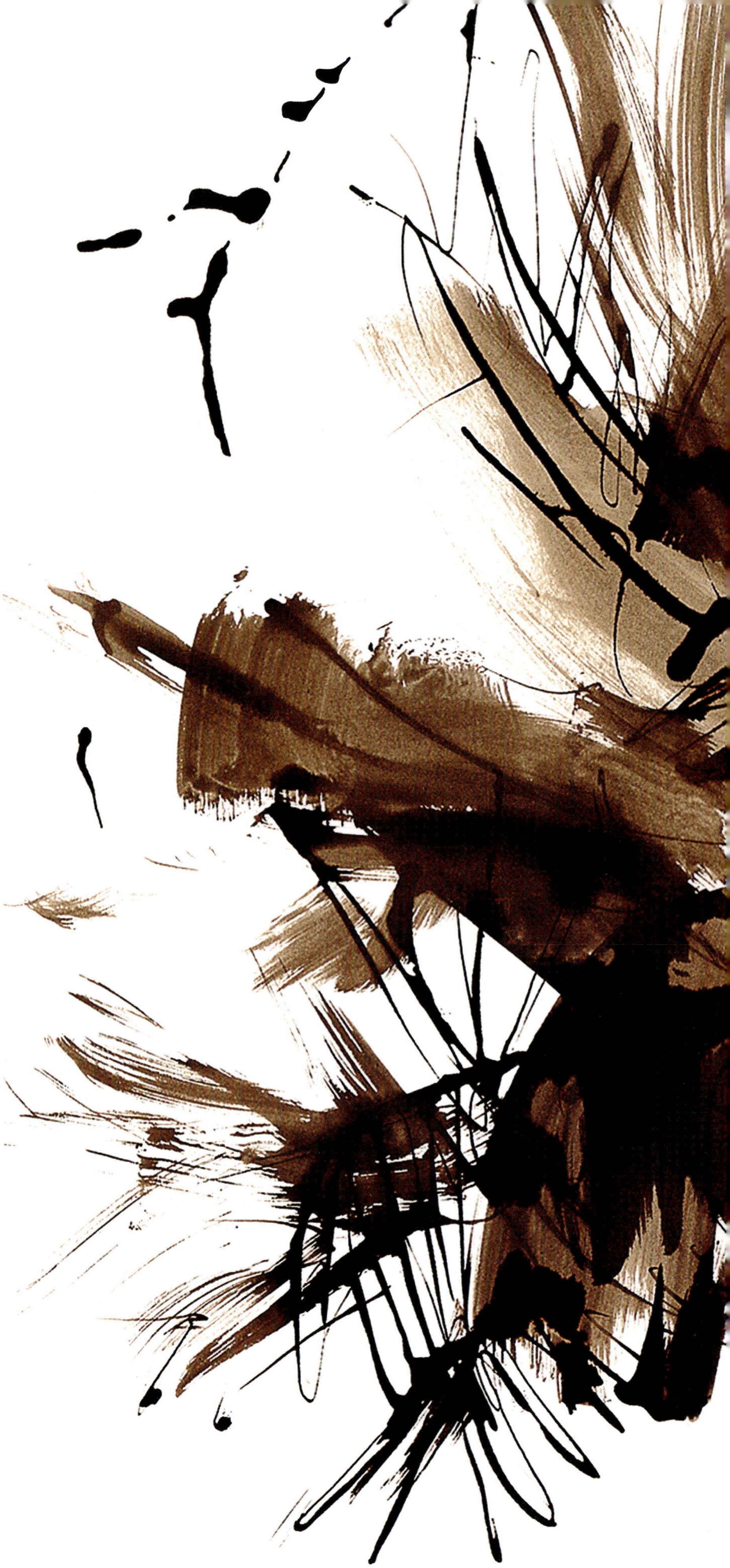

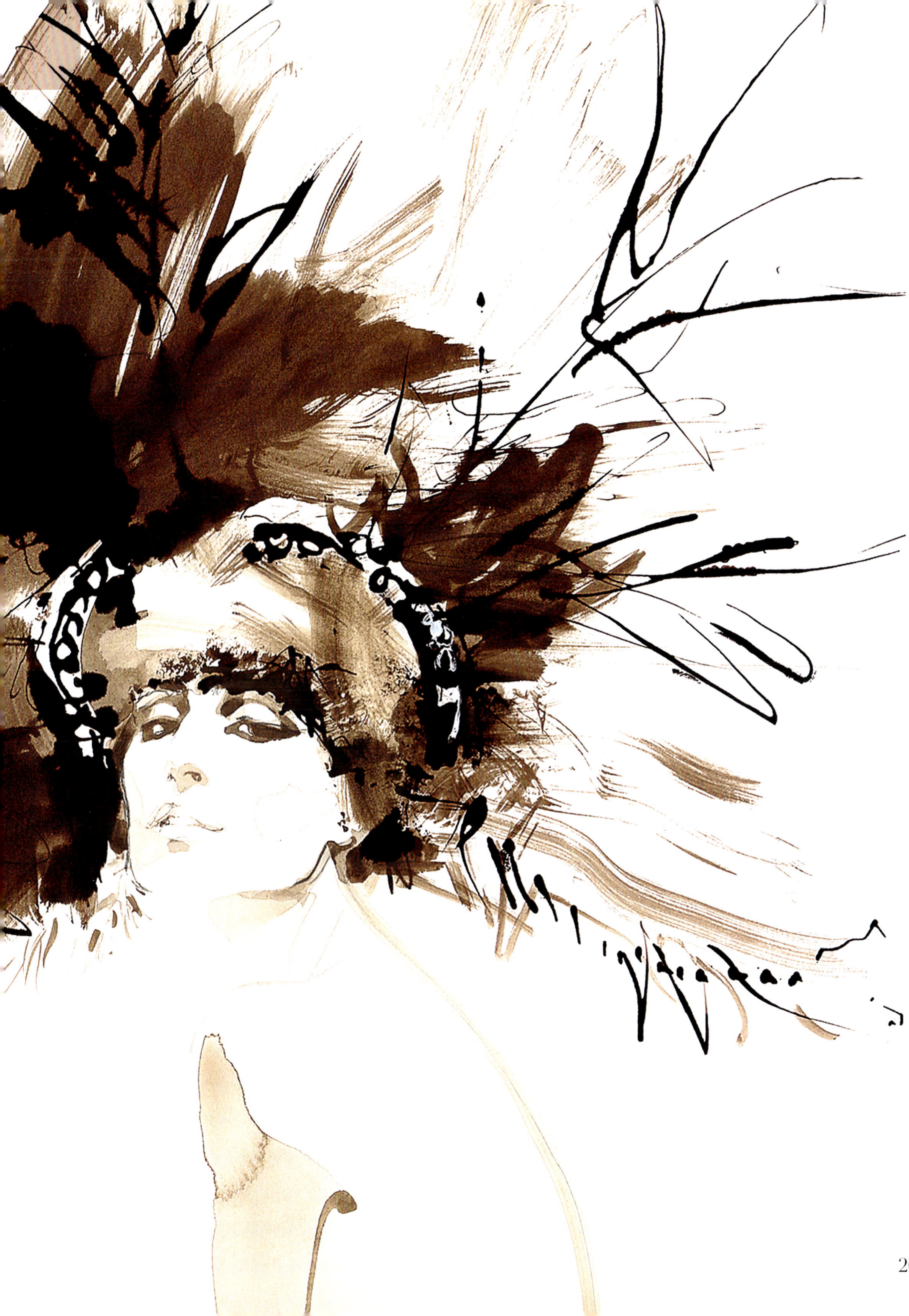

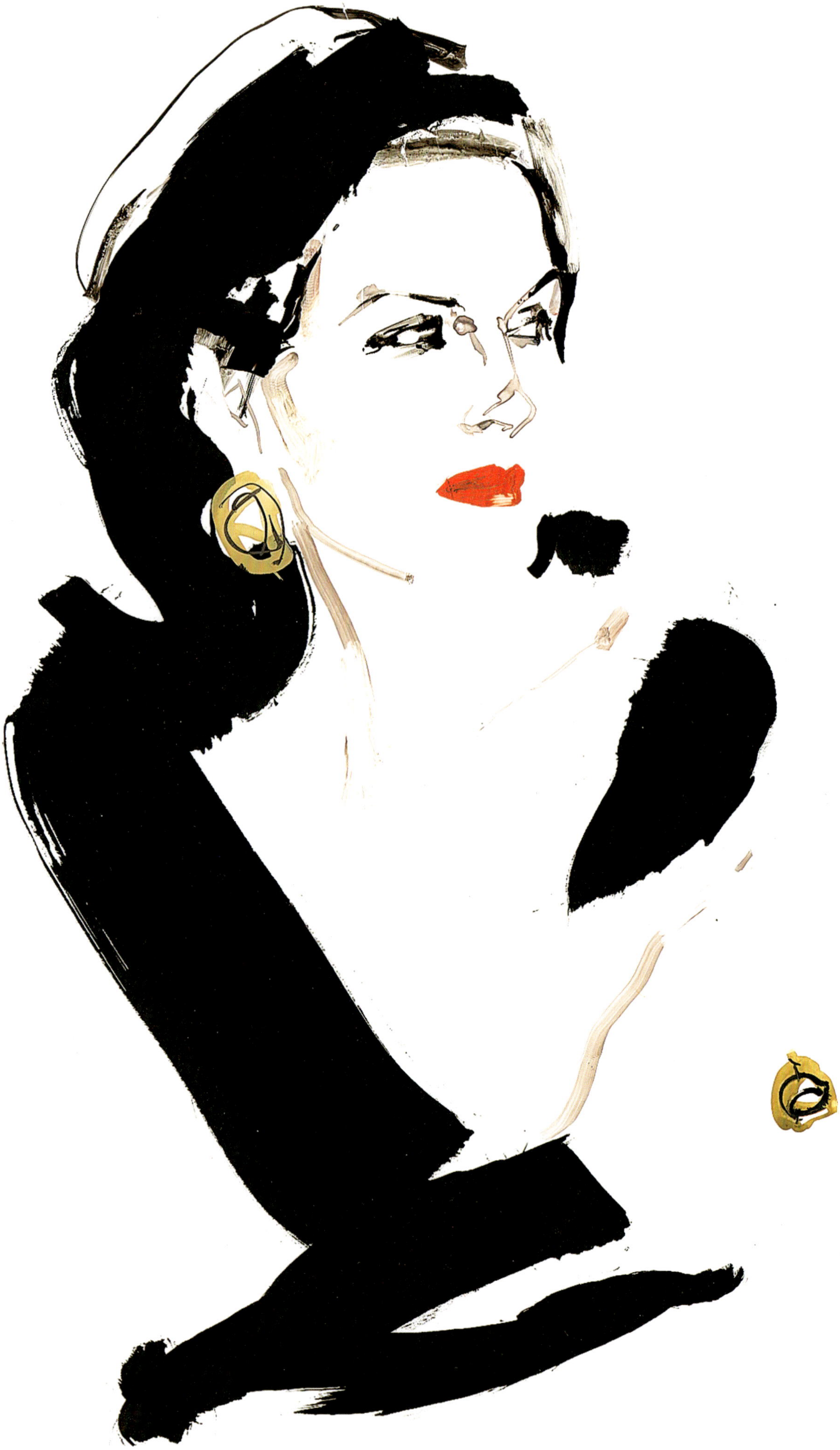

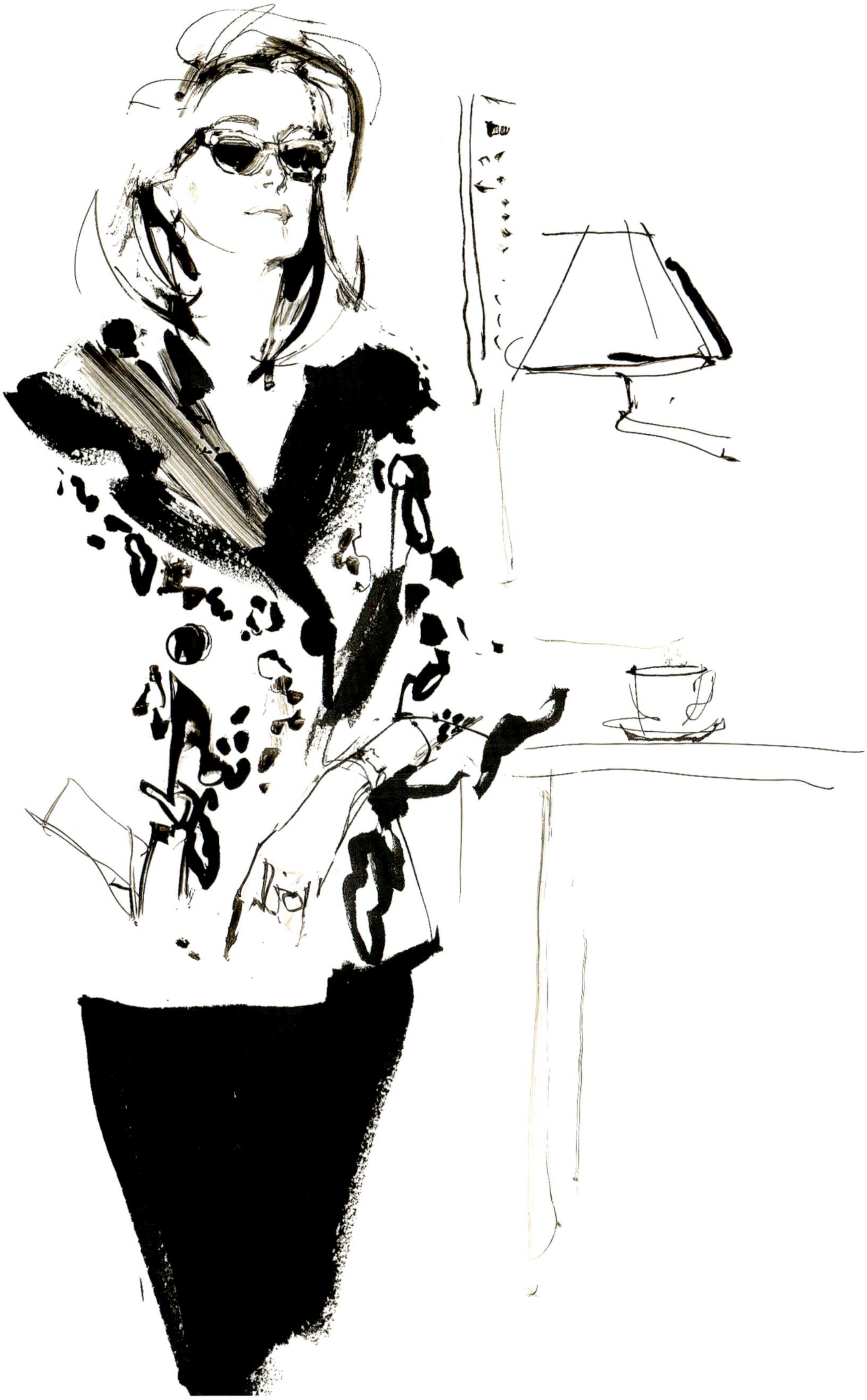

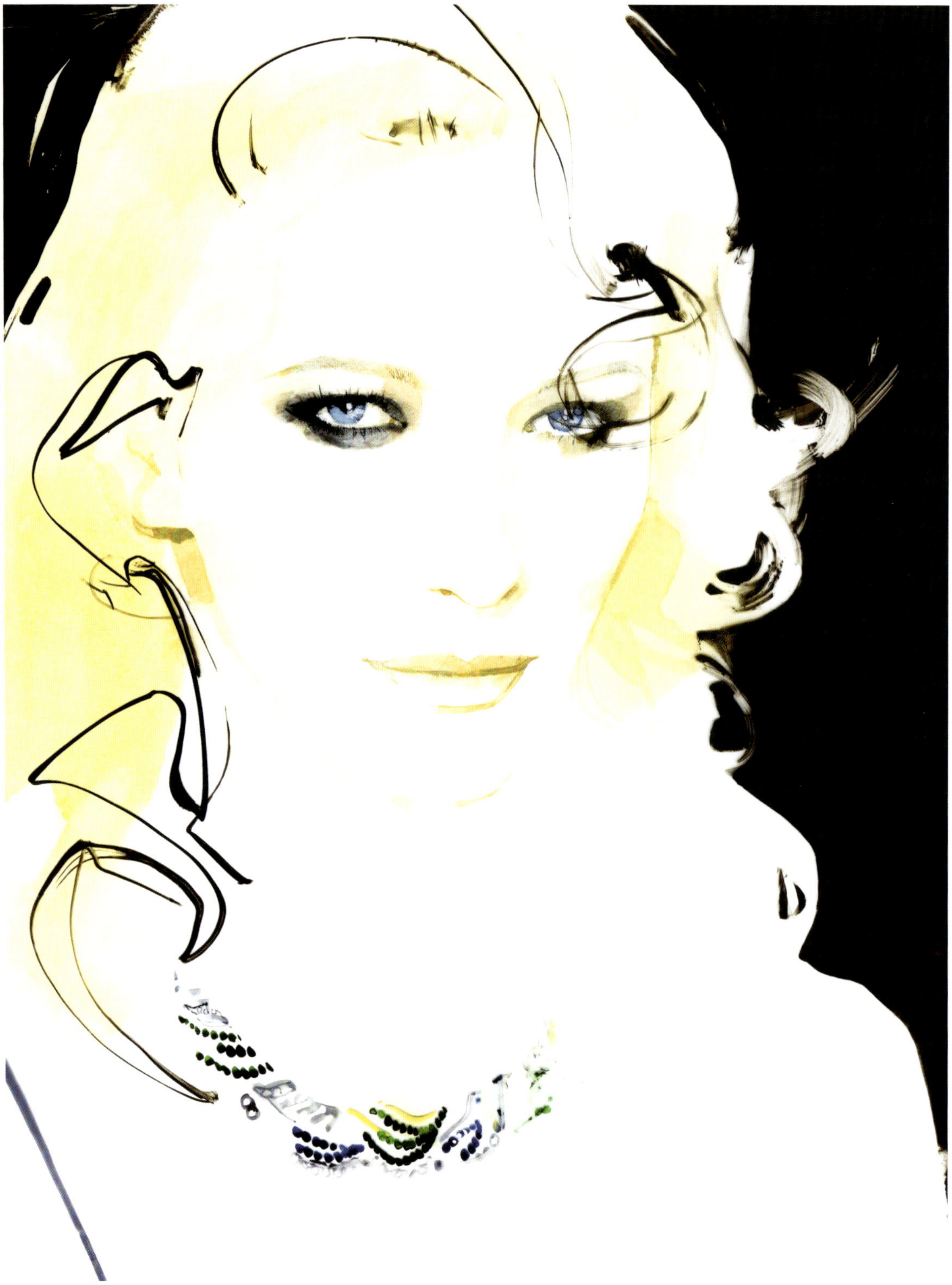

VOGUE

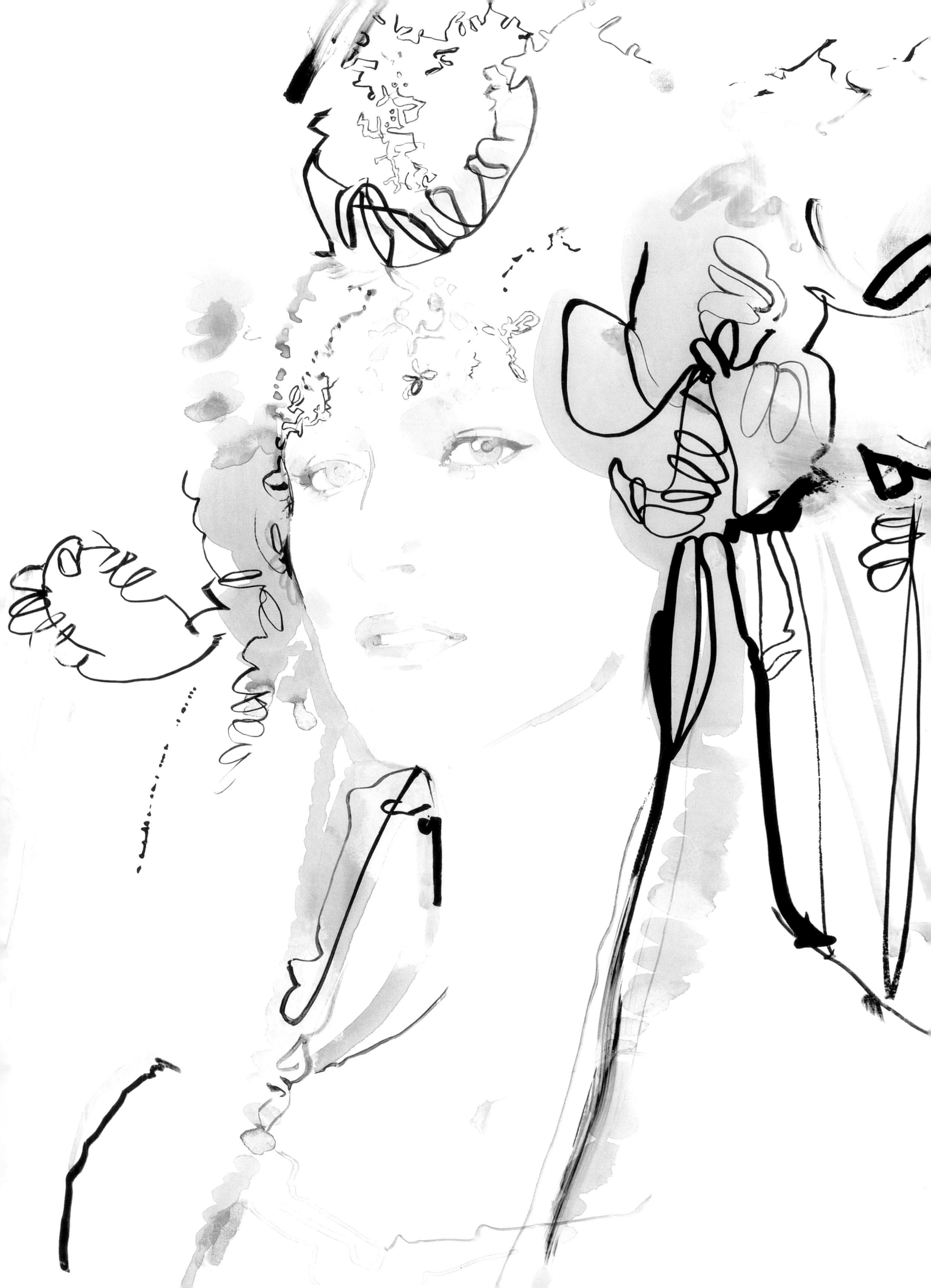

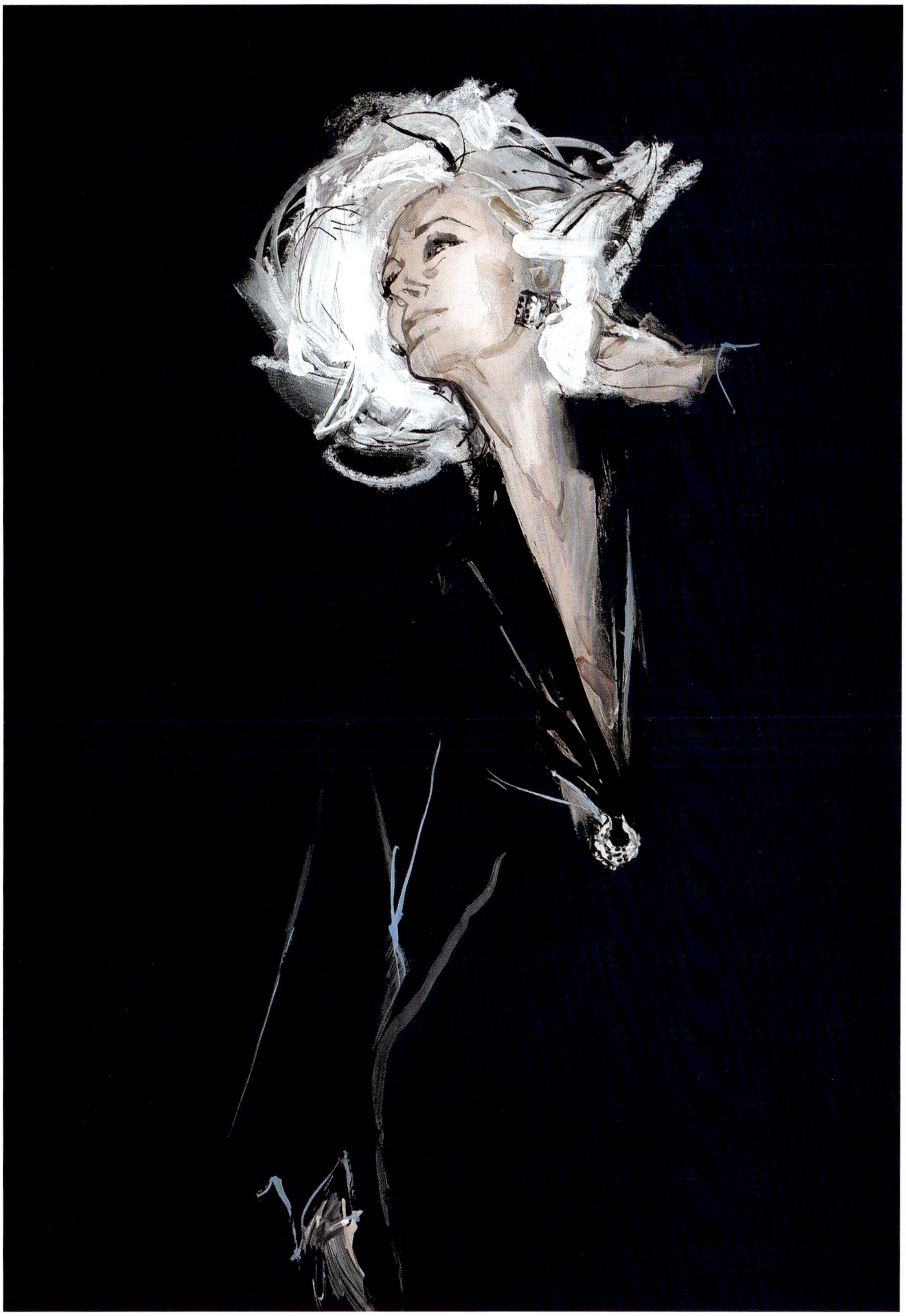

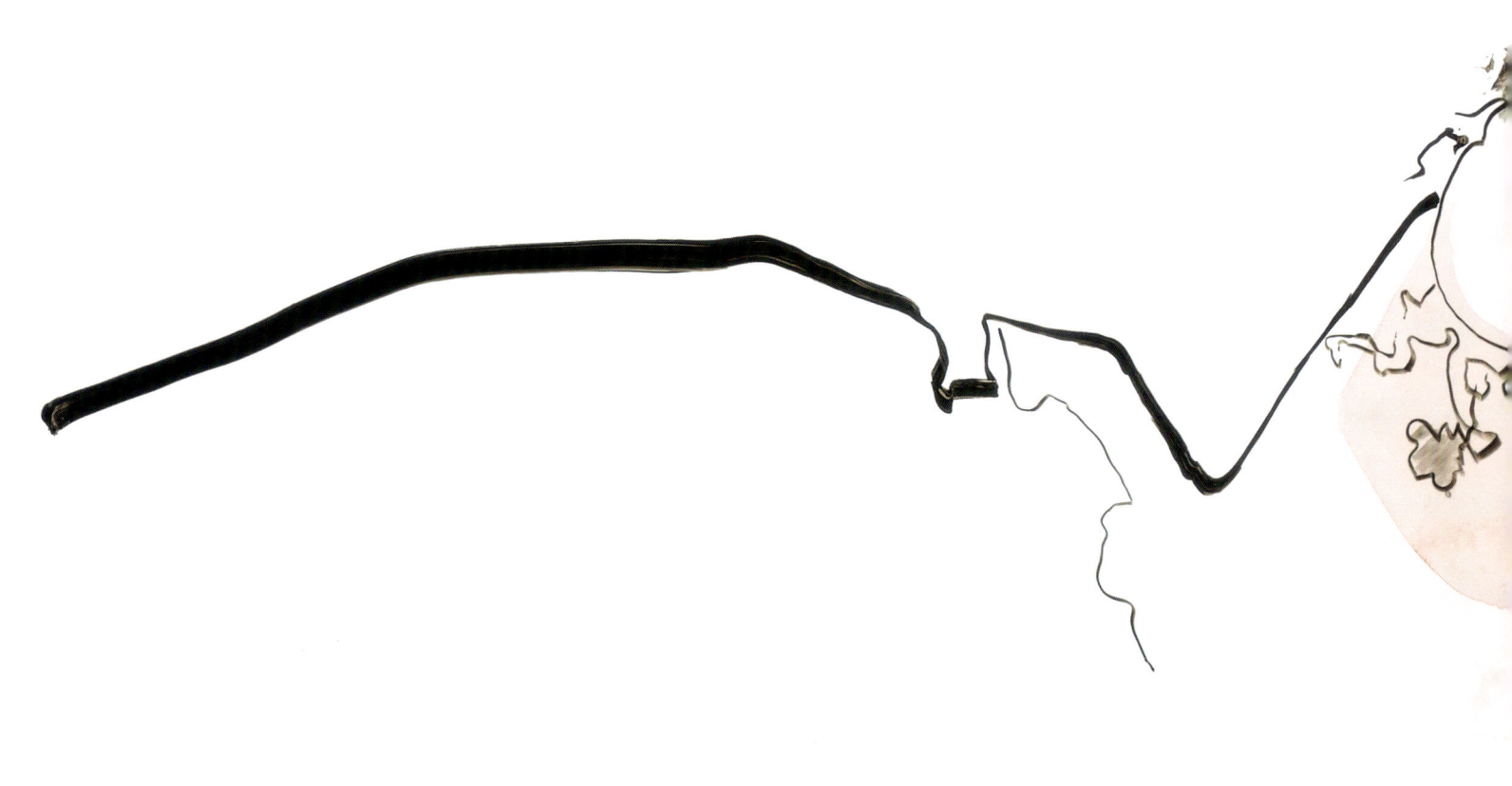

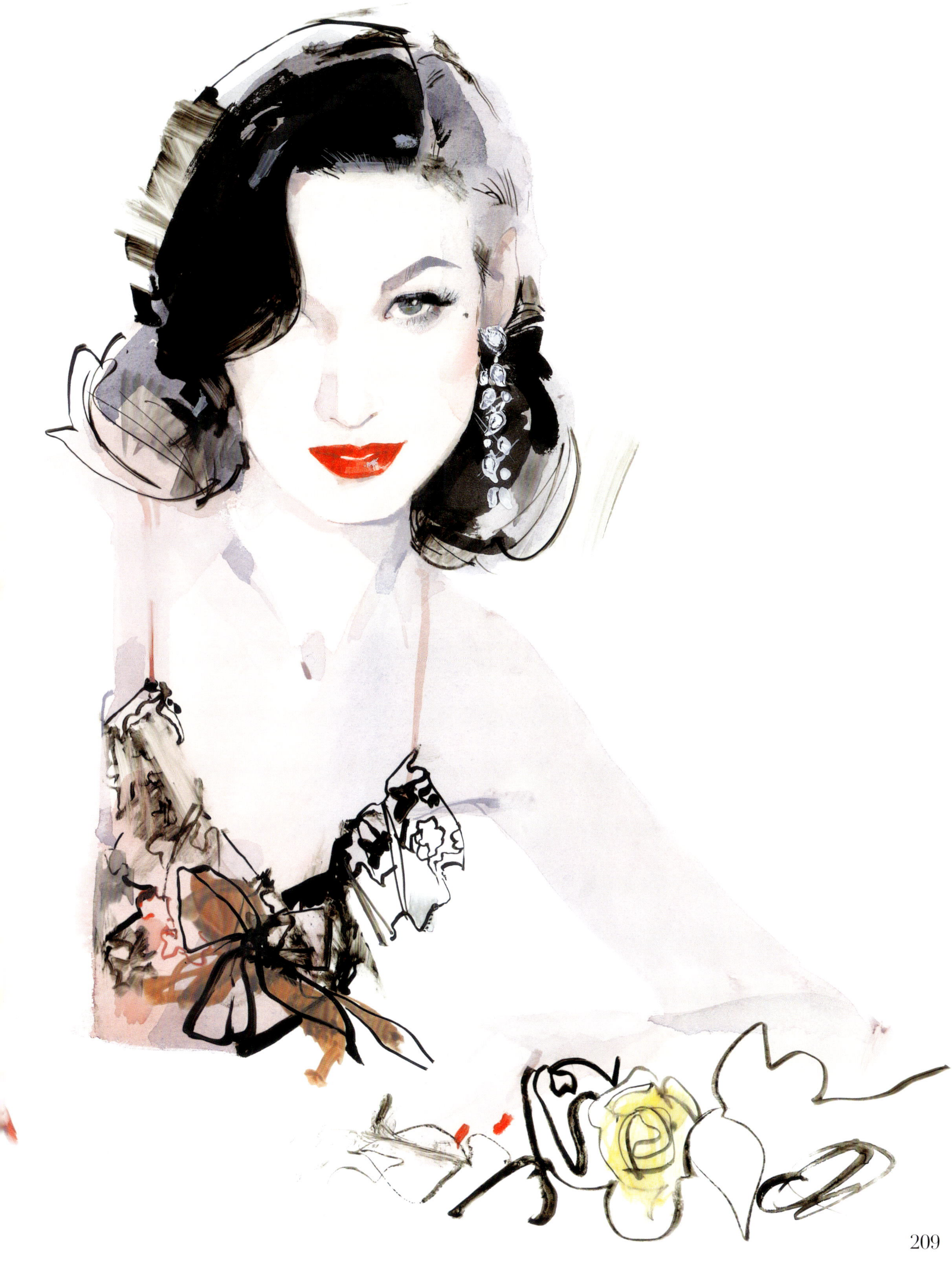

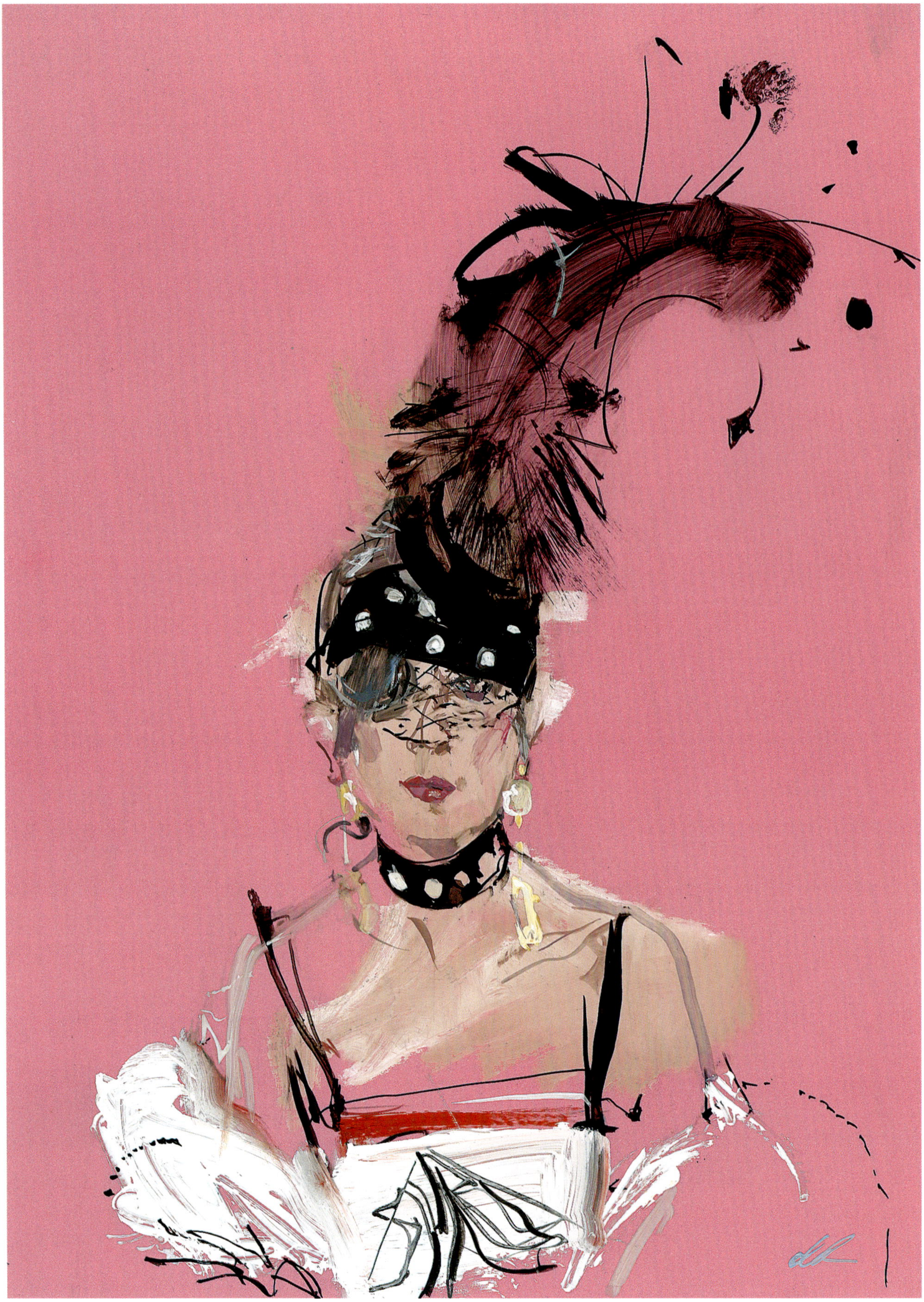

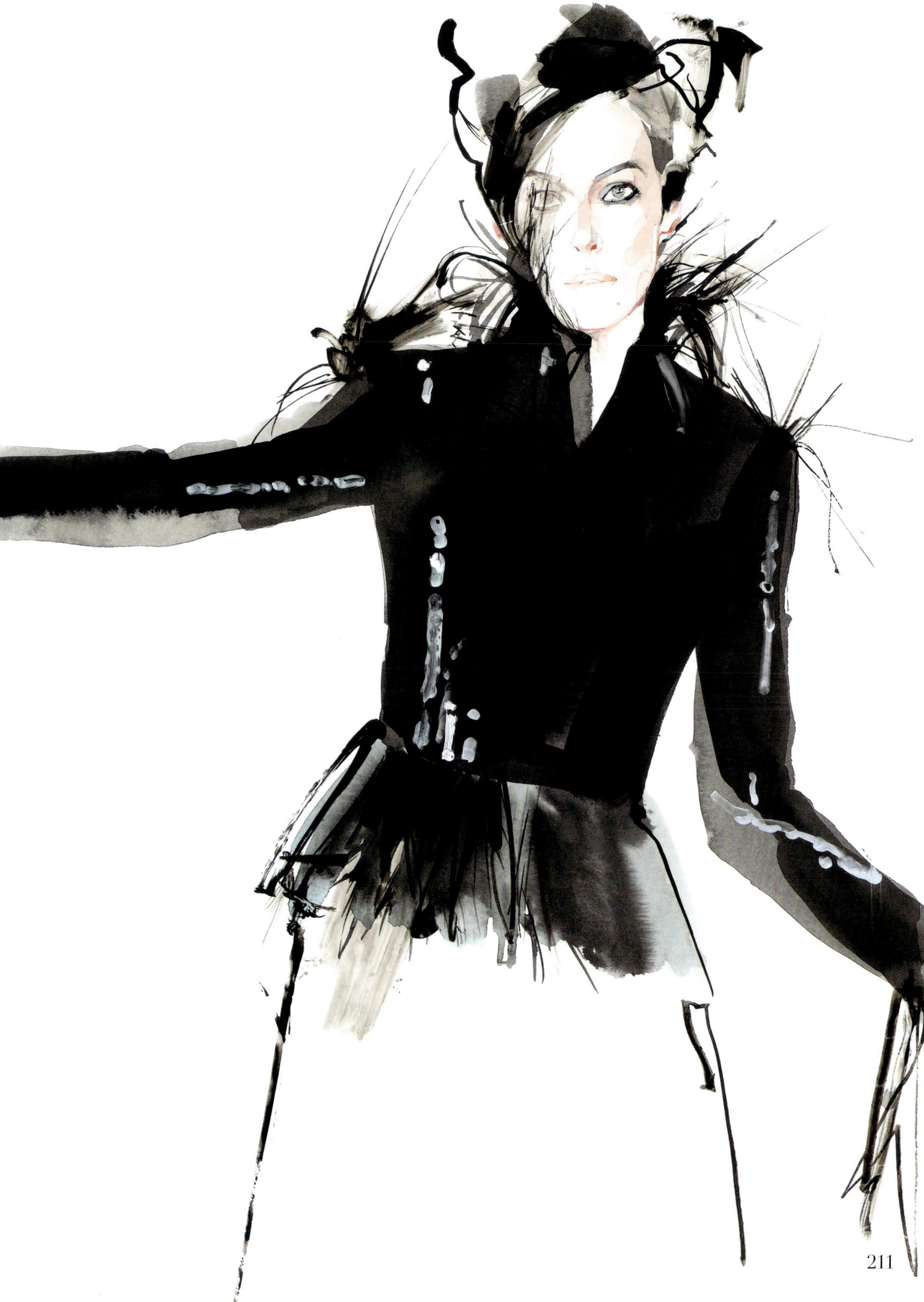

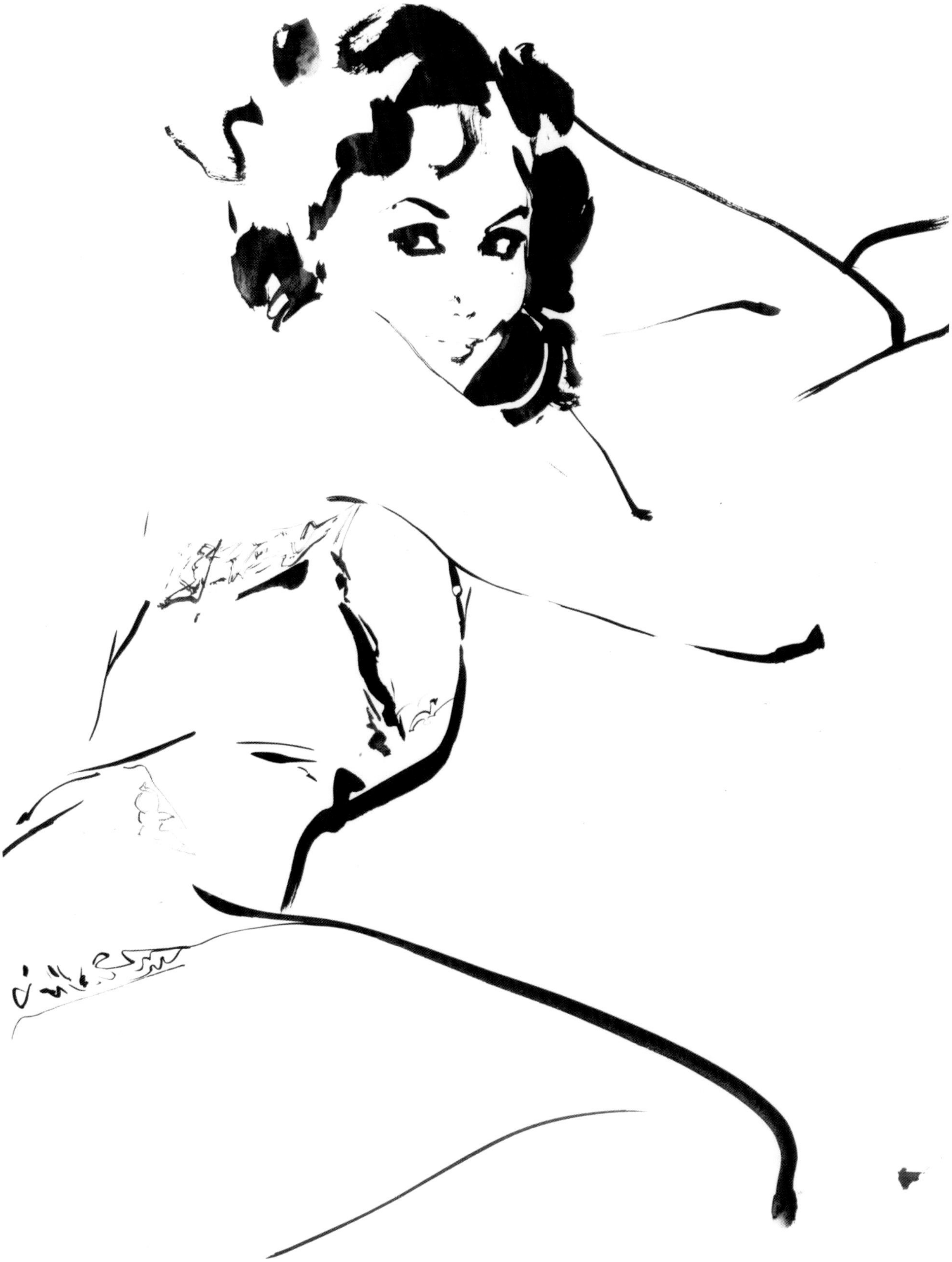

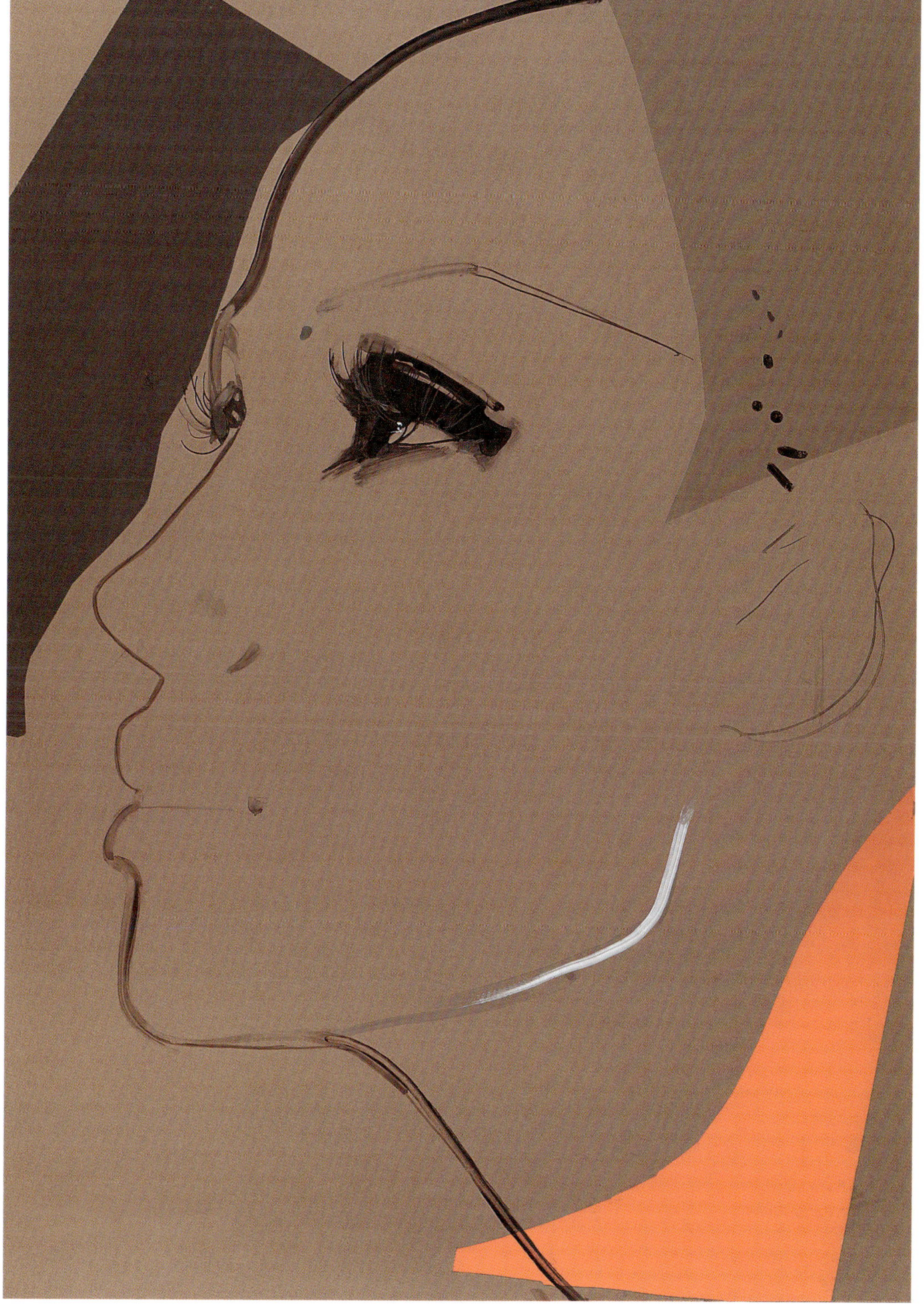

179
YVES SAINT LAURENT
2006. Ink, gouache and charcoal on paper. *Private collection*

180
CHRISTIAN LACROIX
1998. Watercolour on paper. *Private collection*

181
BACKSTAGE AT DIOR
2006. Ink, charcoal and gouache on paper. *LCF collection*

182
CHANEL
2009. Illustration for *Vogue China*. Gouache and ink on paper. Acetate overlay. *Artist's collection*

183
PARIS LONDRES
2007. Drawing commissioned by Chanel. Ink and gouache on paper. *Private collection*

184
BACKSTAGE AT DIOR II
2009. Ink and gouache on paper. *Private collection*

185
DIOR
2009. Ink, gouache, watercolour and charcoal on paper. *Artist's collection*

186
VALENTINO
2008. Portrait of Valentino Garavani commissioned by *Luxure* magazine. Gouache and watercolour on paper. *Artist's collection*

187
VALENTINO FITTING
2005. Drawing commissioned by *Vogue China*. Ink and gouache on paper. Acetate overlay. *Private collection*

188
YVES SAINT LAURENT
2006. Ink and watercolour on paper. *Private collection*

189
GAULTIER PARIS
1999. Ink on paper. *Private collection*

190
SUZY WAITING
2006. Drawing of Suzy Menkes. Ink and gouache on paper. *Private collection*

191
LILY AT LACROIX
2005. Drawing of Lily Cole, backstage at Christian Lacroix, commissioned by *Vogue China*. Ink, gouache and cut paper. Acetate overlay. *Private collection*

192
CHANEL
2006. Drawing commissioned by *ES* magazine. Ink on paper. *Private collection*

193
VERSACE
2006. Acrylic, watercolour and ink on paper. *Private collection*

194
GIAMBATTISTA VALLI
2007. Commissioned by *Madame* magazine, Germany. Oil pastel on paper. Ink and gouache on acetate overlay. *Private collection*

195
DIOR
2007. Commissioned by the *Times*, London. Ink and gouache on paper. *Artist's collection*

196
BACKSTAGE AT SAINT LAURENT
2006. Ink and gouache on paper. *Artist's collection*

199
LINDA EVANGELISTA
2004, Paris. Portrait commissioned for the cover of the *Telegraph Saturday Magazine*. Gouache and watercolour on paper. Hat by Philip Treacy. *Artist's collection*

200
ERIN O'CONNOR
2002, Paris. Watercolour and gouache on paper. Headdress by Stephen Jones for Christian Dior. *Private collection*

202
PALOMA PICASSO
1999, London. Gouache and ink on paper. Acetate overlay. *Artist's collection*

203
CATHERINE DENEUVE
1999, Paris. Ink on paper. Acetate overlay. Jacket by Yves Saint Laurent. *Artist's collection*

204, 205
CATE BLANCHETT
2009, London. Portraits commissioned for the cover of *Vogue Australia*. Ink and gouache on paper. Acetate overlay. Dress by Martin Grant (page 205). *Artist's collection*

206
JADE PARFITT
2005, Paris. Commissioned by *Vogue China*. Watercolour and ink on paper. Acetate overlay. Headdress by Jean Paul Gaultier. *Private collection*

207
CARMEN DELL'OREFICE
2000, New York. Oil pastel on Pantone paper. Ink on acetate overlay. Dress by Thierry Mugler. *Artist's collection*

208
DITA VON TEESE
2008, Paris. Sitting for *Pourquoi Pas?* magazine. Ink and gouache on paper. Acetate overlay. Dress by Christian Lacroix Couture. *Artist's collection*

210
ANNA PIAGGI
2000, Paris. Oil pastel on Pantone paper. Ink and gouache on acetate overlay. *Artist's collection*

211
AMANDA HARLECH
2005, Paris. Portrait commissioned by *Vogue China*. Gouache and ink on paper. Acetate overlay. Clothes by Chanel Couture. *Artist's collection*

212
MARIE HELVIN
1998, London. Ink on paper. Dress by Stella McCartney. *Artist's collection*

213
IMAN
1999, London. Cut paper collage, using Pantone paper. Ink on acetate overlay. *Artist's collection*

214
STELLA TENNANT
1998, New York. Ink on acetate. *Artist's collection*

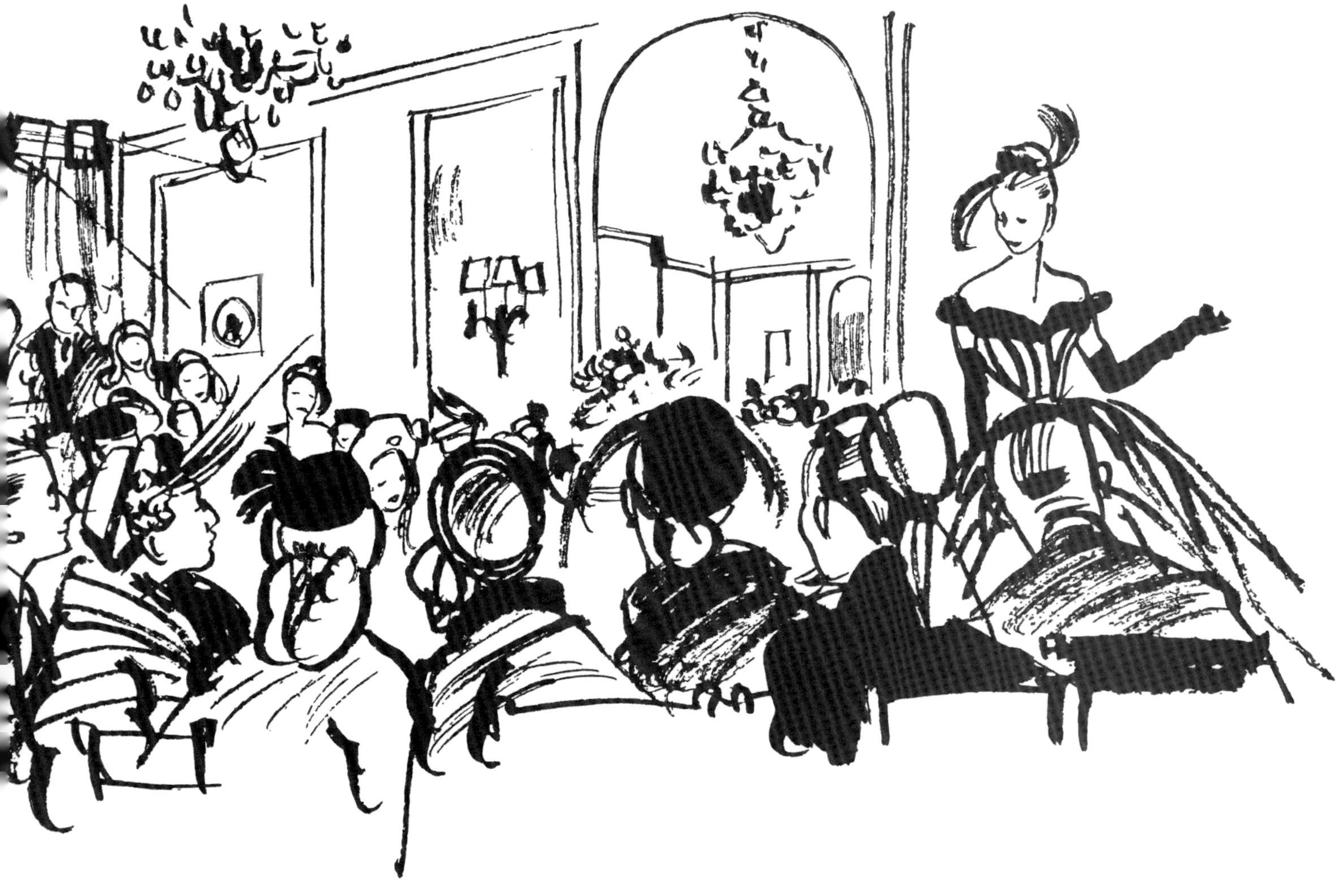

FURTHER READING

100 YEARS OF FASHION ILLUSTRATION by Cally Blackman
Laurence King Publishing Ltd, London, UK in association with Central St Martins College, London 2007

ANTONIO 60•70•80: Three Decades of Fashion Illustration by Antonio *Thames and Hudson, London, UK* 1995

ANTONIO'S GIRLS by Christopher Hemphill
Congreve Publishing Company, New York, USA 1982

ANTONIO'S PEOPLE by Paul Caranicas
Thames & Hudson, London, UK 2004

THE ART OF VOGUE COVERS 1909–1940 by William Packer *Octopus, London, UK* 1980

GEORGE BARBIER The Birth of Art Deco
Edited by Barbara Martorelli *Marsilio Editori, Venezia, Italy* 2008

FRANÇOIS BERTHOUD FACSIMILE by Holly Brubach
Edition Dino Simonett, Zurich 2000

DRAWING FASHION The Art of Kenneth Paul Block by Susan Mulcahy *Pointed Leaf Press, New York, USA* 2007

AN ENGLISHMAN IN NEW YORK by Francis Marshall
The Foley House Press, London, UK 1949

EPHEMERAL BEAUTY: Al Parker and the
American Woman's Magazine 1940–1960
Norman Rockwell Museum, Stockbridge, Massachusetts, USA 2007

ERTÉ: MY LIFE/MY ART An Autobiography
EP Dutton, New York 1989

FASHION DRAWING by Francis Marshall
The Studio Publications, London, UK 1942

FASHION DRAWING IN VOGUE by William Packer
Thames and Hudson, London, UK 1983

FASHION DRAWINGS IN VOGUE: Rene Bouët-Willaumez by William Packer *Webb & Bower in association with Michael Joseph, London, UK* 1989

FASHION DRAWINGS IN VOGUE: Carl Erickson by William Packer *Webb & Bower in association with Michael Joseph, London, UK* 1989

FASHION GALLERY. Edited by Volker Zahm *Germany* 1994

FASHION ILLUSTRATION by Colin Barnes
Macdonald & Co (Publishers) Ltd, London 1988

FASHION ILLUSTRATION IN NEW YORK by Peter Sato
Graphica-Sha Publishing Co, Tokyo, Japan 1985

FASHION PEOPLE by Gladys Perint Palmer
Assouline, New York, USA 2003

THE GLASS OF FASHION by Cecil Beaton
Weidenfeld and Nicholson, London, UK 1954

THE GOLDEN AGE OF STYLE: Art Deco Fashion Illustration by Julian Robinson *Harcourt Brace Jovanovich, New York and London* 1976

GRUAU by François Baudot *Editions Assouline, Paris, France* 1998

GRUAU Introduction by Ulf Poschard *Schirmer/Mosel* 1999

RENÉ GRUAU by Frieda Grafe *Rizzoli, New York, USA* 1984

RENÉ GRUAU by Patrick Mauries
Franco Maria Ricci, Milano, Italy 1984

ILLUSTRATING FASHION by E. Sloane
Harper & Row, New York, USA 1977

J.C.LEYENDECKER: American Imagist
by Laurence S. Cutler, Judy Goffman Cutler and the National Museum of American Illustration *Abrams, New York, USA* 2008

THE SNIPPY WORLD OF NEW YORKER FASHION ARTIST MICHAEL ROBERTS by Michael Roberts
Edition 7L, Paris, France 2005

SUBJECTS by Peter Sato *Parco Co., Ltd, Japan* 1984

ANDY WARHOL: Drawings and Illustrations of the 1950s by Andy Warhol *D.A.P, New York/Goliga Books, Japan* 2000

PRE-POP WARHOL by Jesse Kornbluth
Panache Press at Random House, New York, USA 1988

WWD ILLUSTRATED: 1960s–1990s by Michele Wesen Bryant *Fairchild Publications, Inc., New York, USA* 2004

INDEX

Page numbers in *italic* refer to the illustrations

A

Agnelli, Marella *140, 143*
Alaïa, Azzedine *165*
Antongini, Tom 51
Antonio see Lopez, Antonio
Arden, Elizabeth 82, 98, 136
L'Art de la Mode 91
Ashley, Betty Brader 175
Astaire, Fred 98
Auden, W.H. 143
Avedon, Richard 103

B

Bacall, Lauren *78*
Balanchine, George 78
Balenciaga, Cristóbal *134*, 139
Ballets Russes 23, 39, 58
Barbier, George 40, *45*, 47, 58, 63
Barrios, Pedro 146
Beach, Charles 33, 36
The Beatles 154
Beaton, Cecil 19, 51
Beer, Gustav 40
Benito 64
Bérard, Christian 91, 97, 98
Bergé, Pierre 151
Bernstein, Leonard 143
Berthoud, François 175
Bixby, Jane 175
Blanchett, Cate 177, *204–5*
Block, Kenneth Paul *144*, 145–51, *146–9*, 154, 175, 176
Blossac, Bernard *11, 88*, 89–95, *90–5*, 98
Blumenfeld, Erwin 19
Boldini, Giovanni *24*, 25–31, *27–30*, 47, 135, 154
Bouché, René *12*, 19, 89, 91, 98, 116, 133, *134*, 135–43, *136–43*, 154, 174
Bouët-Willaumez, René 64, 175
Bouret, Alfredo 175
Boutet de Monvel, Bernard 40, *42*
Bowler, Joe 105
Brando, Marlon *121*
Braque, Georges 143
Brissaud, Pierre 40, *43*
Brooks, Jason 175
Brunhoff, Michel de 98

C

Caldaguès, Paul 89
Calder, Alexander 143
Campbell, Lady Colin 29
Capote, Truman 127, 143
Capucci *156–7*
Caranicas, Paul 154
Cardin, Pierre *146*
Cardona, Emilia 31
Carlstedt, Cecilia 176
Cartland, Dame Barbara 86, *87*
Casati, Marchesa *30*, 31
Cassandre 58
Century magazine 34
Chambers, Margaret 82
Chanel *169, 182, 183, 192, 211*
Charles of the Ritz 136
Chase, Edna Woolman 64
Cheret, Jules 34
Cheruit, Madeleine 40
Cocteau, Jean 130, 164
Cole, Lily 191
Colette 74
Colin, Paul 89
Collier's 34
Concha de Ossa, Emiliana 26
Cooper Studios 105–6, 110, 116, 175
Cosmopolitan 106, 116
Coty 70
Creelman, Lee 64, 69

D

Daché, Lily 77
Daily Mail 81, 86
Dalí, Salvador 19
Davis, Sammy, Jr. *143*
De Kooning, Willem 143
de la Renta, Oscar 151, 159
de Mers, Joe 105
de Wolfe, Elsie 51
Degas, Edgar 26, 64
Delhomme, Jean Philippe 175
Dell'Orefice, Carmen *18*, 19, 177, *207*
Deneuve, Catherine *203*
Desses, Jean 98
Diaghilev, Sergei 39
Dick, Elsie 145
Dietrich, Marlene 97, *142*, 143
Diners Club *116*
Dinesen, Isak 143

Dior, Christian *3, 90, 136,* 139, *148–9, 181, 184–5, 194, 200–1*
Dobbs hats 116, *116*
Doeuillet, Georges 40
Dongen, Kees van 64
Doucet, Jacques 40
Downton, David *3, 18,* 19, *174–7, 179–214*
Doze *161*
Drian, Étienne *9,* 25, 44, 46, 47–52, *48–53*
Duran Duran 163

E

École des Beaux-Arts 40
Elle 154
Elvgren, Gil 105
Eric (Carl Erickson) *5,* 19, 20, 25, 47, *62,* 63–70, *64–71,* 89, 91, 98, 136, 175
Erté *54,* 55–8, *56–7, 59,* 63, 174
Esquire 116, 125
Eula, Joe 19, 151
Evangelista, Linda *199*

F

Fairchild, John 146, 151
Falconer, Sir William 26
Fath, Jacques *11, 88*
Femina 51
La Femme Chic 91
Les Feuillets d'Art 51
Fitch, Denise Bouché 139, 175
Fitch, John 110
Fokine, Michel 78
Fredericks, Tina S. 127
Fredman-Chaite Studios 116
Furness, Lady Thelma 52

G
Galliano, John 19
Garbo, Greta 139
Garland, Judy 143, *143*
Gaultier, Jean Paul *189, 206*
Gautreau, Virginie 26
Gazette du Bon Ton 39–44, *40–5*, 51, 73
George V, King 82
George VI, King 82, *82*
Givenchy, Hubert de 139, 151
Glamour 125, 127
Glenville, Tony 174–7
Good Housekeeping 106, *108–9, 111*
Goodman, Lenny 143
Goupil, Adolphe 26
Goya, Francisco de 154
Grant, Martin *205*
Gray, Richard 175
Greenhill, Fred 19
Grés, Madame *137*
Grosz, George 73
Gruau, René 20, 25, 47, 52, 89, 95, 98, 154, 175
Guest, C.Z. 143
Guinness, Gloria 52, 146
Gunzburg, Baron Nicky de 19
Gustafson, Mats 175

H
Halston *150*, 151, *166–7*
Hammerstein, Oscar *84–5*
Harlech, Amanda 177, *211*
Harper's Bazaar 44, 51, *54*, 55–8, *56–7, 59*, 125, 145, 146, 154, 174
Harrison, Lawrence Alexander *28*
Harrison, Rex *120*
Harrods 95
Hearst, William Randolph 58
Hedren, Tippi 107
Helvin, Marie 177, *212*
Hemingway, Ernest 98
Hepburn, Audrey *120*
Hood, Dorothy 175
Horst 103
Huston, John 78
Huxley, Aldous 143

I
L'Illustration 51
Iman *213*
Interview magazine 154
Iran, Shah of 116
Iribe, Paul 39

J
Jackson, Janet 163, 168
Jaeger 82, *83*
Jeanmaire, Zizi 98
Jones, Stephen 164, 168, *200–1*
Le Journal des Dames et des Modes 51

K
Karinska, Madame 97
Kelly, Grace 107
Kennedy, Jacqueline *141*, 143, 146
Kennedy, John F. 143, 146, 174
Keogh, Tom 7, *96*, 97–8, *98–101*, 175
Kim, Willa 97, 98, 175
Klee, Paul 130
Kuppenheimer 36

L
Lacroix, Christian *180, 191, 208–9*
Ladies Home Journal 106
Lagerfeld, Karl 154
Lamarr, Hedy *84–5*
Lanvin, Jeanne 40, *43*
Lanvin, Monsieur *117*
Lee, Gipsy Rose 78
Léger, Fernand 154
Lepape, Georges 39–40, 47, 63, 64
Leyendecker, J.C. *32*, 33–6, *34–7*
Lichtenstein, Roy 154
Lieberman, William S. 143
Lopez, Antonio *8*, 20, 73, 146, *152*, 153–9, *154–61*, 163, 164, 174, 175
L'Oréal 95, *95*

M
McCall's 106
McCall's Patterns 145
McCartney, Stella *212*
Marshall, Francis *80*, 81–6, *82–7*
Martin, Charles 40, *41*
Marty, André-Édouard *4, 38*, 40, 47
Mata Hari 55
Matisse, Henri 130
Menkes, Suzy *52, 190*
Mérode, Cléo de *24*
Millendorf, Rudy 146
Minnelli, Vincent 97
La Mode en Peinture 168
Molyneux, Edward 51, *91*
Montana, Claude 168
Montgomery, Scully 19
Mori, Hanae 168
Motherwell, Robert 143
Mucha, Alphonse 34
Mugler, Thierry *207*
My Fair Lady 120

N
Nast, Condé 64
New York Times 154
Noailles, Vicomtesse Marie-Laure de 98

O
O'Connor, Erin 177, *200–1*
L'Officiel 91

219

P

Paley, Babe 19, 143, 146
Palmer, Gladys Perint 175
Paquin, Jeanne 40, *45*
Parfitt, Jade *206*
Parker, Al 105, 110
Parkinson, Norman 64, 70
Peak, Bob *114*, 115–21, *116–23*, 174, 176
Pearlman, Barbara 175
Peignot, Georges 40
Penn, Irving 19, 103
Persson, Stina 176
Petit, Roland 98
Piaggi, Anna 154, 159, *210*
Picasso, Pablo 31, 58
Picasso, Paloma *8*, 168, *202*
Piguet, Robert 89, *101*
Plaisirs de France 136
Poiret, Paul *38*, 39–44, *41*, 55
Puritan Sportswear *114*, 116, *118*

R

Ramos, Juan 154, 159
Ray, Man 164
Redbook 106, 116, *118–19*
Redfern 40
Rhodes, Zandra 151
Roberts, Michael 175
Rochas 168
Rockwell, Norman 36, 110
Roosevelt, Theodora 97, 98
Rosine Paris *91*
Ross, Diana 55, 168
Russo, Rene 163

S

Saint Laurent, Yves 159, *160, 168, 170, 179, 188, 196, 203*
Saks Fifth Avenue 136
Sargent, John Singer 26, 31, 135
The Saturday Evening Post 110
Scherrer, Jean Louis *10*
Schiaparelli, Elsa 74, *74–5, 77,* 78, *80, 91, 131*
Schiele, Egon 164
Schoenlank, Margo 'Pony' 136, 139
Sem (Georges Goursat) 31, *31*, 73
Shahn, Ben 130
Sinatra, Frank 143
Smith, Fred 70
Snow, Carmel 58
Sorel, Cécile *51*
Sports Illustrated 116
Stipelman, Steven 146
Stork Club, Manhattan *84–5*
Stravinsky, Igor 143
Summer, Donna 163
Sundblom, Haddon 105
Suter, Elizabeth 175

T

Tam, Reuben 110
Tennant, Stella *214*
Testard, Maurice 89
Tice, Bill *144*
Time magazine 116, 135, 143
Timothy Taylor Gallery *130*
Tinkleman, Murray 175
Toulouse-Lautrec, Henri de 26, 74, 78
Toy, Teri *164*
Treacy, Philip *199*

V

Valentino 20, 168, *171, 186–7*
Valletta, Amber 20
Valli, Giambattista *193*
Vanity 156–9, 159
Versace, Gianni 20, *193*
Vertès, Marcel *6*, 19, *72,* 73–8, *74–9,* 91, 97, 98, 174
Viramontes, Tony *10, 162,* 163–8, *164–71,* 174, 175
Vogel, Lucien 40, 51, 55
Vogue 44, *62,* 63–70, *64,* 81–2, 91, 98, *98–9,* 136, 139, 143, 146, 154, 164, 174, 175, 177
Vollbracht, Michael 151
Von Teese, Dita 177, *208–9*
Vreeland, Diana 146

W

W 151
Warhol, Andy 55, *124,* 125–30, *126–31,* 135, 153, 154, 159
Welles, Orson *84–5*
Werboff, Michael 19
Wesley Simpson 79
West, Sir Alfred Cornwallis 26
West, Mae 74
Whistler, James Abbott McNeill 26, 31
Whitcomb, Jon 105
Whitehurst, Audrey 176
Whitmore, Coby *104,* 105–10, *106–13,* 174, 175
Wibout, Constance 175
Winchell, Walter *84–5*
Windsor, Duchess of *52,* 146
Woman's Day 106
Woman's Home Companion 106
Women's Wear Daily 145–51, *148–9,* 154, 176
Worth, Charles Frederick 40, *42*

Z

Zola, Émile 74

PICTURE CREDITS

Every effort has been made to contact the copyright holders, but should there be any errors or omissions, Laurence King Publishing would be pleased to correct them in any subsequent printing of this publication.

Page 3 Courtesy David Downton
Page 4 Courtesy Tony Glenville Collection
Page 5 photograph © 2010 Museum of Fine Arts, Boston
Page 6 Courtesy The Mary Evans Picture Library
Page 7 Private collection
Page 8 © Estate of Antonio Lopez and Juan Ramos/Courtesy Galerie Bartsch & Chariau, Munich
Page 9 © ADAGP, Paris and DACS, London 2010/Courtesy The Collection of Joanne Bergen/Artophile
Page 10 The Estate of Tony Viramontes/Courtesy Anita Viramontes, Ralph Viramontes and Ed Viramontes
Page 11 Courtesy Galerie Bartsch & Chariau, Munich/Mr & Mme Alain Matrand de La Bourdonnaye-Blossac
Page 12 Courtesy Galerie Bartsch & Chariau, Munich
Page 18 Courtesy David Downton
Page 24 Topfoto/The Granger Collection
Page 27 akg-images/Nimatallah
Page 28 akg-images/© Sotheby's
Page 29 © National Portrait Gallery, London
Page 30 Collection: Lord Lloyd Webber
Page 31 Private collection
Pages 32, 34 & 35 © Copyright 2010 National Museum of American Illustration™, Newport RI, www.americanillustration.org. Photo courtesy Archives of the American Illustrators Gallery TM NYC, www.americanillustrators.com
Pages 36 & 37 Courtesy The Advertising Archives
Page 38 © ADAGP, Paris and DACS, London 2010/Courtesy Tony Glenville Collection
Pages 40 & 41 Courtesy Tony Glenville Collection
Page 42 © ADAGP, Paris and DACS, London 2010/Courtesy Tony Glenville Collection
Pages 43, 44 & 45 Courtesy Tony Glenville Collection
Pages 46, 48 & 49 © ADAGP, Paris and DACS, London 2010/Courtesy Tony Glenville Collection
Page 50 © ADAGP, Paris and DACS, London 2010/Private collection
Page 51 © ADAGP, Paris and DACS, London 2010/Courtesy Tony Glenville Collection
Page 52 © ADAGP, Paris and DACS, London 2010/Courtesy The Bridgeman Art Library/© The Sullivan Collection
Page 53 © ADAGP, Paris and DACS, London 2010/Private collection
Pages 54, 56, 57 & 59 Courtesy The Mary Evans Picture Library/National Magazines
Pages 62, 64 & 66 Eric/*Vogue* © The Condé Nast Publications Ltd
Page 65 Eric/*Vogue* © The Condé Nast Publications Ltd/Private collection
Page 67 Courtesy The Condé Nast Archive, NY

Pages 68 & 69 Courtesy The Condé Nast Archive, NY
Page 70 Private collection
Page 71 Courtesy Dean Rhys Morgan Collection
Page 72 Marcel Vertès/*Vogue* © The Condé Nast Publications Ltd
Pages 74 & 75 Courtesy Schiaparelli France SAS/Private collection
Page 76 Marcel Vertès/*Vogue* © The Condé Nast Publications Ltd
Page 77 Private collection
Page 78 top Private collection
Page 78 bottom Courtesy Tony Glenville Collection
Page 79 Private collection
Page 80 Courtesy Volker and Ingrid Zahm Collection/© V&A Images, Victoria and Albert Museum
Page 82 Courtesy Tony Glenville Collection
Page 83 Courtesy The Advertising Archive/Jaeger
Pages 84–85 & 86 Private collection/© V&A Images, Victoria and Albert Museum
Page 87 Courtesy Cartland Promotions
Pages 89 & 90 Mr & Mme Alain Matrand de La Bourdonnaye-Blossac/Courtesy Galerie Bartsch & Chariau, Munich
Pages 91, 92, 93, 94 & 95 Mr & Mme Alain Matrand de La Bourdonnaye-Blossac/Private collection
Pages 96, 98, 99, 100 & 101 Courtesy French *Vogue*/All rights reserved
Page 104 ©1958 SEPS: Licensed by Curtis Publishing, Indianapolis, IN. All rights reserved. www.curtispublishing.com
Page 106 From the Klompen-LaRoche Collection/The Whitmore Family/Featured in *McCall's Magazine*
Page 107 From the LaRoche-Knight Collection/The Whitmore Family/Featured in *McCall's Magazine*
Pages 108–109 From the LaRoche-Knight Collection/The Whitmore Family/with permission of Hearst Magazines
Page 110 From the LaRoche-Knight Collection/The Whitmore Family/with permission of Hearst Magazines
Page 111 Private collection/with permission of Hearst Magazines
Page 112 From the LaRoche-Knight Collection/The Whitmore Family/with permission of Hearst Magazines
Page 113 From the LaRoche-Knight Collection/The Whitmore Family/Featured in *McCall's Magazine*
Pages 115–123 all COPYRIGHT BOB PEAK ESTATE / WWW.BOBPEAK.COM
Pages 124–129 © The Andy Warhol Foundation for the Visual Arts/Artists Rights Society (ARS), New York/DACS, London 2010/Courtesy Corbis
Page 130 top © The Andy Warhol Foundation for the Visual Arts/Artists Rights Society (ARS), New York/DACS, London 2010/Courtesy Corbis
Page 130 bottom © The Andy Warhol Foundation for the Visual Arts/Artists Rights Society (ARS), New York/DACS, London 2010/Private collection/Courtesy Timothy Taylor Gallery

Page 131 © The Andy Warhol Foundation for the Visual Arts/Artists Rights Society (ARS), New York/DACS, London 2010/Private collection
Page 134 Courtesy Estate of René Bouché
Pages 136 & 137 Courtesy French *Vogue*/All rights reserved
Page 138 The Bridgeman Art Library/Musee d'Art Thomas Henry, Cherbourg, France/Giraudon
Page 139 Courtesy Estate of René Bouché
Page 140 Courtesy The Condé Nast Archive, NY
Page 141 Courtesy Estate of René Bouché
Page 142 Courtesy Deutsche Kinemathek – Marlene Dietrich Collection, Berlin
Page 143 top *TV Guide* magazine cover courtesy of *TV Guide* magazine, LLC © 1963
Page 143 bottom Courtesy The Condé Nast Archive, NY
Page 144 Courtesy The Condé Nast Archive, NY/From the archive of Kenneth Paul Block: Photographs by Peter Riesett
Page 146 top Courtesy The Condé Nast Archive, NY/From the archive of Kenneth Paul Block: Photographs by Peter Riesett
Page 146 bottom Courtesy Morton Ribyat/Dean Rhys Morgan Collection
Page 147 Courtesy Morton Ribyat/Dean Rhys Morgan Collection
Pages 148–149 Courtesy The Condé Nast Archive, NY/From the archive of Kenneth Paul Block: Photographs by Peter Riesett
Page 150 Courtesy Morton Ribyat/From the archive of Kenneth Paul Block: Photographs by Peter Riesett
Page 151 From the archive of Kenneth Paul Block: Photographs by Peter Riesett
Pages 153, 154, 155 & 156–157 Copyright Estate of Antonio Lopez and Juan Ramos/Courtesy Galerie Bartsch & Chariau, Munich
Pages 158 & 159 Copyright Estate of Antonio Lopez and Juan Ramos/Courtesy Tony Glenville Collection
Pages 160 & 161 Copyright Estate of Antonio Lopez and Juan Ramos/Courtesy Galerie Bartsch & Chariau, Munich
Pages 162–171 The Estate of Tony Viramontes/Courtesy Anita Viramontes, Ralph Viramontes and Ed Viramontes
Pages 179 & 180 Private collection
Page 181 LCF Collection
Page 182 Artist's collection
Pages 183 & 184 Private collection
Pages 185 & 186 Artist's collection
Pages 187–194 Private collection
Pages 195–199 Artist's collection
Page 200 Private collection
Pages 202–205 Artist's collection
Page 206 Private collection
Pages 207–214 Artist's collection
Pages 216, 219 & 223 Private collection